The BIG Book of Stories, Songs, and Sing-Alongs

Programs for Babies, Toddlers, and Families

Text by Beth Maddigan

Program plans and introductions by Stefanie Drennan

Illustrations by Roberta Thompson

LIBRARIES
UNLIMITED

A Member of the Greenwood Publishing Group

Westport, Connecticut • London

British Library Cataloguing in Publication Data is available.

Library of Congress Catalog Card Number:
ISBN: 1-56308-975-0

First published in 2003

Libraries Unlimited, Inc.
A Member of the Greenwood Publishing, Inc.
88 Post Road West, Westport, CT 06881
www.lu.com

J/REF/ Printed in the United States of America

The paper used in this book complies with the P
ermanent Paper Standard issued by the National
Information Standards Organization (Z39.48-1984).

10 9 8 7 6 5 4 3 2 1

Every reasonable effort has been made to trace the owners of copyrighted materials in
this book, but in some instances this has proven impossible. The author and publisher will be
glad to receive information leading to more complete acknowledgments in subsequent
printings of the book and in the meantime extend their apologies for any omissions.

I would like to dedicate this book to my family for their support and understanding. I would also like to thank my friends of Sunnyside Beach.
Wink and smile,
Berta

My family--my inspiration.
My heart & soul.
My dedication.
Thank you for giving me the wings to fly and for believing I could.
All my love,
Stefanie

To children everywhere and to the adults that delight and encourage them . . .
Beth

Contents

Acknowledgements

We would like to thank our colleagues and friends for providing us with their encouragement and great ideas throughout the writing of this book—Go Team!—as well as the Cambridge Libraries for their continuing dedication to the pursuit of excellence in children's services. We would also like to thank two individuals without whom this project would not have been realised: Barbara Ittner, the editor with a vision, and Robert Pound, for his 24-hour technical support and specialised services.

Introduction

The best thing about being a children's library programmer is that every day your job is new; children change and grow and delight you in unexpected ways. There are new books published constantly and new rhymes and songs written daily. Unfortunately, the same thing that makes our jobs exciting and fun is also the greatest source of time consumption. The greatest challenge facing library programmers is also that every day the job is new: developing, growing, and changing. Sometimes keeping abreast of these changes seems overwhelming. This book is designed to make your life as a programmer easier, and to let you concentrate on the reason you have a job: the children.

There is a wealth of information available for children's programmers: collections of fingerplays, rhymes, and songs; books on child development; activity books for children of all ages; guides for storytimes for preschoolers; and much, much more. Programmers can be overwhelmed by the amount of information, and trying to tie it all together can seem like an insurmountable task. That is what this book is designed to do: gather all the pertinent information together that you will need to start a children's program for preschoolers at any age. We explore the full range of preschool library programs, for children from six months to three years of age, and we highlight what to expect for each age group. At every level there are a series of programs designed specifically for children's developmental needs: rhymes, songs, and activities presented in a format and style best suited to the children's level of development. These programs are presented as reproducible handouts. You can choose some that appeal to you, photocopy them, and give them to caregivers during or after a program. They can also be used to supplement your own repertoire of rhymes, songs, and activities.

The principles of child development, what to expect from children at different ages, are key concepts when designing programs. However, library programmers are not often trained in child psychology. We are trained to focus on the literacy angle: sharing books and developing reading skills. The pages that follow bring those two concepts together into one, achievable objective: book-based programs designed to enhance children's developing skills at every age.

This guide is designed to be used by anyone who is planning a literature-based program, both novice programmers who have never planned and performed a storytime and seasoned programmers looking for new ideas and novel approaches. It refers, specifically, to library programs such as those run in a public library setting. However, the programs themselves and information on children at specific ages can also be used by preschool and kindergarten teachers. Library school students studying children's services will find a wealth of resources and tips. In fact, anyone looking for ways to bring children and books together can benefit from this resource guide: parents, teachers, library staff, and children's literature enthusiasts.

Use this manual in one or many ways: Read it from cover to cover if you are starting from scratch with children's programming or simply refer to the chapter that covers the age group you will be working with, if you have run storytime programs before. If your library has established programs for a limited age range, check out the chapters on programming with babies and toddlers.

Finally, every programmer runs into problems from time to time, and it can be difficult to find advice. Use this source to search out situations similar to your own and read what has worked for us. There are not always perfect solutions, but you'll take comfort and gain confidence from the experiences of people who have run successful programs and sorted out problematic situations. Children are a delight and an exciting challenge; take the leap into programming with the right attitude and use this manual to guide you along the way.

Library Programming: Benefits for Children

Library and literature-based programs are centred around one key concept: sharing stories with children. Reading aloud to children is satisfying for both child and caregiver, and it is now known to improve a child's capacity for learning. Dr. Fraser Mustard is one of the leading Canadian experts on early childhood brain development, and his research has shown that early literacy is related to language development (Ontario Early Years Study, 1999). The theory centres on the fact that children who grow up listening to literature are more likely to become capable readers. Stories do more than assist basic language and brain development, they also engage children's imagination and open them up to a world outside their own limited existence. Through story, children grow beyond their personal understanding of the world around them. Books hold the key to adventure, fantasy, friendships, and new experiences. These are just a few of the numerous benefits of library programming for young children. In the last decade there has been a great deal of research surrounding emergent literacy and fostering child development through literature (Ernst, 2001). And much has been written to emphasise a concept many of us understood long ago: Children and stories belong together.

Many public libraries run programs for children. Preschools and schools also conduct literature-based programs for young children. Before children can read on their own, adults have the exciting job of making reading and sharing stories a magical experience. There are numerous ways to accomplish this goal; as a programmer you are limited only by your imagination and ingenuity. The programs outlined in this book are guidelines, suggestions, and starting points. Use them to inspire, nurture, and develop your own style for programming.

Library Programming: Benefits for the Institution

Literature-based programming is good for children, but what does it do for the workplace? What are the benefits for the library, school, or preschool centre? As a children's programmer, you know intuitively that storytimes are good for children, but how do you tie them to your library or school's focus? Your facility's philosophy should be an integral part of any programming. The design and implementation of your programs will reflect the mission and goals of your institution. Some of the objectives that can be accomplished with the programs presented in this manual may apply to your experience, and you may be able to use them to lobby your administration or governing body to add, enhance, or keep the programming schedule you have developed. Institutional objectives, such as those listed below, can be accomplished through literature-based programming:

- Creating and fostering lifelong literacy

- Increasing exposure in the community

- Creating positive, memorable experiences for children and families

- Increasing circulation of books and other materials

- Expressing your institution's commitment to children

- Enhancing education in a recreational, relaxed environment

- Explaining to participants how the library works and is organised

- Increasing awareness of your facility's services

Accepting the Challenge: Using This Programming Guide

Following this introduction are six chapters designed to give you a practical guide to library-style programming. The first chapter introduces some typical starting points, challenges, and questions related to programming. Subsequent chapters provide a developmental guide to children's programs for specific age groups from babies to toddlers to entire families. Each chapter discusses developmental milestones, challenges, and rewards for age-based programming. Each chapter also includes program outlines and handouts for a variety of theme-based programs. Photocopy these handouts and give them out in your programs, or photocopy one set and laminate them to use over and over at your facility. Each theme showcases books, rhymes, songs, activities, and crafts that are inexpensive and accessible for most libraries and schools. If your institution does not have the budget for crafts and programming materials, you could give these handouts to parents or caregivers to use as follow-up activities at home. The books chosen for inclusion in this guide have all received positive reviews and have been tested by programmers. If you cannot access these titles at your local library, substitute some of your own, or ask to have specific titles ordered from another library. If you do not work in a public library, visit one. The public library is the best resource for children's books and materials related to children's programming (and it's free!).

The rhymes and songs are accompanied by icons indicating the type of activity involved in them, as follows:

Once you have decided that children's programs are in your future, you have taken a great step, not only towards helping children master literacy and access to the advantages of being a reader, but also to a future filled with fun, laughter, and a sense of accomplishment. Congratulations!

Chapter 1

Nuts and Bolts

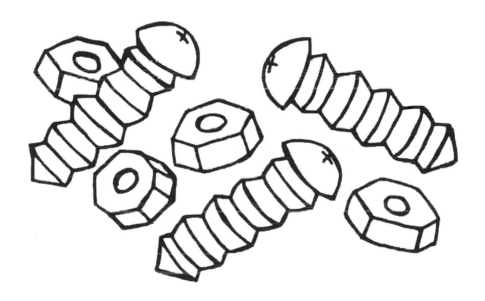

A children's programmer is many things: an entertainer, a nurturer, a teacher, an administrator, and some days . . . even a referee! Literature-based programs are a dynamic mix of the tools children need to get a head start on literacy. The key to success is planning and considering all the basic elements before each series of programs, such as

- Where are you going to run the program?

- When will you run the program, and for how long?

- Who will present the program?

- Whom do you expect to attend?

- What will you need to have on hand?

- How do you manage a group?

If you can answer these questions, you are ready to set up your program. If you aren't sure, read on! Chapter 1 will help you work out the details no matter what age group or type of program you are planning for.

1. Where?

1.1 Finding a Home for Programs

A space of its own is all a preplanned children's program really needs. Storytime can run on the lawn or in the corner of an existing space, but ideally it will be held in a space designed for this purpose. The storytime area should be separate from other communal or public areas. If an entire room is not available, create the space by subdividing a larger room. Program participants may need a little extra help getting focused in a shared space. Distractions should be limited, and the area should be enclosed as much as possible. Large open spaces can be intimidating for some children and cause others to exhibit gregarious behaviour such as running and shouting. Use an area rug or blanket to minimise a large, open space. A divider or screen can also be helpful to eliminate distractions or enclose an area.

The programmer should feel secure and be able to see and engage the entire audience. Stand with your back to a wall or in a space void of people to focus attention and minimise confusion. Avoid standing in front of a mirror or window; the reflections and shadows will be distracting. If your space isn't ideal, help the participants relax and focus by smiling and making eye contact as you read, sing, and rhyme.

The program area should be child-friendly and comfortable. To get a sense of the space, sit on the floor where the children will sit. Check sight lines from the children's view to make sure you will be visible and the focus of their attention. Eliminate distractions, such as pictures or a mural, from behind and on either side of the area where you will be presenting the program. If possible, arrange the seating before the program starts. Organise the group in a circle so children can see from every angle. This also helps cosy the program space with enclosed bodies. Use floor mats to designate each participant's program space. Carpet squares are inexpensive and are a good size for children to establish personal space. Many carpet stores will donate samples from discontinued colours or styles. If no carpet squares are available, simply set up the circle using shapes laid out on the floor or yarn arranged in a large circle. If you aren't sure how many participants will be attending, wait until everyone arrives and have them join hands to form the circle.

2. When?

2.1 Morning, Noon, and Night—When to Run Programs

Now that the program room is set up, when should the program run? To make this decision, consider factors such as

- the age of the children and typical naptime patterns,

- siblings and school dismissal times,

- working parents' schedules,

- opening hours for your school or library, and

- other activities scheduled in your neighbourhood.

In addition to these considerations, programs for children two years and under should take place in the morning because young children are more attentive early in the day and often nap in the afternoon. To accommodate working parents, these programs could also run on the weekends. Another factor will be time for program set-up and clean-up. The programmer will usually need half an hour to get things ready and at least fifteen minutes to clean up.

2.2 How Long Is Story Hour?: Length of Individual Programs

The term *story hour* is used frequently by libraries, but few libraries actually run programs for a full hour. The attention span of the children attending should determine the length of your program. For babies and toddlers, twenty minutes of structured programming is ideal. However, it may be difficult to encourage new parents to bundle up baby and come to the library for a mere twenty minutes. Therefore, organise a program with twenty minutes of structured activity and ten to twenty minutes of informal activity and social time. Two and three year olds will remain focused for slightly longer, allowing for thirty minutes of structured activity.

2.3 Seasons Change: Sessions and Semesters for Programming

Tailor the structure of your programming session to your facility and the community's needs. Programs will usually take place once a week for a number of weeks. Children need a few weeks to establish a routine. Once established, continue the program for a few weeks and then wrap up. Over the course of a year you could run a number of semestered programming sessions. Seasonal sessions are a popular format; people have their lives structured to change with the seasons and will adapt quickly to this routine.

The summer season may require a little more flexibility. Families often take holidays, as do library staff. Also, public libraries frequently run programs aimed at school-aged children in the summertime. One solution would be to offer drop-in preschool programs throughout the summer. The open attendance is more conducive to families' relaxed summer schedules, and it allows you to continue programming for preschoolers year round.

3. Who?

3.1 Programmers

Your personality and style will determine the way you run your programs. Key elements will be consistent from one programmer to the next, but the way you present the elements and make transitions will be completely individual. Take some time to develop your personal style: Think about your interests and personal preferences for music and interpersonal relationships. Are you quiet and calm? Work on developing a gentle style and approach. Are you outgoing or dramatic? Develop a style that is boisterous and energised. Never include activities, rhymes, songs, or books in your program that make you feel uncomfortable. Choose elements that complement and enhance your personal approach; you will feel more confident and connect with your audience.

Your body language is very important in a program. Meet children at their own level and greet them with welcoming facial expressions and a relaxed, open posture. A note of caution on this point, however: Physical contact with any child should be avoided. It may seem natural to hug or touch a child with a hand on the shoulder, but children in our society have been conditioned to fear the touch of a stranger, and by making contact you will likely make the child feel unnecessarily uncomfortable. To avoid any misunderstanding by the child or parent, simply eliminate physical contact.

With relaxed body language and a sense of personal style you will be ready to present your program. However, some aspects of programming may not come naturally to you. We are not all singers, actors, or puppeteers. Involve the audience in dramatic play, if you aren't a natural performer. Try using tapes or sing-along CDs if you tend to sing off key. Karaoke CDs are a worthwhile investment for less-accomplished singers. These will provide the tune of popular songs that you can use to accompany the original words (or adaptations such as those provided in the program plans in the chapters that follow). Children's karaoke CDs, such as the *B-flat the Cat* series, are available at large department and music stores. Another technique that even gifted singers should incorporate in programming is to encourage the group to sing along. Repeatedly remind participants to join in, and soon your voice will be only one among a chorus. If the tune of a song is unfamiliar to you, use it in your program as a rhyme instead, but be sure to include some musical activities during your program; music is a great unifying tool for varied groups of people.

3.2 Participants

Each program will have unique participants. What works for one group may fall a little flat with the next. However, to assist the group dynamic you need to engage the principle on which this book is based: child development. To feel comfortable and confident, children should be surrounded by their developmental peers and should enjoy program elements designed to enhance their growing skills. You may feel pressure to expand or broaden the age of attendees in your session because of time constraints or budgets, but giving in to these pressures will simply undermine the effectiveness of the program. The most beneficial programs have a narrow developmental range. A child that cannot hold a crayon cannot be expected to colour; a child that has learned to read will be bored with simple concept books. By using developmental principles as the guideline for the programs you offer, you are setting up an environment conducive to learning and fun!

The developmental milestones outlined in this book are established norms for children at the designated ages. Agencies such as the Invest in Kids Foundation and the National Network for Child Care were contacted and published materials reviewed to establish these guidelines. For a more detailed investigation of child development, consult some of the sources listed in the child development section of the suggested readings at the end of this book.

Although it is the most important factor, development is not the only consideration for your participants; you must also consider the family's culture, religious upbringing, and language. Language skills, customs, and interpersonal mannerisms vary markedly from culture to culture. Some participants will have customs that are unfamiliar to you. To be sensitive and include everyone in your programming style, use the census and other data on your community to become familiar with the make-up of cultures, religions, and languages in your area. Once you have an awareness, you should adapt and arrange programs to include something for everyone.

3.3 Preregistration Versus Open Attendance

Advance sign-up for any program will allow you to estimate the size of the crowd and the demand for the program. There are other advantages to preregistration as well. With a group of registered attendees you can

- Forecast the number of children/caregivers attending each week,

- Set up guidelines for expected behaviour,

- Establish a relationship with participants,

- Establish a structure and routine for each program,

- Learn what works and what doesn't for the group, and

- Limit the number of unexpected children or children outside the age range for the program.

A registered group works especially well for programs with young children based on developmental principles.

To commit to eight or ten weeks of a program, however, can be difficult for today's busy families. In addition, once the preregistered programs have begun, prospective participants are disappointed to learn they will not be able to attend until the next session. Drop-in programs, therefore, also have some advantages. With open attendance you can

- Encourage participation by newcomers;

- Create an informal, relaxed setting; and

- Welcome infrequent or occasional users.

Ideally, you will be able to arrange for some combination of both registered and drop-in programs to maximise the benefits for your community.

3.4 Sold Out! Maximum Attendance

Every program has an ideal number of participants based on factors such as personal style and available space. To maintain the quality of a program you will need to determine a maximum number of participants while considering factors such as the space devoted to the program, the age of the children attending, and your ability to captivate a large group of people. Some programmers have an entertainment-style delivery that thrives on a large group to respond to their antics. Other programmers have a participatory style; they enjoy engaging individual children and parents in stories, rhymes, and songs. A smaller group of people is more conducive to a participatory style. Keep in mind, however, that no programmer can independently control a *very* large group of children attending without adults. Parent volunteers are excellent assistants and can help if a child needs a bathroom break or becomes upset and wants to see the caregiver waiting outside the program.

The developmental level of the children is also important for the size of the program. For children two years and under there are two people in attendance for every child registered, so you will want to limit the number of attendees. The exception to this rule is the baby programs, often called lapsits (Ernst, 1995). Before children are walking on their own they are held by an adult, and therefore you can register a few more participants than you would for a toddler or two-year-old program, where the activity level is much greater.

Finally, let space be your guide. Keep in mind details that can eat up space, like strollers, winter coats, and boots. If your space holds thirty children comfortably sitting in a circle, then you should register no more than fifteen people in a program for two year olds (adult bodies are larger and each adult also has a child in tow). In this same room, you can register as many as thirty preschool children if your style allows and you have an assistant to help with crowd control.

If your programs do not have preregistration, a first-come, first-served rule for admittance into the program usually applies. If you are constantly reaching your maximum number of attendees, you should consider running an additional program. Alternately, if you often reach your maximum and have to turn disappointed patrons away, consider giving out advance tickets for popular programs and special events. Advance tickets allow you to estimate the crowd that will be in attendance, and patrons that have been turned away at the last minute from a popular program will feel better if they can pick up an advance ticket for another session.

3.5 No Room at the Inn: Waiting Lists

Once a registered program has reached its maximum number of participants, you will need a waiting list. Prospective participants can be moved off the waiting list and into the program as spots open up. Some program participants will call to drop out before the program starts; the first person on the waiting list is then contacted and admitted into the program. Encourage participants to call in advance if they cannot attend the program, so you can address those on the waiting list.

On the first day of a program series you should take attendance of all the participants in your program and contact the people who were registered but did not attend. This will serve as a reminder for participants and may also reveal that some people are unable to attend, allowing someone from the waiting list to gain a coveted program spot. If your programs consistently have long waiting lists, consider running a second, identical program right after the first. You could offer the exact same program for a new group of participants. A little extra effort will allow you to reach a much larger audience.

Programs with free advance tickets often fill, and you will need to turn interested patrons away, but on the day of the event some ticket holders will inevitably not come, leaving you with empty spaces. To minimise this problem you need a way to encourage people to drop by on the day of the program and wait to see if there is available space. Numbered waiting list tickets, given out an hour or so before the performance, are one way to fill the audience. A line-up of non-ticket holders allowed into the program, space permitting, is another option. Whichever method you choose, be sure to encourage patrons who are interested in the program but unable to secure tickets to drop by before the program begins. This will ensure your events are filled to capacity.

3.6 Fee Versus Free: Charging Participants for Admission

Should storytime be free? Some libraries offer a full range of programs and never charge participants. Other libraries and educational centres are run on a for-profit or self-sufficient basis and charge for attendance at any program. You will have to consider the mandate and funding of your institution to decide your position in this debate. You may be in a position to support the fact that children's programs are a core public library service and should be free. Alternately, some institutions endorse the concept that you get what you pay for and charging for programs inherently increases their value for participants. Where you and your facility fall in this debate will depend on many factors, such as your budget for programming, the ability community members have to pay for programs, and the value your administration places on children's programming.

If possible, run some free programs. Children's literature-based programming is an integral tool to assist families with emergent literacy and reading-readiness, and it should be available to everyone. If you offer the program free of charge, you are making it easier for low-income families to attend. Should *all* your programs be free? Not necessarily. Some libraries find it beneficial to charge for special programs such as crafts or professional entertainers. These programs usually draw a crowd and are good for publicising your centre's services. Appropriate fees should be low enough to encourage accessibility but high enough to cover expenses incurred. You may find that a small fee for special event programs will minimise the number of people who pick up tickets but do not attend the program.

What if your centre could not run programs without charging a fee? Then absolutely charge the fees necessary to allow the programs to run in your community. Consider soliciting service clubs or other organisations to sponsor children whose families cannot afford the fees. There are also more and more grant opportunities for centres providing educational programming for young children. Contact your local government representative for more information. Benefits to the institution of charging for programs (Sackowski, 2000) include

- Consistent attendance; ticket holders do not often miss programs they have paid for.

- Recognition of quality; participants feel they get what they pay for, and they will believe your program is more valuable if you charge for participation.

- Greater budget for supplies and extra materials if the fees you are charging go back into the programming budget.

Charging for programs is becoming more commonplace as budgets are stretched to keep up with new technologies. If your facility is forced to charge for programs, do your best to find ways to provide access to as many people in your community as possible.

3.7 To Run, or Not to Run: Program Cancellation

Occasionally you may have to cancel a program session because of circumstances beyond your control, such as lack of interest, bad weather, or illness. You will need guidelines in place for program cancellation so that your participants know what to expect and other staff know what to do in an emergency.

Set a minimum number for a preregistered program to run. You want to be sure all the wonderful programs you have planned will be enjoyed by a group of children. Choose a number below which you feel your program would be unsuccessful and use that as the minimum number of registrants you will accept in a program. Typically, minimum numbers are between six and ten. Choose a number low enough that it is attainable for the vast majority of your programs and high enough that having a regular attendance of that number would still be enjoyable. Check the registration list a few days before the series of programs is set to begin. If the number of participants registered at that point is below your minimum you should cancel the program. If you do have to cancel a preregistered program, give participants ample warning. Call them about forty-eight hours in advance and explain that the program has to be cancelled for lack of response.

If you decide to run a series of drop-in programs and you have advertised them, you should run the entire session, even if the response rate is low. Try to increase awareness of the program and increase attendance by using some of the free publicity and promotion opportunities available in your community, such as community bulletin boards in supermarkets or public service announcements on radio and television stations. Be creative in your advertising approach and you will have little trouble building enthusiasm for your program line-up.

Individual programs occasionally have to be cancelled due to poor weather, illness, or other unforeseen circumstances. Avoid cancelling programs by having a back-up plan in place. This is especially important for drop-in programs, because you cannot anticipate the number of participants or contact them in advance. For registered programs, cancellation is a little easier to control because you have contact names and telephone numbers for all participants. If bad weather is the issue, let participants choose whether or not to come to the program, unless your facility is closed, in which case you should contact each program participant individually. Always announce closures with the local media to give people ample warning.

If the programmer is ill and unable to run the program, have another staff member step in, or allow an assistant to run the group. Always be honest with participants and explain that the regular programmer is unavailable due to illness or emergency. If all else fails, reschedule the program, at the attendees' convenience, if possible.

4. What?

4.1 Set-Up and Programming Essentials

Every trade has tools, and library programming is no exception. Following is a list of things you will want to have on hand for your programs:

- Flannel or felt board and a magnetic board

- Display table for books and other materials available for loan

- Storyteller's chair or stool (high enough so all children can see the story, low enough to be friendly)

- Storyteller's table for books to read aloud in the program, as well as for other program materials (flannel stories, magnet rhymes, etc.)

- Easel or stand to display/read oversized books

- Craft or activity area (if your budget allows) with child-sized tables

Most of these items can be fashioned or borrowed from existing materials you likely have on hand. There is no need to go to great expense in setting up your programming space; children are not harsh critics. They won't notice if your craft tables don't match or if your flannel board is made from a piece of felt attached to cork board.

In each of the chapters that follows you will find eight sample programs. Each program includes two or three pages of reproducible rhymes and songs as well as instructions for a craft or storytime souvenir to make with your group. Crafts are a fun added element for programs but should only be included if your budget allows and need not be included every week. Instead of preparing and doing the craft with your group, copy your favourite storytime souvenir sheets and hand them out to participants with instructions to complete them at home with their own supplies.

If you do plan to use the storytime souvenirs included in this book, however, or to create others of your own design, you will need a standard set of craft, school, and office supplies on hand as you begin each programming session. The list that follows contains the supplies necessary to complete all the storytime souvenirs in this book. The materials can be found at your local school supply store, hardware store, or discount department store.

adhesive tape	masking tape
aluminium foil	paint brushes
bingo dabbers	painting sponges
black chalkboard paint	paper plates
brass fasteners	party blowers
brown paper lunch bags	photocopy paper
buttons	plastic cups
cardstock (64 lb. paper)	plastic lace
chalk	pom-poms (variety of colours)
confetti	Popsicle sticks
construction paper (variety of colours)	poster board (variety of colours)
cotton balls	sandpaper
cotton swabs	satin ribbon
crayons	sticky-backed clear plastic paper
drinking straws (bendable and straight)	string
elastics	thick fuzzy pipe cleaners (variety of colours)
feathers	thin foam sheets
felt (variety of colours)	tissue paper (variety of colours)
gift basket cellophane (variety of colours)	washable tempera paint (variety of colours)
glitter	white school glue
glitter glue	wiggle eyes
glue sticks	yarn
markers	

In addition to the supplies listed, a few speciality items will be needed. These can be found at the grocery store or may be donated by participants and staff: empty cassette cases (or small clear plastic cases), rice, cinnamon sticks, paper towels, paint sticks, bamboo sticks, cereal (e.g., fruit loops), newspaper, toilet paper rolls, paper towel rolls, and paint sticks (available free at your local hardware or paint store).

4.2 On a Scale from 1 to 10: Program Evaluation and Feedback

Feedback is one of those essential elements that can be forgotten in the excitement of setting up a program for the first time. Informal feedback can be solicited from program participants throughout the program, but a formal evaluation structure is also necessary. Evaluation forms should be given to participants in every program during one of the sessions close to the end of the series. Construct your feedback form to include specific questions related to your facility's mandate and include room for general comments. Figure 1.1 is a sample feedback form. Encourage informal feedback by talking to program participants before and after the program to find out what their favourite parts were. Chat with people and allow their opinions to evolve casually. Some of the most useful comments you will receive will be completely unsolicited!

Children's Services Program Evaluation Form

At the Cambridge Libraries we continually strive to improve our children's programs. Your input on the program your child recently attended will assist us with this process.

Program Attended : ☐ Baby & Me ☐ Fun with Ones ☐ Time for Twos ☐ Just Threes ☐ The Story Corner

Please circle the answer that best describes the experience you and your child had with this program:

What was your overall impression of this program? *poor fair satisfactory good excellent not applicable*

What is your opinion of the of books read aloud to your child in this program? *poor fair satisfactory good excellent not applicable*

What was your impression of the books displayed for children to take home? *poor fair satisfactory good excellent not applicable*

What was your impression of the other resources used in this program (flannel stories, props, videos, etc.) *poor fair satisfactory good excellent not applicable*

How would you rate the activities (rhymes, songs, games, crafts, etc.)? *poor fair satisfactory good excellent not applicable*

How would you rate the age-appropriateness of this program? *poor fair satisfactory good excellent not applicable*

Please circle yes or no for the following questions:

Did your child have a positive experience in this program? yes no
If no, why not? _____
_____

Did you take books or other library materials home for your child from this program? yes no
If no, why not? _____
_____

Would you register your child for another library program based on this experience? yes no
If no, why not? _____
_____

Do you feel the total number of children registered for this program was appropriate? yes no
If no, why not? _____
_____

Please add any additional comments:
_____
_____
_____
_____
_____
_____
_____
_____
_____

Figure 1.1. Sample Evaluation Sheet for Caregivers.

5. How (Do You Manage Your Group)?

5.1 Expectations for Children's Behaviour

What is reasonable to expect from a group of fifteen three year olds attending their first independent storytime? You can't expect to instil a code of conduct in children attending a program for the first time; however, you can have a list of expectations for caregivers to make the program run more smoothly. If your program is preregistered, you can provide this list at registration to welcome newcomers to the program (see figure 1.2). If you are running a drop-in program, you can share your expectations with participants in the first program and then reinforce them as situations arise. You can also have the list available for attendees to take with them for future programs.

You should create guidelines for any situation that is routinely problematic for your library or school. Whatever specific guidelines you choose to outline, ask parents to discuss them with children before the program. This is especially important for preschoolers who will be attending storytime on their own; children who come prepared for the situation are usually better able to adapt to the storytime environment.

5.2 Common Problems and How to Avoid Them

Common problems encountered in library programs are detailed below, but the best way to avoid problems is to have a clear set of guidelines and expectations, make people aware of these guidelines, and apply them consistently. Anticipating a situation and how you will handle it allows you to be prepared and confident if the situation arises.

5.2a Latecomers

People occasionally have valid reasons for being late for a program: car trouble, upset baby, missed train, etc. To minimise lateness without penalising the children by denying them access to the program, it is important to express your expectations for arrival to the caregivers before the program. Invite people to arrive ten or fifteen minutes before you begin the structured activities to socialise, get comfortable, and look through books. Express your expectation for early arrival on the handout you give to parents welcoming them to the program (see figure 1.2). If the program is run on a drop-in basis, be sure to explain to people in the first few weeks that interruptions are disruptive for everyone and ask them to please come early.

Occasionally you will have a chronic latecomer in your program. If one individual comes late virtually every week, speak to him or her personally and explain that although you are sympathetic to the fact that it can be difficult to keep up with life's busy schedule, that person's tardiness is disruptive to the program and unfair to the other participants. The individual may have a legitimate scheduling problem, and you may be able to sort out a solution (e.g., he or she could attend a drop-in family storytime later in the day or on the weekend).

5.2b Allergies and Food Restrictions

Today's health-conscious families are aware of their children's allergies and problems with food. To avoid an allergic reaction in your program, be extremely cautious when introducing food as a program element. Only introduce food in programs that are preregistered so you can advise parents in advance, or in programs with parents and caregivers present so they can make decisions on the suitability of the food for their children.

Welcome to the Library's Children's Programs

The goal of all library-run programs is to provide parents and children with an enjoyable library experience based on books and stories. Working together we can ensure that all participants reach this goal.

❏ Please be on time for the program. We want to be able to greet each child properly without disruption for other children once the program has begun.

❏ If participating in the program with your child, please make alternate arrangements for siblings. This is a special time for the adult and the child enrolled in the program.

❏ On days when your child is unable to manage in the program, please feel free to leave the room with your child, rejoining the group again when your child is ready.

❏ We ask you to remain in the Children's Department if your child is attending the program alone. Extra staff are not available to care for an upset child who wishes to leave the room, and in this case the staff member needs to be able to turn the child over to his or her parent or caregiver quickly and return to the program.

❏ If you are unable to attend any of the programs, please call to cancel before the start date of the session. This will allow us to call someone on the waiting list.

We hope that everyone will have a good time at the library. With your help we can develop and nurture your child's love of books and the library. If you have any questions don't hesitate to ask library staff before or after the program.

Child's Name: _____

Program: _____

Dates: _____

Time: _____

Library Location: _____

Library Telephone: _____

Figure 1.2. Expectations for Children Attending Registered Programs.

5.2c Siblings

In programs for babies, toddlers, and twos, where adults attend with the child, a grown-up may request to bring a sibling or friend along to the program. In such cases, encourage the participant to make alternate arrangements for the other child. It may be possible if a number of people attending the program are in a similar situation to arrange to have alternating child care arrangements. The presence of children outside the developmental guidelines can be disruptive and cause the children the program was designed for to be uncomfortable.

5.2d Twins

Parents of twins may want to bring both children to the same program. Suggest to such parents that they bring along an extra person to share the one-on-one experiences that are an integral part of the program. Do not discourage a parent of twins, however, from attending the program if he or she does not have another adult to attend with. The added stresses related to multiple births often leave parents with little time to share stories, songs, and rhymes with their children in a fun, relaxed setting. Even if the program is not ideal for the adult and child, it will provide them with some exposure to rhymes and songs and will give the adult a chance to meet and socialise with parents of children the same age.

5.2e Disruptive Behaviour

Even the most seasoned and energetic programmers find it difficult to conduct a program over a crying baby or a child who demands a monopoly on their attention. Disruptive behaviour is occasionally unavoidable, and you should map out a plan of what you will do when problems arise, so you can be prepared. If a problem occurs in a program where adult and child attend together, gently ask the adult to address the disruption. It may mean he or she has to leave the room for a few minutes with the child; assure the parent that it happens to everyone and they both can come back as soon as the child has calmed down.

If the disruption is caused by a child attending the program independently, assess the severity of the disruption. If the child is bothering the other children or touching them physically, the problem should be addressed. Try techniques such as individual attention or distractions (i.e., a game or toy the disruptive child can manipulate near you while the rest of the children move on with the program's elements). You shouldn't hesitate if you feel it is appropriate to seek out the parent to take over the child's discipline.

5.2f Age or Developmental Discrepancies

It is impossible to ensure that all the children in your program are at the same developmental level. To minimise major discrepancies you may decide to have strict age guidelines. It would be more appropriate to have developmental guidelines (Marino and Houlihan, 1992), but this relies on the objective judgement of parents. Therefore, most libraries opt to have age guidelines. Some libraries require children to be a certain age before the start date of the program. Other libraries require that children be the appropriate age before the programming session ends. Whichever formula you choose, be prepared to stick by it consistently.

Children who have developmental disorders may be better suited to a program with children of a younger age. In these cases, consider allowing exceptions to an age registration rule. Children should be in an environment where it is comfortable to learn and grow, and fostering this by allowing children to attend a program with younger children should not be problematic for the group.

6. Flexibility and a Smile

It is impossible to plan for every eventuality, and no matter how well organised you are, there will be unexpected and unplanned events. Embrace these with a smile! The unplanned excitements and disturbances can often turn into an opportunity to break the ice with a new group. A positive attitude and encouraging atmosphere are two of the most important ingredients of any successful storytime!

Chapter 2
Beginning with Babies

They are the smallest, least judgmental group of children, and yet they are the most intimidating: babies. Infants do not read, sing, or play games. They cannot choose their own library books, and they may not even see the programmer sitting on the far side of the room very well. They do not walk on their own, and they can occasionally be a little disruptive to a library program. And yet programs for children at this age are in great demand in the libraries that offer them. In addition, baby programs, often called lapsits (Ernst, 1995), are among the most valuable a library can offer. Parents and caregivers of children under a year old are often looking for ways to stimulate their children in a situation that is stress free. The library not only offers a fun and friendly introduction to early childhood development, it also gives parents and caregivers the tools to re-create those developmental incentives at home. The media have been flooding the public arena with messages telling us that the earlier we start to develop a child's intellectual potential, the better the chance that child has at success later in life. But parents do not always know how to enhance their child's cognitive growth. Library programs are one answer; adults learn about books, songs, rhymes, games, and activities that their child enjoys and that are developmentally appropriate.

1. What Can Babies Do?: Child Development at Six to Eleven Months

According to child development theory, babies from six to eleven months of age are at a stage called late infancy (Allen and Marotz, 2000). Apart from the basics of survival that children at this stage need (protection from physical danger, nutrition, health care, and adults to bond with), infants also need stimulation: things to look at, touch, hear, smell, and taste; opportunities to explore the world; and appropriate language development. Literature-based programming will provide parents and caregivers with practical ways to give their children the tools they need to enhance development. Developmental markers for eight month olds include

- sitting up independently;

- transferring an object from one hand to the other;

- drooling and chewing on objects;

- recognising familiar voices and sounds;

- a heightened sense of awareness;

- looking for hidden objects;

- touching, shaking, and dropping;

- imitating sounds and actions; and

- enjoying the sensations of being tickled and touched.

Knowing these markers will allow you to achieve successful programs. Stimulate babies and amuse parents with rhythmic language and sensory stimuli. Try not to prepare souvenirs for babies made of paper that will dissolve when popped into the mouth. Instead, introduce games like peek-a-boo with props for adults to hold, and use interactive rhymes allowing caregivers to tickle and nuzzle. Try a variety of sound stimuli: read stories aloud, introduce rhymes, use music and instruments parents can re-create at home, and sing simple, memorable songs. This approach to baby programs goes beyond the traditional "lapsit" (Ernst, 1995). These programs do not consist of adults holding babies on their laps for extended periods of time. This fun and interactive style has adults standing and marching while holding and swooping babies, playing games on the floor, and taking part in group activities.

The babies in your group will be growing and developing at different rates. Some will have achieved the benchmarks listed above and gone on to the next stage of development; others may have months to go before sitting up independently. It is important to keep in mind that these stages are only a guideline for the type of activities to include in your program. While talking to the adults and caregivers in the group, be aware that they are sensitive to their children's development in comparison to other children at the same age and avoid the use of phrases like "by now your child should be . . ." Instead, talk about *why* the program's ingredients are being introduced so that, as an example, parents can see that while they are singing a lullaby, they are also stimulating sense development and encouraging speech.

To keep the babies amused, the program should be fast paced and energetic. To keep the adults amused, the program should be fun, and the leader should model activities and keep the mood and pace light. For this age group, the program is designed as much for the adults as it is for the children. Adults learn, experience, practice, and enjoy positive, nurturing time with their children. Try a variety of activities and use trial and error to get a sense of what works for your group. Repeat favourites and discard ideas that fall a little flat.

The children's physical development determines the basic set-up of any baby program. Ideally the group will consist of approximately ten adults, with one child each, in a circle. The leader will sit at one end of the group with a doll or stuffed animal. Use a doll that has moveable arms and legs to demonstrate the actions, rhymes, and songs the group will do together. This set-up allows everyone to see the group leader but still focus on the child in front of them. The circle can, and in fact should, be broken many times to allow adults and children to stand and move for activities. To encourage the adults to view the circle as the place to play, listen, and sing, the end of the program should bring the group together in a different space for the social time. This space should have library resources available to participants that will help them with their current focus; parenting books, board books, and music are the sorts of things you might choose to display and make available for loan.

2. Baby Programming Guidelines

2.1 Ways to Introduce Baby Programming

If your library currently offers a program for one year olds, then this program for even younger children is a natural step. The program ideally will require preregistration, allowing the programmer some control over the number of people in the space. It will run, on a weekly basis, for several sessions in a row.

If your library or children's centre does *not* offer a program for one year olds, you can still use the unique opportunities a baby program provides. You could run a special "one time only" program once a year and invite new parents and their babies. Or you could invite a group already established with another organisation (e.g., a Moms and Tots Playgroup) in for an introduction to the library. Their introduction could include a program like one of the samples included in this chapter and a tour highlighting the resources pertinent to their needs.

If the current trend for early learning development continues, programming for babies will one day be as established in libraries as preschool storytime is today. After all, what better way to encourage lifelong learning than to begin with the user group that is, quite literally, at the start of their lives?

2.2 Getting Ready

Before you begin, there are some things you need to do to get ready for your group's first meeting. Keep in mind that many of the program's participants will be new parents, and these folks will relish the opportunity for informal chatting and gathering with other parents and caregivers.

2.2a Selecting Books to Share

Choosing the best books is one of the key ingredients for a successful program. Books for children at this age should *sound* appealing. Books that rhyme or have a defined beat will stimulate language development and appeal to babies. Using big books (oversized versions of most classic books are available from publishers) is a great way to involve the group—adults will often read along when they can see the text. The most appropriate books will work well when read aloud to a group. Adults appreciate books that are well written, and the babies will love the sound and cadence of the language. Use one or two books per program, interspersed with more physical activities. A bibliography of books to share with babies appears at the end of this chapter.

2.2b Selecting Books to Display

Display books that will appeal to adults and babies. Books on parenting and baby issues, such as sleeping through the night, or homemade baby food, have great appeal to the parents in the group. Board books will be the most popular to take home and share with baby because they are small, sturdy, and easily manipulated by baby's little hands. Choose board books with one picture and word per page to promote object recognition. Illustrations with thick black borders or black and white pictures are good choices for visual development because babies can distinguish the pictures more easily. Other media, such as magazines, music CDs, or parenting videos, will also be very popular if you have them available for loan.

3. Baby Programs: Format and Routine

To help you run a successful baby program, what follows are a series of tried-and-true examples of successful routines used with babies in library programming. But the most important tip for any programmer about to embark on an adventure with a group of babies is to keep an open mind. Work with your group and get a sense of what they like and enjoy, then use these experiences to mould future programs.

3.1 Program Outline

Find a routine that feels comfortable for you and your group and stick with it each week. Demonstrate actions for rhymes and songs by using a stuffed animal or doll. Make sure to vary the sitting and standing activities, especially if adults are sitting on the floor. Each session should run for approximately half an hour, with twenty minutes of structured activity (rhymes, songs, and stories) and ten minutes of less formalised activities, giving adults a chance to socialise and interact with other caregivers.

3.2 Opening Routine

Establish a routine you can use every week to signal the beginning of the program. There are many, many choices for wonderful greeting songs. Here is one you might like to try:

Welcome, Welcome

(Tune: Twinkle, Twinkle, Little Star)
> Welcome, Welcome everyone,
> Now you're here let's have some fun.
> First we'll clap our hands just so,

(Clap baby's hands.)
> Then we'll bend and touch our toes.

(Touch baby's toes.)
> Welcome, Welcome everyone,
> Now you're here let's have some fun.

EXPERT ADVICE
Use the same welcome song each week to begin your program. It is a great way to establish a routine for your group.

3.3 Program Ingredients

Each week you will have planned ingredients for your program. Sometimes that plan will change depending on the mood of the group. Don't feel you have to stick to the script; add new rhymes and songs, or leave some out. Adults will appreciate having program sheets to use with babies when they return home (see samples at the end of this chapter), and they may even feel adventurous and try ones you didn't demonstrate during the program. Keep a copy of each handout for yourself so you can make a note of favourites to repeat in the weeks that follow.

3.4 Quiet Time

Gentle, quiet time is essential for the development of a bond between baby and caregiver. Participants should be encouraged to share kisses and affection with their baby. Studies have proven that babies need genuine expressions of love and affection (Ernst, 2001). This need is as fundamental as the need for food and shelter; babies learn how to deal with the world at large by, at first, dealing with the parents and caregivers that love them. Adults should be encouraged to express their affection for their baby in ways that are comfortable for them. In different cultures this expression will manifest itself in different ways. Regardless of the form of expression, it is useful to remind caregivers that even though they are busy with diapers, feedings, sleepless nights, and laundry, it is very important to take time to cuddle, kiss, and love their baby.

3.5 Closing Routine

End the program the same way you began, with a routine activity. Here is another song that is catchy and easy for participants to remember from week to week:

It's Time to Say Goodbye

(Tune. She'll Be Coming 'Round the Mountain)
Oh, it's time to say goodbye to our friends,
Oh, it's time to say goodbye to our friends.
Oh, it's time to say goodbye,
Make a smile and wink an eye . . .
It's time to say goodbye to our friends.

4. Baby Programming Techniques and Activities

Certain elements belong in every baby program. Some activities can be adapted for use with babies; songs, dances, and rhymes used with older children can be manipulated and reworked for use with babies. For example, the *Hokey Pokey* is a dance many people are familiar with; it involves standing in a circle and gesturing towards the centre of the circle with parts of your body as they are named in the song. This song can be done with babies by having the adults hold their babies around the waist in front of them and gently hold out the named body part on the baby, while gesturing towards the centre of the circle.

4.1 Bouncing

Babies love to bounce—you should incorporate bounces into each program to liven the mood. Repeat favourites from week to week during a bouncing medley. To bounce with their babies, adults can sit with their legs extended in front of them and the baby facing them, or they can sit in a chair with the baby on their lap—whichever feels more comfortable. Do a number of bouncing rhymes in a row; it will allow the group to get into a groove and the rhymes are usually so short you can complete two or three of them in a minute.

4.2 Tickle Rhymes

Sensory stimulation is very important for babies. These rhymes, which focus on touching the baby, also make a wonderful bonding experience between baby and caregiver. The best position for tickle rhymes is to have the baby lying on the floor in front of the adult. However, some babies may prefer sitting to lying down, and caregivers should be encouraged to do what feels natural for them. Tickle rhymes are popular and easy to follow because the actions are usually obvious from the words in the rhyme.

BRIGHT IDEA

Have a set of receiving blankets on hand for participants to use for tickle rhymes with baby on the floor. Blankets are quite inexpensive and are available at many discount and department stores. Contact a local business—they may even be willing to donate a class set!

4.3 Action Rhymes and Songs

Babies love to be swung, rocked, and gently thrown in the air. All songs used in baby programs can be done with some sort of action. Adults can hold their babies on their laps and rock or clap the baby's hands together in rhythm. Intersperse action rhymes throughout your program to allow caregivers and babies a chance to change positions and move around. This will help you keep the group's focus and attention.

Music and singing are integral parts of all book-based programs, from babies to school-aged children. But for babies the sound of their parent or caregiver's voice in song will be pleasing regardless of the ability of the adult to carry a tune, so encourage adults to join in on every song, rhyme, and lullaby.

EXPERT ADVICE

Stand-up action rhymes are popular with the babies, but don't do too many in a row because they are a workout for the adults!

4.4 Special Activities and Storytime Souvenirs

Target baby's physical, emotional, and educational development with activities that will be fun for both baby and caregiver. Include sensory and gross motor activities that will stimulate and be enjoyable for the baby. Have the adults take an active role in the preparation of the activity; this will help them learn about things they can repeat and modify for the baby at home. Set up paint in trays for caregivers to dip the baby's feet in, or have a stick puppet put together with all but the cotton balls or feathers left to glue on. By allowing adults to take an active role in part of the preparation, it will give some of the more insecure participants the confidence to try things at home. The process will also allow caregivers time to chat with the person next to them.

4.5 Music and Noise

Babies love to listen and make noise. Rattles, bells, and musical mobiles are very popular with this age group. One of the sample programs included in this chapter focuses exclusively on music, noise, and movement, but rhythm and music are elements of every baby program. Explain to caregivers that the music is a way to stimulate the left side of the baby's brain and thereby encourage creativity and open expression. If possible hand out bells (at Christmastime jingle bells are available from craft and department stores; after Christmas these items will go on sale at greatly reduced rates), shakers, and musical instruments for babies to hold, shake, and listen to.

4.6 Repetition

The program plans included in this manual have new rhymes and songs detailed for each week. However, an important element of any program for young children is repetition. Be sure to repeat favourite songs and rhymes from week to week. Gauge the mood and participation level of your group. Pull out a favourite action rhyme to elevate the activity level of a sluggish group, or repeat a favourite lullaby to soothe or calm participants in a session that has gotten a little unfocused. Repetition is good for young children, and it also helps the adults memorise the words of the rhymes and songs. If caregivers know the rhymes well, they will be more likely to repeat them at home.

CONFIDENCE BOOSTER

The groundwork for familiarity begins with a solid foundation. Use rhymes, songs, and books that you are comfortable with. Also, use some you think the group may be familiar with. Nursery rhymes, for example, are an excellent choice because they will be familiar to people from many cultures. Using familiar resources will make you more confident as a programmer and the audience more comfortable as a group.

4.7 Circle Games and Rhymes

Some of the rhymes introduced in this section work quite well as circle games. Begin the rhyme by having participants move in a circle, follow-the-leader style. Actions can be done by stopping the group and facing into the centre of the circle. Repeat circle rhymes at least twice, depending on the reception you get from participants. Explain that these rhymes can be done while standing in place, but it is fun to take advantage of having a group together by adding the circle time. Many of the program plans that follow in this and subsequent chapters include rhymes and songs that can be adapted to a circle if your group has fun with the format.

4.8 Reading Aloud

Some programmers find reading aloud difficult with a group of babies and caregivers. Encourage adults to read along to their babies, especially with books that include rhyme or repetition. Babies will respond very favourably to the sound of a familiar voice. Sometimes the books suitable for sharing with babies are available in a format too small to use with a large group; this is especially true of board books, which are often specifically designed to fit into small hands. You can solve this dilemma in a number of ways:

- If your budget allows, purchase class sets of favourite baby books and give them out to participants to read aloud together.

- Purchase "big books"—oversized softcover books specifically designed for sharing with a large group. Oversized editions are available from the publishers of the original classic. If you have a favourite read-aloud story, check the publication information. Contact the publisher to see if an oversized version of your favourite book is available for purchase.

- Make your own oversized books. Some baby favourites are not available in large-sized format, but publishers will often grant permission for the development of homemade large-sized books to groups such as libraries or schools. To create the large-sized version you could scan the images on a digital scanner and enlarge them to the largest printable size (usually on 11-by-17-inch paper). Or use your photocopier to enlarge the image. If that type of equipment is not available, contact your local printer or business supply store. They may have a scanner, computer, and printer available for this type of job. Alternately, enlist the help of a talented artistic co-worker, or photocopy the images onto an overhead transparency and trace them onto poster-sized pages.

Program 1

Baby and Me: Baby Favourites

The first program we'll start with is "Baby Favourites." Not every program you'll do needs to have a specific theme name. Sometimes having a more general theme enables programmers to have more flexibility in their programming. "Baby Favourites"—just by using this title, or one similar to it, you can use any song or rhyme that you feel comfortable with.

Books to Share

More, More, More Said the Baby, by Vera Williams

Read to Your Bunny, by Rosemary Wells

I Touch, by Rachel Isadora

More books to share with babies can be found in the bibliography at the end of this chapter.

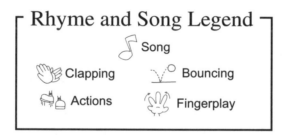

Baby and Me: Baby Favourites

Rhymes and Songs

Little Cat

 (Suit actions to words.)
> Creeping, creeping, creeping,
> Comes the little cat.
> Meow, meow, meow, meow
> Just like that!

(With baby lying in front of you, begin at his or her toes and creep fingertips up baby's legs. Tap fingertips on baby's tummy as you say "meow.")
> Creeping, creeping, creeping
> Comes the little bunny.
> Hop, hop, hop, hop
> Do you think that's funny?

(Continue creeping fingertips up baby's tummy. Tap fingertips on baby's neck and under baby's ears as you say "hop.")

Diddle, Diddle, Dumpling

 (Sing along and follow the actions below.)
> Diddle diddle dumpling my son John
> Went to bed with his trousers on
> One shoe off, one shoe on,
> Diddle diddle dumpling my son John!

(Bounce baby on your knees, and hold up baby's feet alternately as you say "one shoe off" and "one shoe on.")

Little Mouse

 (With baby seated in your lap, creep fingers up baby's back. Tickle baby's neck as you say, "there oh there.")
> See the little mouse
> Creeping up the stair
> Looking for a warm place
> There oh there.

Tick Tock

 (Stand and follow the actions below.)
> Tick tock, tick tock, I'm a little cuckoo clock.
> Tick tock, tick tock, now it's almost one o'clock.

(Hold baby under his or her arms and swing back and forth gently in front of you.)
> Cuckoo!

(Swoop baby up in front of you as the cuckoo chimes.)
> Tick tock, tick tock, I'm a little cuckoo clock.
> Tick tock, tick tock, now it's almost two o'clock.

(Hold baby under his or her arms and swing back and forth gently in front of you.)
> Cuckoo! Cuckoo!

(Swoop baby up in front of you twice as the cuckoo chimes.)
> Tick tock, tick tock, I'm a little cuckoo clock.
> Tick tock, tick tock, now it's almost three o'clock.

(Hold baby under his or her arms and swing back and forth gently in front of you.)
> Cuckoo! Cuckoo! Cuckoo!

(Swoop baby up in front of you three times as the cuckoo chimes.)

21

Jack in the Box

(Start this rhyme standing and follow the actions below.)

> Jack in the box,
> Jack in the box,
> I crouch so very low.
> Turn the handle,
> Round and round,
> And up and up I go.

(Hold baby under his or her arms near the floor and slowly rise.)

> Jack in the box,
> Jack in the box,
> Turn the handle,
> And up I pop!

(Swoop baby up in the air as the jack –in –the box pops.)

One Little Baby

(Follow along with the actions below.)
> One little baby rocking in a tree

(Rock baby back and forth in your lap.)
> Two little babies splashing in the sea

("Splash" baby's hands in front of you.)
> Three little babies crawling on the
> floor

(Make crawling motion with baby's hands.)
> Four little babies knocking on the door

(Make knocking motion with baby's fist.)
> Five little babies playing hide and seek

(Cover baby's eyes gently with your hands.)
> Keep your eyes closed tightly now
> Until I say . . . Peek!

(Sweep hands away as you say "peek.")

When You're One

(Suit actions to words.)

> Oh, when you're one, one, one,
> Tap on your thumb, thumb, thumb.
> Oh, when you're two, two, two,
> Tap on your shoe, shoe, shoe.
> Oh, when you're three, three, three,
> Tap on your knee, knee, knee,
> Oh, when you're four, four, four,
> Tap on the floor, floor, floor.
> Oh when you're five, five, five,
> You do the jive, jive, jive!

(With baby lying in front of you, tap on each part as it is mentioned in the rhyme. "Dance" baby's legs back and forth as you say "jive.")

The Grand Old Duke of York

(Adults march in time and hold babies up or down as appropriate.)

> The grand old Duke of York,
> He had ten thousand men
> He marched them up to the top of the
> hill
> And then marched them down again
> And when they're up, they're up
> And when they're down, they're down
> But when they were only half way up
> They were neither up nor down!

Storytime Souvenir

For the first week, a storytime souvenir is not really necessary because you will spend the informal time at the end of the program with an icebreaker exercise. After approximately twenty minutes of structured bouncing, singing, and reading, have the adults introduce themselves and their babies. After introductions are finished, allow time for caregivers to chat amongst themselves and look at the resources laid out for them. Have age-appropriate toys on the floor for babies (toys can be donated by staff whose children have grown beyond the baby stage, or you could solicit donations from local businesses). The programmer should spend this time circulating throughout the room, chatting with individuals and answering questions. This free time will allow everyone to get to know one another. Friendly and familiar participants will be more relaxed and more likely to enjoy and benefit from the experience the program offers.

If you would like participants to have something to take home from their first week in the program, you could try writing to the publisher of your favourite book to share with babies and ask for a donation of bookmarks, posters, or other freebies they might have available. Let the publisher know you will pass out the freebies to parents and caregivers in your program, along with the suggestion that they buy the book you have recommended. We have never had a publisher turn down a request for this type of donation.

Program 2

Baby and Me: Bees and Butterflies

Babies are naturally attracted to things with wings. Anything that flutters or flies within eyesight of your little one is sure to grab the baby's attention. That's what makes bees and butterflies such a great theme to do with this age group. The storytime souvenir for this program, Peekaboo Bee, is a great resource to use while singing. The pop-up motion of the bee will help to keep the baby's attention right where you want it, on the caregiver.

Plan Ahead Note

One way to extend your songs and fingerplays is by having different props to accompany them. In all of our chapters there are detailed illustrations to match with the songs we have chosen. Any of these can be photocopied, coloured, and used in your program. One idea for this particular program would be to photocopy, colour, and stick the caterpillar to your thumb (using masking tape) to be used as a focal point while singing.

Books to Share

Bumble Bee, by Margaret Wise Brown

Buzz, Buzz, Buzz, Went Bumblebee, by Colin West

Who Am I?, by Alain Crozon

More books to share with babies can be found in the bibliography at the end of this chapter.

Baby and Me: Bees and Butterflies

Rhymes and Songs

Bumble Bee

(Start this rhyme standing and follow the actions below.)

> Bumble Bee, Bumble Bee,
> Flying through the air.

(Swing baby up high.)

> Bumble Bee, Bumble Bee,
> Landing in my hair.

(Swing baby down and kiss hair.)

> Bumble Bee, Bumble Bee,
> What should I do?

(Swing baby up high.)

> Bumble Bee, Bumble Bee,
> BUZZ BUZZ BOO!

(Swing baby down and hug close to chest.)

Flutter, Flutter Butterfly

(Tune: Twinkle, Twinkle, Little Star)

> Flutter, flutter butterfly,
> Floating in the summer sky.
> Floating by for all to see,
> Floating by so merrily.
> Flutter, flutter butterfly,
> Floating in the summer sky.

(Have baby sit in adult's lap and rock gently back and forth.)

Can You Move with Me?

(Tune: Do Your Ears Hang Low?)
(Bounce baby up and down gently and end with a hug.)

> Can you wiggle like a worm?
> Can you squiggle? Can you squirm?
> Can you flutter? Can you fly like a
>   gentle butterfly?
> Can you crawl upon the ground?
> Like a beetle that is round?
> Can you move with me?
> Can you flip? Can you flop?
> Can you give a little hop?
> Can you slither like a snake?
> Can you give a little shake?
> Can you dance like a bee?
> Who is buzzing 'round a tree?
> Can you move with me?

Fuzzy Bumblebee

(Bounce baby up and down and gently tap appropriate body parts.)

> Fuzzy, fuzzy, fuzzy bumble-bee,
>   bumble-bee, bumble-bee
> Fuzzy, fuzzy, fuzzy bumble-bee,
>   bumble-bee . . .
> Landing on my toes
>
> Fuzzy, fuzzy, fuzzy bumble-bee,
>   bumble-bee, bumble-bee
> Fuzzy, fuzzy, fuzzy bumble-bee,
>   bumble-bee . . .
> Landing on my nose

Additional verses:

> Landing on my tum . . . bum
> Landing on my ear . . . hair

Bumble Bee, Bumble Bee

(Tune: Jingle Bells)
(Have bee prop or fingers fly through the air and touch baby as appropriate.)

Bumble Bee, Bumble Bee,
Buzzing all around,
Bumble Bee, Bumble Bee,
Buzzing on the ground.
Bumble Bee, Bumble Bee,
Buzzing up so high,
Bumble Bee, Bumble Bee,
Buzzing in the sky.
Bumble Bee, Bumble Bee,
Buzzing past your toes,
Bumble Bee, Bumble Bee,
Buzzing on your nose.
Bumble Bee, Bumble Bee,
Buzzing on your chest,
Bumble Bee, Bumble Bee,
Stopping for a rest.

A Bee Is on My Toe

(Tune: Farmer in the Dell)
(With baby sitting or lying in front of you, blow gently on each body part as it is mentioned throughout the song.)

A bee is on my toe,
A bee is on my toe,
Heigh-ho just watch me blow,
A bee is on my toe.

Additional verses:
On my nose
On my head
On my ear

Insect Song

(Tune: Wheels on the Bus)
(Follow along with the actions below.)

The firefly at night goes blink, blink,
blink.
Blink, blink, blink. Blink, blink, blink.
The firefly at night goes blink, blink,
blink.
All through the town.

(Tap baby's face on "blink.")

Additional verses:
Bees in the flowers go buzz buzz buzz

(Tickle baby's arms on "buzz.")
Ants in the grass go march march
march

(Move baby's legs or feet on "march.")
Crickets In the leaves go chirp chirp
chirp

(Tickle baby's stomach on "chirp.")

Caterpillar Chant

(Suit actions to words.)
A caterpillar looks so small.

(Hold up caterpillar.)
It's hardly even there at all.
It munches on green leafy treats.
And it gets bigger as it eats.
It eats and eats 'til pretty soon.
It wraps up tight in a cocoon.

(Wrap arms around baby.)
When it wakes up it blinks its eyes,
And says, "Now I'm a butterfly!"

(Hold up butterfly.)

Fuzzytail Bee

Instructions to make tiny fuzzy bees that can be used as props and to tickle babies during songs.

Materials

1½ black, 10-inch or 25 cm fuzzy pipe cleaners per person

1 yellow, 10-inch or 25cm fuzzy pipe cleaner per person

4 inches or 10 cm of (¼ inch) black satin ribbon per person

Pencils

Instructions

1. Twist the two full pipe cleaners together. Wrap them around a pencil to create the body of the bee. Slide it off the pencil.

2. Take the remaining half of the second black pipe cleaner, fold it in half, and twist the ends to look like antennae. Put the antennae through the same hole in the body the pencil was in and bend the antennae to keep the body in place.

3. Attach the satin "tail" by lacing one end of the ribbon through the bottom end of the antennae and glue that short end to the longer end to form a small loop.

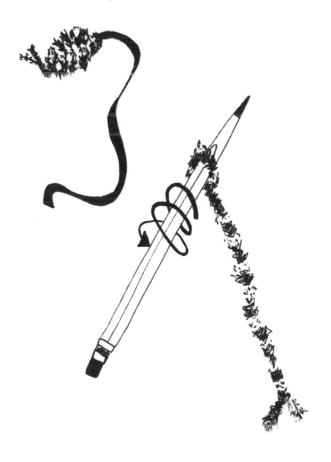

Peekaboo Bee

Instructions to make pop-up bees used to play peek-a-boo with babies.

Materials

1 photocopied bee (see below for image to copy) per person

1 Popsicle stick per person

1 plastic yellow beverage cup per person

Masking tape

Instructions

1. Photocopy the bee on white or yellow paper.

2. Back it onto cardstock or construction paper to make the bee more sturdy.

3. Tape a Popsicle stick onto the back of the bee using masking tape.

4. Take the yellow plastic cup and cut a triangular shaped hole in the bottom of the cup to allow the Popsicle stick to move the bee up and down inside.

Program 3
Baby and Me: Shake, Rattle, and Roll

This theme incorporates plenty of clapping, movin', and groovin' for everyone. Although some songs will be seen as familiar favourites, some will not. Those that are new are sure to become favourites, with practice, in no time! That's why it is important to include the new and the old in each program you do. Caregivers and babies alike are sure to have a rockin' good time in this session.

Plan Ahead Note

The craft for this program requires the programmer to complete all of the steps ahead of time. One added extra is using glitter in the tape cassette with the rice. The glitter catches and reflects light, and that is sure to attract babies' attention.

Books to Share

Black on White, by Tana Hoban

Clap Hands, by Helen Oxenbury

Pots and Pans, by Patricia Hubbell

More books to share with babies can be found in the bibliography at the end of this chapter.

Baby and Me: Shake, Rattle, and Roll

Rhymes and Songs

Good Morning Toes

(Lay baby in front of you and touch each of baby's body parts as you sing along.)

Good morning toes,
Good morning toes,
And how are you today?
I trust you had a good nights sleep,
And now you're ready to play.

Additional verses:

Good morning knees
Good morning tummy
Good morning hands
Good morning cheeks

If You're Happy and You Know It

(Sing along and do the actions using baby's body parts.)

If you're happy and you know it clap your hands,

(Clap, clap.)

If you're happy and you know it clap your hands,

(Clap, clap.)

If you're happy and you know it, and you really want to show it,
If you're happy and you know it clap you're hands.

(Clap, clap.)

Additional verses:

Stamp your feet
Shout hooray
Do all three

Let's Tap

(Tune: The More We Get Together)
(Suit actions to words.)

Lets tap our feet together, together, together.

(Gently tap baby's feet.)

Let's tap our feet together because it's fun to do.

Additional verses:

Clap our hands
Touch our nose
Blink our eyes

Clap Your Hands

(Suit actions to words.)

Clap your hands, one, two, three,

(Clap with baby.)

Play a clapping game with me.
Now your hands have gone away,

(Hide your hands behind your back.)

Bring them back so we can play.
Tap your hands, one, two, three,

(Tap your hands on your thighs.)

Play a tapping game with me.
Now your hands have gone away,

(Hide your hands behind your back.)

Bring them back so we can play.
Wiggle your fingers, one, two, three,

(Wiggle your fingers with baby.)

Play a wiggling game with me.
Now your fingers have gone away,

(Hide your fingers behind your back.)

We'll play this game another day.

We're Going to Kentucky

(This is a great song for getting up and moving with baby. Start off standing and do as the actions indicate.)

We're going to Kentucky,

(March in a circle holding baby in your arms.)

We're going to the fair,
To see the señoritas
With roses in their hair.
So shake it baby, shake it,

(Gently shake with baby.)

Shake it all you can.
Shake it like a milkshake,
Shake it in a can.

Rumba to the bottom,

(Slowly crouch to the floor.)

Rumba to the top.

(Slowly stand back up.)

Turn around and turn around,
Until we holler STOP.

Did You Ever See a Baby

(Tune: Did You Ever See a Lassie)
(Suit actions to words.)

Did you ever see a baby, a baby, a
    baby?
Did you ever see a baby go this way
    and that?

(Holding baby on your lap, gently sway from side to side.)

Go this way and that way, and this way
    and that way.
Did you ever see a baby go this way
    and that?

Did you ever see a baby, a baby, a
    baby?
Did you ever see a baby bounce this
    way and that?

(Holding baby, gently bounce up and down.)

Bounce this way and that way, and this
    way and that way.
Did you ever see a baby bounce this
    way and that?

I Can Make My Baby Smile

(Tune: The Muffin Man)
(Lay baby on the floor in front of you while singing.)

I can make my baby smile,
My baby smile, my baby smile.
I can make my baby smile,
When I tickle his [or her] toes.

(Tickle baby's toes.)

I can make my baby laugh,
My baby laugh, my baby laugh.
I can make my baby laugh,
When I tickle his [or her] nose.

(Tickle baby's nose.)

Additional verses:
    Tickle his or her tummy
    Tickle his or her feet

Clap, Clap, Clap

(Tune: Row, Row, Row Your Boat)
(Suit actions to words.)

Clap, clap, clap your hands,
Clap them high and low.

(Clap hands above your head and close to the floor.)

Clap them all around the room,

(Clap your hands in a circular motion.)

Whichever way you go.

Clap, clap, clap your hands,
Clap them left and right.
Clap them all around the room,
Clap them out of sight.

(Hide hands behind your back.)

Shake-a-Shaker

Make rattle-type shakers ideal for babies to hold and shake along with songs and music.

Materials

1 empty tape cassette case per person

1-2 tablespoons of rice per cassette case

Gift basket cellophane wrap (plain or patterned)

Scissors

Adhesive tape

Instructions

1. Open the cassette case and put approximately 1–2 tablespoons of rice inside.

2. Close the case and secure it with tape.

3. Wrap the cassette with the cellophane (like wrapping a present) and tape the cellophane edges securely in place to finish.

1.

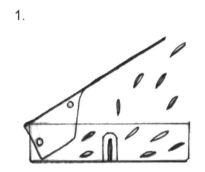

2.

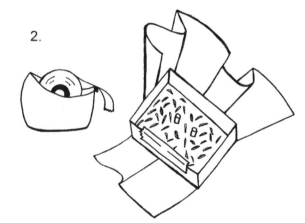

3.

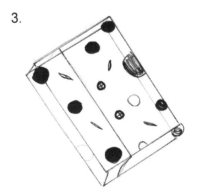

Program 4

Baby and Me:
Wiggle, Jiggle, and Bounce

Just as the title implies, get ready to wiggle (your baby's hands, fingers and toes that is!)

Although singing to babies is wonderful, never forget the importance of touch. Of all a baby's senses, touch is the most crucial. Cuddling a baby shows him or her how much he or she is loved and provides the baby with comfort. This program is sure to be a hit because it combines the best of singing and cuddling and puts them into one great session.

Plan Ahead Note

This craft requires the programmer to do all of the preparation ahead of time. Wiggle E. Worm can be left for the caregivers to colour as they wish.

Books to Share

All Fall Down, by Helen Oxenbury

Tickle, Tickle, by Helen Oxenbury

Watch Me Dance, by Andrea Pinkney and Brian Pinkney

More books to share with babies can be found in the bibliography at the end of this chapter.

Baby and Me:
Wiggle, Jiggle, and Bounce

Rhymes and Songs

Ride to Town

(Tune: Row, Row, Row Your Boat)
(Gently bounce baby up and down on your knees.)

Ride, ride, ride to town,
Ride to town today.
First we shop,
Then we'll stop,

(Stop bouncing.)

And then we'll ride away.

(Bounce a little more quickly.)

Home, home, home we go.
We had so much fun.
We shopped until the sun went down,

(Slowly stop bouncing.)

And now the day is done.

(Stop.)

Merry-Go-Round

(Suit actions to words.)

Merry-go-round,
Merry-go-round,
We go riding all around.
First we're up and then we're down,
We go riding all around.

(Move baby up and down on your knee.)

Off to town,
Off to town,
We go riding off to town,
Hold on tight and don't fall down,

(Gently lean to one side.)

We go riding off to town.

I Have 10 Fingers

(Tune: Do Your Ears Hang Low?)
(Suit actions to words.)

I have ten little fingers
And they all belong to me.
I can make them do things,
Would you like to see?

I can shut them up tight,
Or open them all wide.
I can put them all together,
Or make them all hide.

I can make them jump high,
I can make them fall down low.
I can make them clap loudly,
Or clap them soft and slow.

Touch

(Touch each part of baby as named in the poem.)

Touch your nose,
Touch your chin,
That's the way this game begins.
Touch your eyes,
Touch your knees,
Now pretend you're going to sneeze!
ACHOO!
Touch your hair,
Touch one ear,
Touch your two red lips right here.
Touch your elbows where they bend,
That is how this game will end.

34

3 Fat Sausages

  (Use your fingers to represent the sausages and do as the actions indicate.)

3 fat sausages
Frying in the pan,
One went POP!

(Clap hands softly.)

The other went BAM!

(Clap hands a little more loudly.)

2 fat sausages
Frying in the pan,
One went POP!
The other went BAM!

1 fat sausage
Frying in the pan,
It went POP!
When it should have gone BAM!

This Little Piggy

(Wiggle baby's toes one by one, starting with the big toe and ending with the pinkie toe.)

This little piggy went to market,
This little piggy stayed home.
This little piggy had roast beef,
This little piggy had none.
And this little piggy cried
"Wee, wee, wee, wee,"
All the way home.

Rickety Rickety Rocking Horse

 (Sit baby on your knees and bounce baby gently up and down.)

Rickety, rickety, rocking horse
Over the fields we go.
Rickety, rickety rocking horse,
Gitty up! Gitty up!
Whoa!

Wiggle Your Toes

 (Tune: Row, Row, Row Your Boat)
(Suit actions to words.)

 Wiggle, wiggle, wiggle, your toes

(Wiggle baby's toes.)

 Wiggle them up and down,
Wiggle them here; wiggle them there,
Wiggle them all around.

Additional verses.

Clap your hands
Stomp your feet

Wiggle E. Worm

Make a worm mobile to dangle above baby while rhyming or singing.

Materials

1 small jingle bell per person

String (various colours)

Cardstock or construction paper

Instructions

1. Photocopy Wiggle E. Worm (to 4-inch or 10 cm in length), then back it onto cardstock or construction paper and cut it out.

2. Cut a length of string approximately 12 inches or 30 cm in length.

3. Using approximately 2 inches or 5 cm of the string, tie a loop in the piece of string large enough so that the loop can fit your finger.

4. Tie the bell at the top of the string near the loop.

5. Take Wiggle E. Worm and, using a hole punch, make a hole in the middle of the worm.

6. Lace the string through the hole and tie a knot in the sting to secure it in place.

7. Put the loop over your finger and watch Wiggle E. Worm dance as you gently move your finger or thumb up and down.

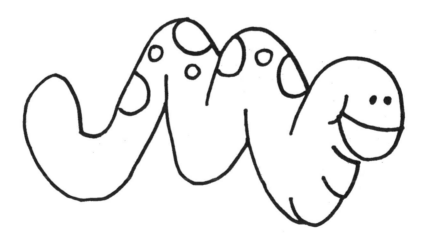

Program 5

Baby and Me: Nursery Rhyme Time

Once again, familiarity will become one of the tools you come to count on the most. One of the most common complaints we may receive as programmers is that participants wish we would repeat our songs and rhymes more often in our programs. Although you may have favourites of your own, it is important to remember that your audience will have their favourites, too. The theme "Nursery Rhyme Time" enables you to revisit some old songs and introduce new ones.

Plan Ahead Note

Some songs in this program call for the use of bells. You may want to warn your participants ahead of time if you've never used the bells before. Some children may not like the sound, whereas others will love it.

This craft also requires that the programmer do all of the preparation ahead of time, but you can get your parents involved in the craft process right from the start. Photocopy the birds onto white paper and give each parent a blue crayon at the beginning of the program. They can then colour the bluebirds as a program icebreaker once they're settled.

Books to Share

Clap Your Hands, by Lorinda Bryan Cauley

Peanut Butter & Jelly, by Nadine Bernard Westcott

Ladybug, Ladybug, by Ruth Brown

More books to share with babies can be found in the bibliography at the end of this chapter.

Baby and Me: Nursery Rhyme Time

Rhymes and Songs

Row, Row, Row Your Boat

 (Gently sway forward and backward with baby on your lap while singing this song.)

Row, row, row, your boat,
Gently down the stream.
Merrily, merrily, merrily, merrily,
Life is but a dream.

(Gently sway side to side with baby on your lap for this verse.)

Rock, rock, rock the boat,
Sway from side to side,
Merrily, merrily, merrily, merrily,
What a bumpy ride!

2 Little Bluebirds

 (Use your hands for the two bluebirds.)

Two little bluebirds sitting on a wall,
One named Peter and one named Paul,
Fly away Peter,

(Put one hand behind your back.)

Fly away Paul.

(Put your second hand behind your back.)

Come back Peter,

(Bring one hand out and wiggle your fingers.)

Come back Paul.

(Bring out other hand and wiggle your fingers.)

Additional verses:

Sitting on a fence—Fred and Spence
Sitting on a hill—Jack and Jill

Baby's Fingers

 (Point to each of baby's body parts as it is named in the poem.)

These are baby's fingers,
These are baby's toes,
This is baby's belly button,
Round and round it goes.

(Circle baby's belly button with a finger.)

These are baby's ears,
This is baby's nose,
This is baby's belly button
Round and round it goes.

Eensy Weensy Spider

 (Do as the actions indicate.)

The eensy weensy spider climbed up
the waterspout,

(Creep your fingers up baby's arm.)

Down came the rain and washed the
spider out.

(Creep your fingers down baby's arm.)

Out came the sun and dried up all the rain,

(Using your arms make a large circle over your head.)

And the eensy weensy spider went up
the spout again.

(Creep your fingers back up baby's arm.)

10 Fingers on My Hand

(Suit actions to words.)
    1 little, 2 little, 3 little fingers,
    4 little, 5 little, 6 little fingers,
    7 little, 8 little, 9 little fingers,
    10 little fingers on my hand.

    They wiggle and they wiggle and they
       wiggle
    All together,
    They wiggle and they wiggle and they
       wiggle
    All together,
    They wiggle and they wiggle and they
       wiggle
    All together,
    10 little fingers on my hand.

Additional verses:
    Clap all together
    Crawl all together
    Hide all together

10 Little Fingers

(Touch each of baby's body parts as it is named in the poem.)
    10 little fingers,
    10 little toes.
    2 little eyes,
    And 1 little nose.

    2 little cheeks,
    1 little chin,
    And 1 little mouth,
    Where the treats go in!

Shake Your Bells

(Suit actions to words.)
    Shake your bells in the air, in the air,
    Shake them here and everywhere.
    Shake them up,
    And shake them down,
    Shake them all around the town.
    Shake your bells in the air, in the air.

Additional verses:
    Clap your hands

Trot Trot to Boston

(Stand to say this poem, holding baby in your arms.)
    Trot trot to Boston,
    Trot trot to Lynn,
    Careful when you get there,
    That you don't fall in!

(Gently dip baby.)
    Trot trot to Boston,
    Trot trot to Dover,
    Careful when you get there,
    That you don't fall over!

(Sway to one side.)
    Trot trot to Boston,
    Trot trot to town,
    Careful when you get there,
    That you don't fall down!

(Sit down gently with baby.)

Birds of a Feather

Make two bluebird props to use for the rhyme *Two Little Bluebirds*.

Materials

Photocopy paper (any colour)

Cardstock or construction paper

4 feathers (2 for each bird) per person

Scissors

Glue

Masking tape

Instructions

1. Photocopy two bluebirds for each caregiver. (They should be the size of an adult fist.)

2. Glue them onto cardstock or construction paper and cut them out.

3. Tape two feathers on each one for a tickly tail.

Use these with the *2 Little Bluebirds* rhyme mentioned earlier in this program.

Program 6

Baby and Me: Head to Toe

Although the storytime souvenir in this program cannot be used as a prop, it does make a great reminder for the parents and caregivers of the quality one-on-one time they were able to spend with their baby (it also makes a great addition to a keepsake box, photo album, or scrapbook). This theme incorporates songs and rhymes that focus on every part of the baby from head to toe. If you take the time to get to know the songs and rhymes before you present them, you will feel much better about singing them in front of a group.

Plan Ahead Note

You may want to warn your caregivers ahead of time that you will be using paint in this program. It is washable, but caregivers will still want to be and should be told. In our experience caregivers (especially those caring for young children) see paint as one thing: Messy . . . messy . . . messy. So some may be a little apprehensive about this souvenir. But by giving them advance warning you can answer any questions or concerns ahead of time.

Books to Share

Where Is Baby's Belly Button?, by Karen Katz

Eyes, Nose, Fingers, Toes, by Judy Hindley

I See Me, by Pegi Deitz Shea

More books to share with babies can be found in the bibliography at the end of this chapter.

Baby and Me: Head to Toe

Rhymes and Songs

Head and Shoulders

 (Touch each body part on baby as it is named in the song.)
> Head and shoulders, knees and toes,
> Knees and toes, knees and toes.
> Head and shoulders, knees and toes,
> I love my baby!

(Tickle baby.)
> Eyes and ears and mouth and nose,
> Mouth and nose,
> Mouth and nose.
> Eyes and ears and mouth and nose,
> I love my baby!

(Tickle baby.)

Where Is Thumbkin?

 (Dance your hands in front of baby while singing this song.)
> Where is thumbkin? Where is
> thumbkin?

(Hide hands behind your back.)
> Here I am! Here I am!

(Bring thumbs out.)
> How are you today sir?
> Very well I thank you.
> Run away. Run away.

(Hide thumbs behind your back.)

Additional verses:
> Where is Peter Pointer?
> Where is Toby Tall?
> Where is Ruby Ring?
> Where is Baby Finger?
> Where is Finger Family?

This Is the Way

 (Do as the actions indicate, using baby's body parts.)
> This is the way we clap our hands,

 (Clap baby's hands.)
> Clap our hands, clap our hands.
> This is the way we clap our hands,
> So early in the morning.

Additional verses:
> Tap our toes
> Touch our nose
> Stomp our feet

Tommy Thumb

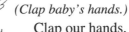 *(Dance your hands in front of baby while singing this song.)*
> Tommy thumb is up and Tommy
> thumb is down,

(Hold thumbs up and bring thumbs down.)
> Tommy thumb is dancing all around
> the town,

(Dance thumbs in the air.)
> Dance him on your shoulders,
> Dance him on your head,
> Dance him on your knees and tuck him
> into bed!

(Tuck thumbs under your arms.)

Additional verses:
> Peter Pointer
> Toby Tall
> Ruby Ring
> Pinkie Finger
> Finger Family

Hokey Pokey

  (Stand and bounce with baby gently while singing this song. Move baby's body parts in, out, and around as mentioned in the song.)

You put your right hand in,

(Put baby's right hand out in front of you.)

You take your right hand out,

(Pull right hand back towards you.)

You put your right hand in,

(Put right hand back in.)

And you shake it all about.

(Shake baby's hand.)

You do the hokey pokey,

(Sway with baby from side to side.)

And you turn yourself about,

(Turn around.)

And that's what it's all about!

(Clap baby's hands.)

Additional verses:
Left hand
Right foot
Left foot
Whole self

They're a Part of Me

  (Tune: The Wheels on the Bus)
(Suit actions to words.)

 I can make my hands go clap, clap, clap,
Clap, clap, clap. Clap, clap, clap.
I can make my hands go clap, clap, clap,
They're a part of me.

Additional verses:
Toes go tap, tap, tap
Feet go stomp, stomp, stomp
Hands wave bye, bye, bye

Hands on Hips

 (Suit actions to words.)

Hands on hips,
Hands on knees,
Put them behind you,
If you please.

Touch your shoulders,
Touch your nose,
Touch your ears,
And touch your toes.

Where Is Baby?

(Tune: Frere Jacques)
(Do as the actions indicate.)

Where is baby? Where is baby?

(Hold your hands in front of your face,)

There he [or she] is! There he [or she] is!

(Open your hands quickly.)

I'm so glad to see you.
I'm so glad to see you.
Peek-a-boo!
Peek-a-boo!

44

Sweet Feet

Keep an adorable footprint souvenir of your baby's feet by completing this activity.

Materials

1 sheet of black construction paper per person

White washable tempera paint

1 paper plate per person

White chalk

Sponges (cut into quarters)

Instructions

1. Provide each caregiver with a sheet of black construction paper, a paper plate with white paint on it, and a piece of sponge.

2. Instruct each caregiver to dip the child's left foot in the white paint, or swab it on using the sponge, and press the foot gently onto the black paper.

3. Repeat with the right foot.

4. Use the white chalk to write each child's name on his or her paper while the caregiver cleans the baby's feet.

Program 7

Baby and Me: Barnyard Banter

What program would be complete without parents and caregivers "oinking" and "quacking" like barnyard animals? This theme is great for introducing baby to the farm and its unique sounds. Some caregivers may feel a bit shy or embarrassed about having to sing in front of others. Remind them that playing with the baby while singing will help to keep the baby's attention. This will also help to keep their minds off the fact that there are other grown-ups in the room.

Plan Ahead Note

This is a program that requires caregiver notification because it is another craft that will be messy, and also because you will be using a food product. Allergies are always a concern for young children, and caregivers should be notified ahead of time so that they can choose whether or not to participate.

Books to Share

Moo, Baa, La La La, by Sandra Boynton

To Market, to Market, by Anne Miranda

How Big Is a Pig?, by Clare Beaton

More books to share with babies can be found in the bibliography at the end of this chapter.

Baby and Me: Barnyard Banter

Rhymes and Songs

Cows in the Barn

 (Tune: The Wheels on the Bus)
(Sing along with baby bouncing on your knee.)

The cows in the barn go moo, moo, moo
Moo, moo, moo; moo, moo, moo.
The cows in the barn go moo, moo, moo,
All day long.

Additional verses:

Ducks in the pond go quack, quack,
quack
Sheep in the field go baa, baa, baa
Piggies in their pens go oink, oink, oink

Eight Baby Pigs

 (Use your fingers to represent the pigs.)
Two little pigs lived in a pen,

(Hold up thumbs.)

Each had four babies and that made
ten.

(Wiggle fingers on both hands.)

These four babies were black and
white.

(Wiggle fingers on one hand.)

These four babies were black as night.

(Wiggle fingers on the other hand.)

All eight babies loved to play,

(Wiggle all fingers.)

And they rolled and they rolled in the
mud all day!

(Roll hands.)

10 Wild Horses

 (Gently bounce baby up and down on your knees.)

10 wild horses came galloping through
town,
5 were white and 5 were brown.
They galloped up,
And they galloped down.
They galloped away,
And out of town.

Old MacDonald

 (Sing along while holding baby on your lap.)
Old MacDonald had a farm, E-I-E-I-O
And on this farm he had a cow,
E-I-E-I-O
With a moo-moo here, and a moo-moo
there,
Here a moo,
There a moo,
Everywhere a moo-moo.
Old MacDonald had a farm, E-I-E-I-O.

Additional verses:

Duck, quack, quack
Sheep, baa, baa
Horse, neigh, neigh

47

1 Is a Cat

 (Hold fingers up one by one.)

1 is a cat that says "Meow"
2 is a dog that says, "Bow, wow"
3 is a hen that says "Cluck, cluck"
4 is a squirrel that says "Chuck, chuck"
5 is a donkey that says "Hee, haw"
6 is a crow that says "Caw, caw"
7 is a sheep that says "Baa, baa"
8 is a goat that says "Maa, maa"
9 is a cow that says "Moo, moo"
10 is a rooster that says
   "Cock-a-doodle-doo!"

Out in the Barnyard

 (Tune: Down by the Station)
(Use your hands and fingers as the animals.)

Out in the barnyard,
Early in the morning,
You can hear the piglets

(Wiggle your fingers.)

Squealing up a storm.
Here comes the farmer,

(Wiggle your other hand.)

He will feed those piggies,
Oink, oink, oink, oink,
On the farm.

Additional verses:

Chickens clucking
Roosters crowing
Kittens meowing

When Cows Get Up in the Morning

 (Sit baby on your knees and bounce gently up and down when you say the words "good day.")

When cows get up in the morning
They always say "good day"
When cows get up in the morning
They always say "good day"
Moo, moo, moo—that's how they say
   "good day"
Moo, moo, moo—that's how they say
   "good day"

Additional verses:

Pigs, oink, oink, oink
Cats, meow, meow, meow
Dogs, woof, woof, woof
Sheep, baa, baa, baa

3 Pigs in a Bed

 (Do as the actions indicate.)

3 pigs in a bed
And the little one said,
"Roll over, roll over"

 (Gently sway side to side with baby.)

So they all rolled over and one fell out!

(Lean to one side.)

2 pigs in a bed
And the little one said,
"Roll over, roll over"

(Gently sway side to side with baby.)

So they all rolled over and one fell out!

(Lean to one side.)

1 pig in the bed
And you know what he said?
"I've got the whole mattress to myself,
I've got the whole mattress to myself,
I've got the whole mattress to myself,
The whole mattress to myself!"

This Little Piggy

Let babies enjoy messy painting as they spread pudding over the pig.

Materials

1 sheet of pink construction paper per person

Chocolate pudding (premade, enough for your group)

Paper plates (enough for your group)

Damp and dry paper towels (enough for your group)

Cotton swabs, sponges, or paint brushes (enough for your group)

Instructions

1. Photocopy one pig for each child onto pink construction paper (to fit an 8½-by-11-inch sheet).

2. Give each caregiver the pig, a plate with a small amount of pudding on it, a sponge, and a cotton swab

3. Caregivers and children can spread, sponge, or fingerpaint pudding onto their pigs to make them look muddy.

Program 8

Baby and Me: Hush Little Baby

To finish off our baby chapter, we have chosen a bedtime theme. "Hush Little Baby" is a calmer, more quiet approach to programming for babies than the programs you've seen previously in this book. The songs and rhymes listed here are meant to be used as facilitators for caregivers to cuddle and hold their children. We also feel that this makes for a happy ending when bringing your "Baby and Me" sessions to a close.

Plan Ahead Note

The craft for this program requires that the programmer cut out the doorhangers ahead of time. Also, the song titles and nighttime clip art need to be photocopied and cut out before the program. This will help to minimise confusion and make craft time run a little more smoothly.

Books to Share

Goodnight Moon, by Margaret Wise Brown

Time for Bed, by Mem Fox

Sleepytime Rhyme, by Remy Charlip

More books to share with babies can be found in the bibliography at the end of this chapter.

Baby and Me: Hush Little Baby

The Kissy Game

 (Kiss baby's body as each part is mentioned.)
Kissy, kissy fingers,
Kissy, kissy toes.
Kissy, kissy baby
On your kissy, kissy nose.

I love to kiss your fingers,
I love to kiss your toes,
I love to kiss my baby,
On his or her kissy, kissy nose.

The Moon Is Round

 (Suit actions to words.)
The moon is round,
As round can be.

(Circle baby's face with finger.)
Two eyes,
A nose,
And a mouth like me!

(Point to each part in baby, and then to self.)

Mama's Little Baby

 (Lay baby in front of you as you sing.)
Mama's little baby a kiss can blow,

 (Blow a kiss to baby.)
And rub noses just like so.

(Rub noses with baby.)
Two little hands can clap, clap, clap,

(Clap hands with baby.)
And ten little toes can tap, tap, tap.

(Tap baby's toes.)

You're My Little Baby

 (Tune: I'm a Little Teapot)
(Suit actions to words.)
 You're my little baby,
So soft and sweet.
Here are your hands,

(Touch baby's hands.)
Here are your feet.

(Touch baby's feet.)
I'll watch you clap your hands,

(Clap baby's hands.)
And tap your feet.

(Tap baby's feet.)
I love you baby,
So soft and sweet!

(Tickle baby's tummy.)

Stretch Up High

 (Suit actions to words.)
Stretch up high,
As tall as a house.

(Reach in the air.)
Curl up small,
As small as a mouse.

(Bend low to the floor.)
Now pretend you have a drum,
And beat it like this,
Rum, tum, tum.

(Pat the floor.)
Shake your fingers,
Stamp your feet,
Close your eyes,
And go to sleep!

(Pretend to be sleeping.)

Twinkle, Twinkle Little Star

(Sway baby back and forth gently as you sing this song.)

Twinkle, twinkle, little star,
How I wonder what you are.
Up above the world so high,
Like a diamond in the sky.
Twinkle, twinkle, little star
How I wonder what you are.

Rickety Crickety

(Suit actions to words.)
Rickety, crickety, rockety chair,

(Gently rock baby back and forth as baby stands.)
Sitting alone at the top of the stair,

(Sit baby on your lap.)
Waiting for someone to stop for a
    minute,

(Hug baby and hold still.)
And rickety, crickety, rock in it.

(Rock baby again while sitting.)

The Kissing Rhyme

(Swing baby up and down as indicated in this song.)
Up, up, up in the sky like this,

(Lift baby high in the air.)
Down, down, down, for a great big
    kiss,

(Bring baby down for a kiss.)
Up like this, down like this,

(Lift and lower baby.)
You're my special baby!

(Hold baby close and cuddle.)

53

Baby's Sleeping Doorhanger

Materials

1 doorhanger (made from template) per person

Coloured photocopy paper

Cardstock or construction paper

Nighttime clip art pictures (samples on the next page)

Lullaby song titles (e.g., "Twinkle, Twinkle Little Star")

Glue

Instructions

1. Print out various lullaby song titles on assorted colours of paper.

2. Cut out the song titles.

3. Enlarge the doorhanger template from the next page on the photocopier.

4. Trace and cut out a doorhanger and back it onto cardstock or construction paper to make it more sturdy.

5. Provide song titles and clip art for caregivers to glue onto their doorhangers.

6. Bibliography of Books to Share

Beaton, Clare. 2000. *How Big Is a Pig?* New York: Barefoot Books.

Boynton, Sandra. 1995. *Moo, Baa, La, La, La.* New York: Little Simon.

Brown, Margaret Wise. 1999. *Bumble Bee.* New York: HarperCollins Juvenile Books.

Brown, Margaret Wise. 1991. *Goodnight Moon.* New York: HarperCollins Juvenile Books.

Brown, Ruth. 1992. *Ladybug, Ladybug.* Toronto: Penguin Books of Canada.

Cauley, Lorinda Bryan. 1997. *Clap Your Hands.* East Rutherford, NJ: Putnam Publishing Group.

Charlip, Remy. 1999. *Sleepytime Rhyme.* New York: Greenwillow.

Crozon, Alain. 1998. *Who Am I?* San Francisco: Chronicle Books.

Fox, Mem. 1997. *Time for Bed.* San Diego: Harcourt.

Hindley, Judy. 2002. *Eyes, Nose, Fingers, Toes.* Cambridge: Candlewick Press.

Hoban, Tana. 1993. *Black on White.* New York: Greenwillow.

Hubbell, Patricia. 1998. *Pots & Pans.* New York: HarperCollins Juvenile Books.

Isadora, Rachel. 1998. *I Touch.* Cambridge, MA: Candlewick Press.

Katz, Karen. 2000. *Where Is Baby's Belly Button?* New York: Little Simon.

Miranda, Anne. 1997. *To Market, to Market.* San Diego: Harcourt Brace.

Oxenbury, Helen. 1999. *All Fall Down.* New York: Little Simon.

Oxenbury, Helen. 1999. *Clap Hands.* New York: Little Simon.

Oxenbury, Helen. 1999. *Tickle, Tickle.* New York: Simon & Schuster.

Pinkney, Andrea, and Brian Pinkney. 1997. *Watch Me Dance.* San Diego: Harcourt.

Shea, Pegi Deitz. 2000. *I See Me.* New York: HarperCollins Juvenile Books.

Wells, Rosemary. 1998. *Read to Your Bunny.* New York: Scholastic Trade.

West, Colin. 1996. *Buzz, Buzz, Buzz Went Bumblebee.* Cambridge, MA: Candlewick Press.

Westcott, Nadine Bernard. 1992. *Peanut Butter & Jelly; A Play Rhyme.* London: Penguin.

Williams, Vera. 1997. *More, More, More Said the Baby.* Dorset, VT: Tupelo Books.

Chapter 3
Wonderful Ones

For children, the time between twelve and twenty-three months is an enormous developmental span. A program with one-year-old participants will concentrate on walkers, children who have mastered taking a few confident steps on their own. Many children begin walking at approximately twelve months; however, some children will not begin to walk until fourteen or sixteen months. There is no perfect solution to grouping children developmentally. The best approach is to be sensitive to your group and provide options for the level of participation; most rhymes and action songs can be done in a number of different ways: with adults manipulating the child's limbs, with the child moving independently, or some combination of both. This will allow caregivers and their children to enjoy the program and tailor it to their own needs. If your facility plans to run a program for one year olds, you should be aware that some participants will not have started walking. Programmers can be sensitive to this and give alternate directions for activities that require the tots to stand and move independently. Another option is to limit the program registration to walkers and to assign pre-walkers to another program with younger children (Marino and Houlihan, 1992). This option may give rise other issues; children who have developed rapidly physically may not have developed as quickly cognitively. Although there is no perfect solution, keep an open mind and be flexible about the needs of your group.

Running a program for one-year-old children is an exciting challenge. Little ones at this age are active, curious, and moody. Tots can be wonderfully fun and lighthearted, but they can also be stubborn and independent. They will be drawn to interesting sounds, images, and any sort of commotion. Programmers who prefer structure, formality, and an organised set-up may be frustrated when they start a program for one year olds. These children seem involved in a world all their own, and in some ways that is exactly where they are. But they also have the capacity to enjoy the program on many different levels. A child who is distracted and inattentive may seem to be getting little from the program but in fact may be the very one who imitates the program leader at home. Parents and caregivers should be encouraged to participate in and enjoy all the program's activities, even if their child does not seem interested. A one-year-old child may not actively participate in all the storytime activities, but he or she quickly becomes aware if the caregiver grows uninterested and agitated.

To make your program with one year olds a positive experience, it should be fast paced, energetic, flexible, and activity based. Children at this age have brains that are growing and expanding at a phenomenal rate; new neurons are firing and laying neural pathways, and children can begin to explore the world around them in exciting new ways. Library programming can assist in this development in countless ways, including

- language development,

- sensory stimulation,

- gross and fine motor tuning,

- cognitive development,

- creative expression,

- bonding experiences for adult and child, and

- parent/caregiver education.

More than any other age group, one year olds are misunderstood. They are often thought to be disruptive and out of control. In fact, they are curious sponges, exploring and experiencing the world all the time. Sometimes they explore in a very boisterous, energetic way; sometimes they become fixated; and sometimes they will be overstimulated and become grumpy and distressed. Programmers should be sensitive to one year olds' needs, and they should also be prepared to educate caregivers on what to expect from their tots. Keep an open mind and don't be discouraged by minor disruptions; look at the program as a whole and try to keep the energy level high and the mood light.

1. What Can Walkers Do?: Child Development at Twelve to Twenty-three Months

One-year-old children are busy and determined. They like to explore and investigate; they are full of energy and require constant supervision. Programs for one year olds can provide these energetic tots with new ways to stimulate, entertain, and focus some of their energy. Rather than trying to tame these explorers, programs should be focused on ways to nurture their investigation and should give tots exciting challenges for their cognitive and sensory development.

Developmental markers for sixteen month olds include

- grasping small objects;

- using a finger to poke and point;

- copying sounds and actions;

- responding to music and rhythm with the body;

- understanding simple commands;

- using gestures or motions to indicate need;

- pushing, pulling, and dumping things;

- walking without support;

- turning the pages of a book;

- looking for objects that have moved out of sight;

- waving "hi" or "bye" when prompted;

- performing and responding to applause;

- pulling off socks or hat;

- scribbling with oversized crayons; and

- crumpling paper or stiff tissue.

The wide range of skills the children have begun to acquire demonstrates how varied a program for one year olds can be. There must be lots of movement and interactive play, and after each successful activity a round of applause will make everyone feel proud.

2. One Year Old Programming Guidelines

2.1 Starting a Program for One Year Olds

Programs for one year olds are a great enhancement to the for a library's line-up of activities. The children need the extra tools for learning and development, and often caregivers need to understand that their child's behaviour is normal and acceptable. Many parents and caregivers are astounded by how quickly their cuddly baby became an energetic walker. Some parents try to constantly curb, slow, and soothe their children. Instead, they should be shown how to respond to their children's moods and signals, how to give their children appropriate cognitive, physical, and sensory stimulation when they indicate a need for it.

Programs for one year olds, properly advertised, are usually quite popular as adults look for new ways to entertain their children. Programming for one year olds is also beneficial for the library because it cements the institution's importance in the life of the family. If families use the library with their one year olds, they are more likely to keep coming again and again as their children grow older. They will see the variety of benefits your facility may have to offer them and will come to appreciate your institution's importance to the community and to individuals of all ages and backgrounds.

2.2 Getting Ready

To be ready for your group of one year olds you must be optimistic and enthusiastic. The children and parents will feel your energy and excitement and mimic it. You should also take some extra time to prepare the room before the group begins. The entire area needs to be safe. Eliminate sharp edges and any materials that would be dangerous if ingested by a little one.

2.2b Books to Share

Books to read to a group of one year olds must be visually attractive. Large, distinct shapes or illustrations on a contrasting background work well for children to appreciate the images. Use books that focus on the world these young children are learning to explore. Stories with a plot can be introduced at this age, but they must be simple and easy to follow. Rhymes and musical books still work very well, and these one year olds will have learned to appreciate the rhythm and may imitate the intonation or a repeated chant. Books with obvious repetition lend themselves to participation, and adults can chime in and repeat expected lines. Choose books with illustrations that the children will be able to appreciate and understand. Favourites include pictures or photographs of other children, common household objects they may have encountered, and animals or pets.

BRIGHT IDEA

If you have a suitable story for a group of one year olds, but the original book is not a suitable size, make large-scale visuals and print the story on the back. Contact the book's publisher to obtain permission to reproduce the book in this manner. Share the story by holding the visual up in front of you and reading the corresponding text (printed on the reverse side). Programmers without drawing ability can make large visuals by tracing and using the zoom function on the photocopier or by using an overhead projector to project traced images, on a larger scale, onto the wall. Tack paper or bristol board to the wall and trace over the lines of the projected images.

2.2c Books to Display

You can display books suitable for the children to use on their own, especially those with cardboard pages (board books). Picture books, suitable for a bedtime story or for parents and caregivers to read aloud to children, are also great choices. Finally, include a selection of books that adults can use to help them with their active one year olds, including subjects like nutrition, feeding, sleep habits, and temper tantrums. Collections of rhymes, fingerplays, and toddler activities are also excellent resources for adults to continue the storytime experience at home. Display books out of the toddlers' reach so they are not pulled down during the program.

EXPERT ADVICE

In the first few weeks of the program, ask the group about things they are most interested in, problems they are having, and favourite books. These suggestions will make it easier to choose books to display in future weeks that will spark the group's interest.

3. Programs for One Year Olds: Format and Routine

The following section provides examples of program routines and structures that have worked well with one year olds. Adapt these routines to your individual style, then practice and use these strategies and suggestions to make your programs successful.

3.1 Format

A program for children twelve to twenty-three months old will follow a similar format to a program for babies: twenty minutes of follow-the-leader style rhyming, bouncing, movement, singing, and reading. The major difference will be the pace of the program. A typical baby program may include one book and six or seven rhymes and songs. The transitions between activities will be slow and casual as parents and caregivers chat and settle their infants. In your program for one year olds, your transitions will be seamless and quick. You will be able to read two stories and may complete ten or more rhyming and singing activities. The group will not move along together in a slow, easy fashion, and you will not be able to wait for the entire group to be ready to begin an activity or song. The longer the pauses and transitions, the more the tots will become distracted and find other things to occupy their busy minds. Some caregivers may miss the beginning of a new rhyme while they settle or chase after their little one. It is therefore important to repeat each rhyme, even favourites, at least twice. New and unfamiliar rhymes can be repeated three times.

Movement is very important in a program for one year olds. Bouncing, fingerplays, tickling, and dancing are all suitable types of activities to do with this group. Vary the activities in a consistent manner to help the group get used to the routine and format of the program. For example:

- Begin your program with a standard greeting.

- Follow with a few bouncing rhymes.

- Next read a story.

- Immediately follow the story with a stand-up action rhyme or song.

- Continue movement activities with a little dancing.

- Read another story.

- Again, follow the story with a stand-up action rhyme or song.

- Complete the fast-paced twenty minutes with a few touch and tickle rhymes.

- Sing a soft calming song for the final group activity.

- Break your circle to complete the special activity in another area of the room, if possible.

- Finish your program with a standard closing.

3.2 Opening Routine

Toddlers enjoy individual attention, and many have come to recognise their own names. To help you (and other adults in the program) address the children and their caregivers by name, you will need some sort of identifier. If you run a drop-in program, include large self-adhesive labels with permanent, non-toxic markers for adults to write their names and the name of their child. Adorn large plain labels with simple, colourful stickers to make them more friendly and fun.

If you run a preregistered program, having the list of regular attendees will allow you to establish identifiers that you hand out. The process of repeating the children's names each week at the beginning of the program will help to cement them in your mind. Toddlers tend to put things in their mouths, so name tags that hang around the neck and can be reused from week to week may not be practical. One alternative is to hand out labels with each child's name printed clearly, one per label. Sing a song to identify each child, and hand the adult the label to affix to the child's clothing. If you have a computer program that allows you to print labels, you can set up a template and print off labels each week. Otherwise, purchase a permanent, nontoxic marker and plain labels from a discount store, print the children's names, and adorn the labels with a colourful sticker. Explain to adults that when they hear their child's name, they should raise a hand or gesture to indicate their child's presence. In alphabetical, or some other predictable order, sing the following song, inserting each child's name as appropriate:

Where Are My Friends?

 (Tune: Where Is Thumbkin?)

Where are my friends?
Where are my friends?
Who is here today?
Who is here today?
Let us come and find them,
Let us come and find them,
Then we'll play.
Then we'll play.

Where is _____ *(child's name)?*
Where is _____ *(child's name)?*
I see you.
I see you.
How are you today friend?
How are you today friend?
Peek-a-boo.
Peek-a-boo.

Repeat the line with the child's name and the verse that follows as often as necessary. As you approach each child, hand the sticker to the adult to place on the child's forearm, chest, or shin. If a child is absent, after you sing, "Where is _____ *(child's name)?*" and repeat, you will get no response. Then, simply sing "Not here today" twice and move on to the next child.

This opening routine is meant to be fun and provide a few moments of individual attention for each child at the beginning of the program while stragglers are coming in and the group is getting settled into the circle. Don't worry about mispronouncing children's names in the first couple of weeks—when the adult corrects you, write the phonetic spelling on a piece of paper and learn it for the next time.

3.3 Program Ingredients

Spend some time before your program deciding on the routine you think will work for you and the group. In many ways, presenting this program is like performing in front of an audience: There is lots of interaction and participation, but the group will look to you to lead them on to the next activity. Have all your activities gathered and planned.

BRIGHT IDEA

Decide on all your program ingredients and the order you would like to perform them. Write them on index cards and arrange them in order. Having different colours for individual activities will help you differentiate program segments. Include more rhymes and songs than needed to give you some flexibility within your program.

3.4 Teaching New Rhymes and Songs

A group of caregivers with one year olds will have their minds and bodies in two places at once. They will be trying to keep after their little ones while at the same time absorbing all the exciting activities and tips they are learning. To make it easier for caregivers to catch on and learn the words to rhymes and songs, it is helpful to repeat the activity more than once. The first time the programmer should demonstrate; the second time the group should attempt to do it together; and for longer or unfamiliar rhymes and songs, the activity should be repeated for a third time. Visuals are excellent ways for some adults to join in on the fun. Some people will need to see the words to a rhyme or song before they feel comfortable joining in. Post large scale versions of the rhymes that adult participants can use to read along.

> **BRIGHT IDEA**
>
> Make poster-sized visuals for rhymes and songs by typing the text in a large font on letter or legal sized white paper. Post these on an easel or a wall at a height that is easy to read for adults sitting on the floor. Check the angle by sitting on the floor and making sure the words are easily deciphered.

3.5 Focus Activities

Throughout the twenty minutes of structured activity with one year olds you will need to use techniques to focus the group as you make a transition to a new type of activity. One technique is to use action rhymes or songs that end with the child in a sitting position. Another technique involves the use of repetitive music or chanting, such as snapping your fingers or clapping your hands in rhythm until the entire group is doing it along with you. A simple rhythmic chant, such as the nonsense phrase "gooli gooli" or "ding dong ding," repeated over and over until everyone has joined in, works as well. Once you have the focus of the group, quickly make the transition to the next element.

3.6 Closing Routine

A simple, memorable song to close the program is a great way to wrap up the group's activities. Using the same tune as the opening song will also add familiarity.

Goodbye Everyone

(Tune: Where Is Thumbkin)
Goodbye everyone.
Goodbye everyone.
Now we're done.
Now we're done.
Come again next week.
Come again next week.
We'll have fun.
We'll have fun.

4. One Year Old Programming Techniques and Activities

4.1 Music and Movement

Activities such as dancing to music, ringing bells, and marching to the beat of a drum are very popular with one year olds. Choose an age appropriate, social activity to fill the last ten minutes of your program. If you have chosen to use themes to guide the direction of your program, don't feel you have to choose activities that match your theme. At this age, themes are for the programmer; they should *not* restrict the inclusion of a favourite activity or game. Play peek-a-boo, or have the children dance with scarves. Play music and blow bubbles while the children dance and pop them. Activities should be developmentally appropriate and should allow for social interaction.

> **BRIGHT IDEA**
>
> Purchase filmy scarves (available at discount and department stores) and hand out one to each adult participant. Play music and have adults drop scarves while the children dance and play. Some children will giggle as the scarf drops onto them, other children will scoot out of the way, and some children will want to hold the scarf and dance or play peek-a-boo.

4.2 Special Activities and Storytime Souvenirs

Activities suitable for one year olds should require little fine motor skill. Children at this age can scribble with large crayons, affix stickers, dab stamps or dabbers, and fingerpaint or paint with sponges. Therefore, simple crafts with only a few pieces are suitable activities. The crafts should be sturdy and not easily pulled apart. They must be completely nontoxic, as all elements and ingredients of the program should be, if they are to be touched or manipulated by the children.

4.3 Props

One-year-old children can be stimulated visually with props and visuals. Use some of the illustrations provided and photocopy them onto cardstock. Affix felt or magnets on the back of the storytime pieces and use them on the flannel or magnet board to accompany a rhyme or song. Have a class set of soft stuffed animals or sensory toys. Sensory toys are those that have bells, shakers, or Velcro attached; they are designed to stimulate toddlers in ways that are appropriate to their developing skills. Hand these out during one of your programs and give parents tips on how to use them to play with their children. Make a class set of your own sensory objects and pass them out for adults and children to use together.

> **CONFIDENCE BOOSTER**
>
> Sensory stimuli are simple but extremely effective additions to a program with one year olds. Make "smelly bags" by inserting spices, vanilla beans, or coffee in cotton pouches. Sew the top together or close firmly with cloth ribbon. Have children test the smell of each bag. One way to provide a visual stimulus is to make looking glasses with coloured mylar. Purchase coloured mylar from a craft store and frame with cardboard. Have children peer through the looking glass to see the world in a whole new way. Stimulate the children's sense of touch with fabric, cotton, and sandpaper samples affixed firmly to cardboard. These are a few examples of ways to use simple objects to provide sensory stimulation. Adults will be impressed and excited to try similar ideas at home.

Program 1

Fun with Ones:
Mother Goose Is on the Loose

It's wonderful to be one! Mother Goose is such a versatile theme, we have chosen to include it in various programs with a variety of age groups. The songs you will use with your baby group, you may or may not choose to repeat with your group of one year olds. Remember that this is a different age group altogether, so different rules apply here. You can start to expand what you do in your programs as your group of children gets older. So, with that in mind, in this program you should feel free to include more movement and action than you've done previously with the babies.

Plan Ahead Note

The craft in this program requires the programmer to complete all of the assembling before the program. As an added extra, you can cover the ends of the brass fastener with a 2-inch or 5 cm strip of masking tape. Also, some of the songs in this program require the use of bells. You may want to inform caregivers a week before that the next session may get a little loud. Some children may not like the noise and it may upset them a little, so informing the caregivers ahead of time gives them time to prepare the children at home.

Books to Share

Little Red Hen, by Byron Barton

Humpty Dumpty and Other Nursery Rhymes, by Lucy Cousins

Ten in the Bed, by Anne Geddes

More books to share with one year olds can be found in the bibliography at the end of this chapter.

Rhyme and Song Legend

♪ Song

👏 Clapping   ⌄○ Bouncing

🖐 Actions   🖐 Fingerplay

Fun with Ones:
Mother Goose Is on the Loose

One Is a Giant

 (Suit actions to words.)
One is a giant who stomps his feet,

(Stomp feet loudly on the floor.)
Two is a fairy so light and neat.

(Sway gently from side to side.)
Three is a mouse who crouches small

(Crouch down low into a ball.)
And four is a great big bouncing ball.

(Jump up and down.)

This Is the Way We Shake Our Bells

 (Suit actions to words.)
This is the way we shake our bells,
Shake our bells, shake our bells,
This is the way we shake our bells,
So early in the morning.

Additional verses:
This is the way we shake our arms
This is the way we shake our feet

Grandma, Grandma

 (This is a great song to use with shakers or bells.)

Grandma, grandma you're not sick,
All you need is a peppermint stick.
Hands up . . . shake, shake, shake.
Hands down . . . shake, shake, shake.
All around . . . shake, shake, shake.
Put them down.

Colour Mittens

 (Use coloured felt mittens to accompany this rhyme.)
My poor little kitten lost her mitten,
And started to cry, "boo hoo"
So I helped her look for her mitten,
Her beautiful mitten of blue.

I found a mitten just right for a kitten,
Under my mother's bed.
Alas, the mitten was not the right mitten,
For it was coloured red.

I found a mitten just right for a kitten,
Under my father's pillow.
Alas, the mitten was not the right mitten,
For it was coloured yellow.

I found a mitten just right for a kitten,
Under the laundry so clean.
Alas the mitten was not the right
   mitten,
For it was coloured green.

I found a mitten just right for a kitten,
Inside my favourite shoe.
And this time the mitten was just the
   right mitten,
For it was coloured blue!

My Hands

(Suit actions to words.)

My hands upon my head I'll place.
Upon my shoulders, on my face,
At my waist and by my side,
And then behind me they will hide.
Then I'll raise them way up high,
And let my fingers fly, fly, fly,
Then clap, clap, clap and 1, 2, 3,
Just see how quiet they can be.

To Rhyming Land We Go

(Tune: Farmer in the Dell)
(Suit actions to words.)

To Rhyming Land we go,
To Rhyming Land we go,
High-ho the derry-o,
To Rhyming Land we go.
King Cole wears a crown,

(Pretend to place a crown on your head.)

King Cole wears a crown,
High-ho the derry-o,
King Cole wears a crown.

Additional verses:

Jack and Jill fall down

(Tip over to one side.)

Bo-Peep has lost her sheep

(Place hand over your eyes and pretend to look for sheep.)

Boy Blue is fast asleep

(Place hands under your chin and pretend to sleep.)

The cat can play a tune

(Pretend to play a fiddle.)

The cow jumps over the moon

(Make jumping motion with one hand over the other.)

A star shines in the sky

(Open and close your hands while they are over your head.)

And now we'll say goodbye

(Wave goodbye.)

Mother, Father, and Uncle John

(Sit child on your outstretched legs facing you and bounce gently up and down.)

Mother, Father and Uncle John,
Went to town one by one.
Mother fell off and . . .

(Lean to one side.)

Father fell off, but . . .

(Lean to the other side.)

Uncle John went on and on . . .

(Bounce quickly but gently up and down.)

Criss, Cross, Applesauce

(Have the children sit in front of caregivers with their backs to them. Caregivers should do as the actions indicate to the child.)

Criss, Cross, Applesauce

(Draw an "X" with your finger on the child's back.)

Spiders crawling up your back.

(Wiggle your fingers up the child's back.)

Tight squeeze,

(Give a big hug.)

Cool breeze,

(Blow gently on the child's neck.)

Now you've got the shiveries!

(Tickle child.)

The Cow That Jumped Over the Moon

Make a moveable prop to use with the rhyme *Hey Diddle Diddle*.

Materials

1 photocopied cow (to fit a 4-by-4-inch or 10-by-10 cm piece of white paper) per person

1 photocopied moon (to fit on an 8½-by-11-inch piece of yellow paper) per person

1 brass fastener (enough for your group)

1 cardstock strip (approx. 8 inches or 20 cm)

Masking tape

Instructions

1. Photocopy the cow template onto white paper.

2. Photocopy the moon template onto yellow paper.

3. Back both onto cardstock or construction paper to make them more sturdy.

4. Attach the strip of cardstock to the bottom of the cow with tape and measure it to the centre of the moon.

5. Attach the fastener through the bottom of the strip of cardstock and through the middle of the moon.

6. Flatten the tabs on the fastener. Your cow, when moved, should appear to be jumping over the moon.

Program 2

Fun with Ones:
Here Comes Peter Cottontail

What toddler doesn't love bunnies? "Here Comes Peter Cottontail" is a great theme to get your toddler up and hopping! The little ones in your program won't be able to resist joining in the fun. The "Cottonball Bunny" storytime souvenir will also provide a great visual and sensory aid to your session. Try to remember that simple crafts work best for little hands as they begin to explore the world of crayons, colouring, and fine motor skills. This is just as new to them as it may be to you.

Plan Ahead Note

This week's storytime souvenir requires little preparation. Photocopying and gluing are the two major components for the programmer, colouring and gluing for the crafter. This is craft time simplified.

Books to Share

Ten Little Bunnies, by Robin Spowart

Bouncing Bunnies, by Bob Bampton

Busy Bunnies, by Lisa McCue

More books to share with one year olds can be found in the bibliography at the end of this chapter.

Fun with Ones:
Here Comes Peter Cottontail

I Had a Little Bunny

 (Use your fingers to represent the bunnies.)
> I had a little bunny

(Hold up one finger.)
> One day she ran away.

(Make fingers "run.")
> I looked for her by moonlight,
> I looked for her by day.
> I found her in the meadow
> With her babies 1, 2, 3.
> So now I have four rabbit pets,
> To run and jump with me!

Here Is a Bunny with Ears So Funny

 (Suit actions to words.)
> Here is a bunny with ears so funny

(Hold up two fingers to look like bunny ears.)
> And here is his hole in the ground.

(Join your thumbs and fingers to make a circle.)
> When a noise he hears,
> He pricks up his ears

(Hold fingers up straight)
> And he jumps in his hole in the ground.

(Put rabbit ears in hole.)

Five Humpty Dumptys

 (Suit actions to words.)
> Five Humpty Dumptys sitting on a
>   wall,
> Five Humpty Dumptys sitting on a
>   wall,
> And if one Humpty Dumpty should
>   accidentally fall . . .
> CRACK!
> There'll be four Humpty Dumptys
>   sitting on the wall . . .

(Repeat until there are no eggs left.)

Sleeping Bunnies

 (Have the children lie down on the floor and pretend to be the sleeping bunnies.)

> Look at all the bunnies sleeping,
> 'Til it's nearly noon.
> Come and let us gently wake them,
> With a merry tune . . .
> Oh, how still . . . are they ill?
> Wake up soon. . . .
>
> Hop little bunnies, hopping, hopping,
> Hop little bunnies hop, hop, hop.
> Hop little bunnies hopping, hopping,
> Hop little bunnies, hop and stop.

If I Were a Bunny

(Suit actions to words.)
    If I were a bunny,
    I'd have ears this tall.

(Stretch your arms over your head.)
    I could twitch my whiskers and wiggle
      my nose

(Wiggle your nose.)
    But that isn't all—
    I'd be the friskiest bunny,
    That you ever could find.
    I'd hippity hop all around,
    With my cotton tail behind.

(Put hand behind back and wave.)

Little Bunny

(Use a bunny finger puppet or hand puppet or simply bend your fingers to look like bunny ears.)
    There was a little bunny who lived in
      the wood,
    He wiggled his ears like a good bunny
      should.
    He hopped by a squirrel,
    He hopped by a tree,
    He hopped by a carrot,
    And he hopped by me.

    He stared at the squirrel,
    He stared a the tree,
    He stared at the carrot,
    And he stared at me.

    He waved at the squirrel,
    He sniffed at the tree,
    He munched on the carrot,
    And he smiled at me.

See the Bunny?

(Use a finger puppet or hand puppet or simply bend your fingers to make them look like bunny ears.)
    See how the bunny hops along,
    Hops along, hops along.
    See how the bunny hops along,
    On a sunny morning.

Additional verses:
    Flops his ears
    Flops his tail

5 Happy Bunnies

(Photocopy the bunny pictured above to make the five bunnies to use with the rhyme.)
    5 happy bunnies from the corner pet
      store,
    I gave one away, then I had 4.
    4 happy bunnies, cute ones to see,
    I gave another one away, now there are
      3.
    3 happy bunnies, what did I do?
    I gave one more bunny away, then
      there were 2.
    2 happy bunnies, having lots of fun,
    I gave another to my friend, then there
      was just 1.
    1 happy bunny, my story is almost
      done,
    I kept this bunny for myself,
    And now there are none!

Cottonball Bunny

Make a bunny puppet to use with all sorts of rabbit rhymes and songs.

Materials

1 photocopied bunny (any colour) per person

1 Popsicle stick per person

Cotton balls (enough for your group; any colour)

Masking tape

Construction paper or cardstock

Instructions

1. Photocopy the bunny to approximately 5 inches or 13 cm in size.

2. Glue the bunny onto cardstock or construction paper to make it more sturdy.

3. Using masking tape, tape a Popsicle stick onto the back of the bunny.

4. These bunnies can be coloured and cotton balls can be glued on to make them fluffy.

Program 3

Fun with Ones: Things That Go

Ask any one year old what a car says and you're almost certain to hear the words "Beep! Beep!" or "Honk! Honk!" That's why including a transportation theme with a group this young seems fitting. One year olds are curious by nature and are constantly taking in everything around them. Cars, buses, and trucks (to name a few) are a part of everyday life, so why not make them fun to learn about?

Plan Ahead Note

The craft for this program requires that the programmer do all of the preparation ahead of time. It may be a good idea to cover the ends of the brass fasteners, once the wheels have been attached to the bus, with a 1-inch or 3 cm strip of masking tape. This isn't necessary, but it will help to prevent those little fingers from prying or getting poked by the ends.

Books to Share

Beep! Beep!, by Anne Miranda

My Car, by Byron Barton

Wheels on the Bus, by Rosanne Litzinger

More books to share with one year olds can be found in the bibliography at the end of this chapter.

Fun with Ones: Things That Go

Beep! Beep!

 (A great song to sing with bells!)
I'm a little piece of tin,
Nobody knows what shape I'm in.
Got four wheels and a running board,
I'm a four door, I'm a Ford.
Honk, honk, rattle, rattle, crash, beep,
    beep.
Honk, honk, rattle, rattle, crash, beep,
    beep!

Wheels on the Bus

(Suit actions to words.)
The wheels on the bus go round and
    round,
Round and round, round and round.
The wheels on the bus go round and
    round,
All through the town.

Additional verses:
People on the bus—up and down
Doors on the bus—open and shut
Money on the bus—clink, clink, clink
Babies on the bus—cry, cry, cry
Mommies on the bus—shh, shh, shh

Pete the Pilot

 (Tune: Old MacDonald)
(Pretend to be driving each of the vehicles by doing each of the actions indicated.)
Pete the pilot has a plane
Zoom, zoom, zoom, zoom, zoom.
And on that plane there are some
    wings,
Zoom, zoom, zoom, zoom, zoom.
With a zoom, zoom here,
And a zoom, zoom, there,
Here a zoom, there a zoom,
Everywhere a zoom-zoom,
Pete the pilot has a plane,
Zoom, zoom, zoom, zoom, zoom.

Additional verses:
Dan the driver has a car,
Beep, beep, beep, beep, beep

Train conductors drive the train,
Chug, chug, chug, chug, chug.

10 Little Fingers

 (Point to each body or facial part as it is named in the rhyme.)

I have 10 little fingers and 10 little
toes.
2 little arms and 1 little nose.
1 little mouth and 2 little ears.
2 little eyes for smiles and tears.
1 little head and 2 little feet,
1 little chin, that's me, complete!

Choo-Choo Train

 (Pretend to be a train by following the actions below.)

This is a choo-choo train,

(Bend arms at elbows.)

Puffing down the track,

(Rotate forearms in rhythm.)

Now it's going forward,

(Rotate arms forward.)

Now it's going back.

(Rotate arms backward.)

Now the bell is ringing,

(Pull pretend bell cord.)

Now the whistle blows,

(Hold fist near mouth and blow.)

What a lot of noise it makes,

(Cover ears with hands.)

Everywhere it goes.

(Stretch out arms.)

Little Red Wagon

 (Sit your child on your knees and bounce gently up and down.)

 Bumpin' up and down in my little red
wagon,
Bumpin' up and down in my little red
wagon,
Bumpin' up and down in my little red
wagon,
Won't you be my darlin'?

Additional verses:

One wheel's off and the axle's broken
Freddie's gonna fix it with his hammer
Laura's gonna fix it with her pliers
Bumpin' up and down in my little red
wagon

Down by the Station

 (Do as the actions indicate.)

Down by the station,
Early in the morning,

(Place hand over eyes and pretend to be searching.)

See the little pufferbellies,
All in a row?

See the station master,
Pull the little handle,

(Make pulling motion with one hand.)

Puff puff toot toot
Off we go!

I Have

 (Point to each body part as it is named.)

I have two eyes to see with,
I have two feet to run.
I have two hands to wave with,
And a nose, I have but one.

I have two ears to hear with,
And a mouth to say Good-day.
And two red cheeks for you to kiss,
Before I run away!

Big Yellow Bus

Make a bus with wheels that move.

Materials

1 bus photocopied on yellow paper (to fit an 8½-by-11-inch piece of paper) per person

2 black construction paper wheels (cut to fit the wheel space of the bus) per person

2 brass fasteners per person

Cardstock or construction paper

Masking tape

Instructions

1. Photocopy the template of the bus and back it onto cardstock or construction paper (to make the bus more sturdy), then cut it out.

2. Cut two circles from black construction paper to make the wheels for the bus.

3. Punch the fasteners through the middle of the black wheels and then through the bottom of the bus where the "X" indicates.

4. Let the children decorate the bus with crayons or markers or any other decorating material available.

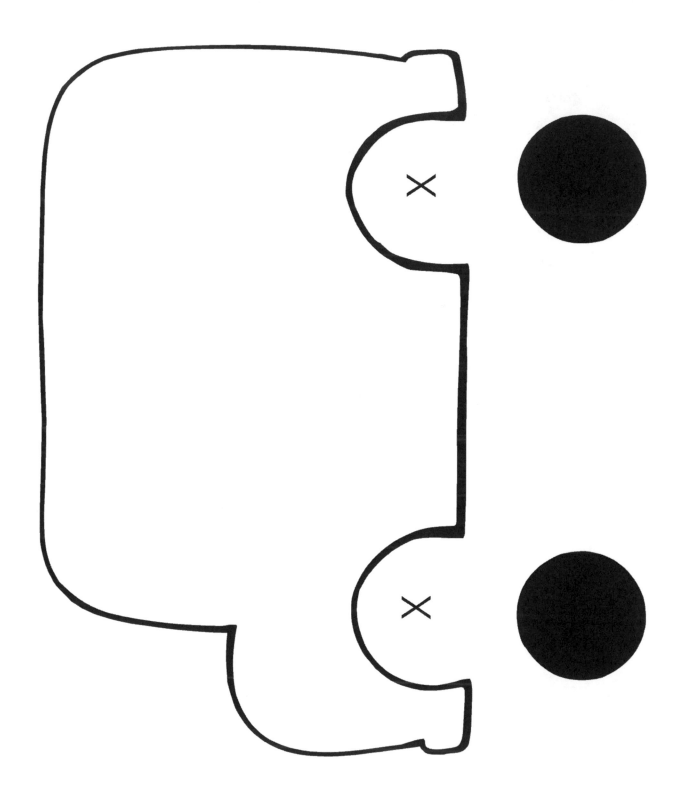

Program 4

Fun with Ones: Going to the Zoo

In this program you'll find some new songs sung to the tune of some old favourites. The songs and rhymes used here are meant to encourage the children to sing or growl along with you. "Silly" is the name of the game when you have a group of children together at any age, and this is a time when we as programmers want the children in our group to join in. Whether it's waddling like a penguin or roaring like a lion, it's all about one thing: F-U-N!

Plan Ahead Note

The *100 Animals* rhyme in this chapter requires the programmer to do his or her homework. We recommend that you have as many pictures as you can to accompany your songs and rhymes. By having pictures of the animals for the *100 Animals* rhyme you can enhance and build on the knowledge of the children in your group.

Books to Share

Color Zoo, by Lois Ehlert

Peekaboo Zoo, by Susan Hood

Zany Zoo, by Derek Matthews

More books to share with one year olds can be found in the bibliography at the end of this chapter.

Fun with Ones: Going to the Zoo

Rhymes and Songs

100 Animals

 (It's a great idea to have pictures accompany a rhyme. You don't need to have ten pictures of each of these animals. You could use one picture to represent all ten.)

I went to the zoo and what did I see?
100 animals looking at me.
There were 10 tall giraffes eating from
    the trees,
10 silly monkeys scratching on their
    knees.
10 sleepy snakes lying in the sun,
10 elephants munching on peanuts one
    by one.
10 leaping tigers performing in the
    shows,
10 pink flamingos standing on their
    toes.
10 grouchy bears trying to get some
    sleep,
10 happy hippos in the water deep.
10 roaring lions walking two by two,
10 galloping zebras . . .
All living at the zoo!

The Monkeys at the Zoo

 (Tune: The Farmer in the Dell)
(Pretending to be the monkey in this rhyme will be tons of fun if you let the children show YOU what monkeys do.)

The monkeys at the zoo,
The monkeys at the zoo,
Heigh-ho they laugh and play,
The monkeys at the zoo.

The monkeys run and hide,
The monkeys run and hide,
They like to play, then run away,
The monkeys at the zoo.

The monkeys love to swing,
The monkeys love to swing,
They love to swing, they love to sing,
The monkeys at the zoo.

Zoo Rhyme

 (This is a great rhyme that would be even better if there were pictures to accompany it.)

Penguin and hippo and elephant too.
Add a lion and a monkey—then you
    have a zoo!

My friend penguin loves to play,
He waddles and he swims, but he
    never flies away.

My friend hippo spends time in the water,
He's smaller than a whale, but bigger
    than an otter.

My friend elephant has a long trunk,
He smells lots of stuff with it, especially
    skunks!

My friend lion has a curly mane,
He loves to run and prance and play,
    even when it rains!

My friend monkey loves to swing all
    the time,
He's the last silly animal in this silly
    rhyme!

Giddy Good Morning

(Slap your thighs and clap your hands as you sing.)

Giddy giddy giddy good morning,
Good morning, good morning.
Giddy giddy giddy good morning,
Good morning to you!

(Roll the child's hands forward.)

Minny mac minny mac
Minny minny minny mac.
Minny mac minny mac minny moe.

(Roll the child's hands backward.)

Minny mac minny mac
Minny minny minny mac.
Minny mac minny mac minny moe.

(Slap your thighs and clap your hands.)

Giddy giddy giddy good morning,
Good morning, good morning.
Giddy giddy giddy good morning,
Good morning to you!

I Went to the Zoo

(Tune: London Bridge)
(Suit actions to words.)

I went to the zoo one day, zoo one day,
zoo one day,
I saw a lion in a cage and this is what
he said—ROAR!

Additional verses:

Snake—hiss
Monkey—ooh ooh ahh
Tiger—grrrr

I'm a Little Monkey

(Tune: I'm a Little Teapot)
(Suit actions to words.)

I'm a little monkey in the tree,
Swinging by my tail so merrily.
I can leap and fly from tree to tree,
I have lots of fun you see.

I'm a little monkey watch me play,
Munching on bananas every day.
Lots of monkey friends to play with
me,
We have fun up in the trees.

Animals in the Zoo

(Tune: Wheels on the Bus)
*(Get the children involved by letting them tell
you what noises the animals make.)*

The monkeys at the zoo say ooh ooh
ahh, ooh ooh ahh, ooh ooh ahh,
The monkeys at the zoo say ooh ooh
ahh,
All day long.

Additional verses:

Parrots say squawk
Tigers say grrr
Lions say ROAR

Swing, Swing

*(Have everyone stand in a circle holding hands
with their children while you recite this poem.)*

Silly little monkeys swinging in the
tree,
All hold hands and swing with me.
Swing up high,
Swing down low,
Swing in the tree now don't let go!
Swing high, swing low, swing like I
do,
Swing like monkeys in the zoo!

Silly Swinging Monkey

Make a funny monkey mobile to hang and amuse young children.

Materials

1 sheet brown construction paper per person

1 sheet yellow construction paper per person

2½ brown pipe cleaners (approx. 10 inches or 12 cm each) per person

2 medium wiggle eyes per person

1 small pom-pom per person

1 drinking straw per person

Glue sticks (enough for your group)

Instructions

1. Using the templates, cut out brown and yellow circles from construction paper.

2. Glue the medium yellow circle to the large brown circle (this is the monkey's body and tummy).

3. Glue the small yellow circle to the medium brown circle (this is the monkey's head and face).

4. Glue the head to the body.

5. Glue on the two wiggle eyes and the pom-pom nose.

6. Cut the two large pipe cleaners in half (these are the arms and legs) and tape them to the body of the monkey. Tape the last half pipe cleaner on the back for the tail curl.

7. Wrap the ends of the pipe cleaner arms around the straw and bend the ends of the legs to look like feet.

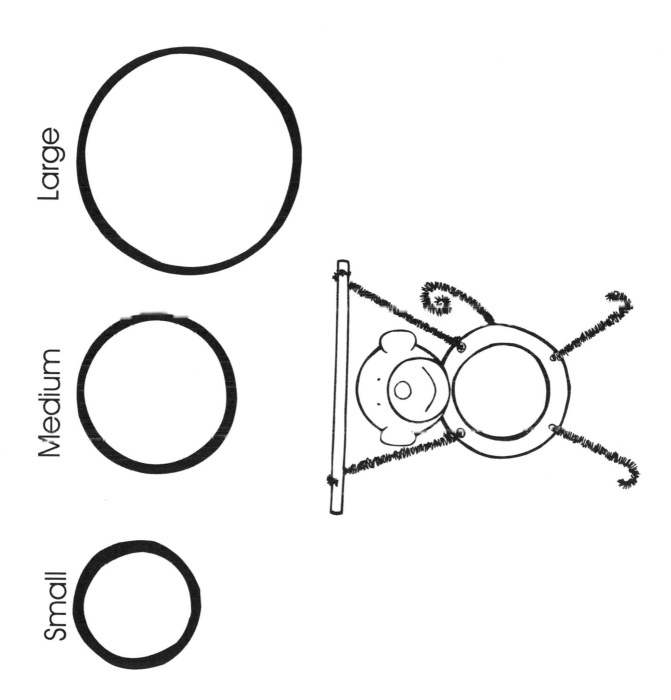

Large

Medium

Small

Program 5

Fun with Ones: Jungle Jamboree

As we introduce this program, you may be wondering, why so many animal programs? The answer is, there are so many wonderful songs, rhymes, and books available that we are always trying to include what we think are the best of the best into our programs. Children seem to have a natural connection with animals. Their sounds and actions are the things that children learn first. Knowing an animal's proper name comes later. So why not build on the knowledge that children already posses and allow their minds to grow?

Plan Ahead Note

As an extension for the *One Elephant* song, before your program, make a circle on the floor (big enough so that all the children can sit around it comfortably) using string. The children can then take turns being the elephant.

Books to Share

Walking Through the Jungle, by Debbie Harter

Jolly Jungle, by Derek Matthews and Dug Steer

But What Does the Hippopotamus Say?, by Francesca Simon

More books to share with one year olds can be found in the bibliography at the end of this chapter.

Fun with Ones: Jungle Jamboree

Rhymes and Songs

3 Little Monkeys

(Use your fingers to represent the monkeys in this song.)

3 little monkeys swinging in the tree,
Along came a crocodile quiet as can be.
The first monkey said, "You can't catch me"
SNAP!

2 little monkeys swinging in a tree . . .

1 little monkeys swing in the tree,
Along came a crocodile quiet as can be.
The last monkey said, "You can't catch me. . . .
MISSED ME"

Once I Saw

(Show the children the actions when you say this rhyme the first time. Repeat this rhyme a second time so the children can do the actions with you.)

Once I saw a little bird come,
Hop, hop, hop,

(Hop up and down.)

I cried, "Little bird won't you
Stop, stop, stop."

(Stop jumping.)

I went to the window saying,
"How do you do?"
But he shook his little tail,

(Shake hips.)

And away he flew.

(Flap arms like a bird.)

One Elephant

(Use your fingers to represent the elephants.)

One elephant went out to play,
Upon a spider's web one day.
He had such enormous fun,
That he called for another elephant to come.
Two elephants went out to play,
Upon a spider's web one day.
They had such enormous fun,
That they called for another elephant to come.

Three elephants went out to play,
Upon a spider's web one day,
They pranced and they danced and they put on a show,
'Til one little elephant had to go.

Two . . . One . . .

Do Your Ears Hang Low?

(Suit actions to words.)
Do your ears hang low?

 (Pretend your arms are your ears.)
Do they wobble to and fro?

(Wiggle arms.)
Can you tie them in a knot?

(Pretend to tie a knot)
Can you tie them in a bow?

(Pretend to tie a bow)
Can you throw them over your shoulder,

(Throw arms over your shoulder.)
Like a continental soldier?

(Stand like a soldier.)
Do your ears hang low?

Underneath the Monkey Tree

(Tune: The Muffin Man)
(Do as the actions indicate.)

Come and play a while with me,

(Tap thighs.)

Underneath the monkey tree,
Monkey see and monkey do,
Just like monkeys in the zoo.

Swing your tail, one, two, three,

(Swing hips from side to side.)

Underneath the monkey tree.
Monkey see and monkey do,
Just like monkeys in the zoo.

Clap your hands, one, two, three,

(Clap your hands.)

Underneath the monkey tree.
Monkey see and monkey do,
Just like monkeys in the zoo.

Sit down on the ground the with me,

(Sit down.)

Underneath the monkey tree.
Monkey see and monkey do,
Just like monkeys in the zoo.

Five Grey Elephants

(Use your fingers to represent the elephants.)

5 grey elephants marching through a glade,

(March fingers of right hand.)

Decide to stop and say that they are
having a parade.
The first swings his trunk and
announces that he'll lead.

(Swing arm like trunk.)

The next waves a flag which of course
they need.

(Wave hand over head.)

The third grey elephant trumpets a song,

(Blow through your hand.)

The fourth beats a drum as he marches
along.

(Pretend to beat a drum.)

While the fifth makes believe that he's
the whole show,
He nods and he waves to the crowd as
they go.

(Nod head left to right and wave one hand.)

5 grey elephants marching through the
glade,
Having lots and lots of fun during their
parade.

The Elephant's Trunk

*(Show the children the actions for this rhyme as
you say it.)*

The elephant has a great big trunk,

(Pretend your arm is a trunk.)

That goes swinging, swinging, so.

(Swing trunk.)

He has tiny, tiny, eyes that show him
just where to go.

(Point to eyes.)

His huge long ears go flapping,
flapping, flapping up and down.

(Pretend your hands are ears.)

His great big feet go stomping,
stomping, stomping, on the ground.

(Stomp feet loudly.)

Elmo Elephant

Make a friendly elephant to take home and put up on your toddler's wall.

Materials

2 adult-sized paper plates per person

2 large elephant ears, enlarged and photocopied from template (slightly larger than the size of the plate) per person

1 strip of grey construction paper (approx. 8 inches or 20 cm in length) per person

Pencils

Instructions

1. Cut out two large elephant ears (slightly larger than a paper plate).

2. Glue elephant ears on either side of a paper plate right side up.

3. Glue the second paper plate to the first one (bottoms facing out) and let dry.

4. Take a strip of construction paper and curl it around a pencil.

5. Glue or tape this strip onto the middle of the top paper plate to create the elephant's trunk.

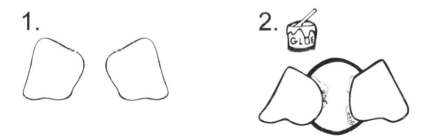

Program 6

Fun with Ones: Pet Parade

This next program will bring you out of the jungle and take you on a trip to the pet shop. "Pet Parade" is a theme that can be related to on a personal level. Almost every child has had an experience of one kind or another with a common household pet (either by owning one or a stuffed animal that closely resembles one). As stated previously, familiarity is a terrific back-pocket tool. Even though some of the songs may not be familiar to many, the animals will be. This alone will allow your group to reach a certain level of comfort, because the caregivers have a general knowledge or understanding of the theme.

Plan Ahead Note

The storytime souvenir for this program requires the programmer to measure each child's head individually. You may want to plan to give the children and caregivers a few extra minutes at craft time. Fitting each head band can be a time-consuming process, and your caregiver may have plans or appointments for after your program ends. One way to streamline the process is to have pre-torn strips of masking tape (enough for your group) on the wall, table, or whatever surface you choose, available for attaching the ends of the head bands. The caregivers can grab their own tape and help the child(ren) they are with.

Books to Share

Happy Snappy Pet Parade, by Dug Steer

Hide-and-Seek Puppy, by David Crossley

Kitty's Colors, by Dick McCue

More books to share with one year olds can be found in the bibliography at the end of this chapter.

Fun with Ones: Pet Parade

Rhymes and Songs

Little Puppies and Kitties

 (Use both hands to represent the pets in this rhyme.)

One little, two little, three little kittens,

(Hold up three fingers on one hand.)
Were napping in the sun.

(Place hands under your chin and pretend to sleep.)
One little, two little, three little puppies,

(Hold up three fingers on the other hand.)
Said "C'mon let's have some fun!"
Up to the kittens the puppies went creeping,

(Creep one hand up to the other.)
As quiet as quiet could be.
One little, two little, three little kittens,
Went scampering up a tall tree.

(Move one hand away quickly.)

This Kitty

 (Start by holding up all 5 fingers. At each line take one away. On the last line have the final finger run through a hole made by the left hand.)

This kitty said, "I smell a mouse."
This kitty said, "Let's hunt through the house."
This kitty said, "Let's go creep creep."
This kitty said, "Is the mouse asleep?"
This kitty said, "Meow, meow, meow, meow,
I saw him go through this hole just now."

Rags

 (Do as the actions indicate.)
I have a dog and his name is Rags,
He eats so much that his tummy sags,

(Put arms in front of your body to show a big tummy.)
His ears flip-flop and his tail wig wags,

(Use hands for ears and tail.)
And when he walks, he goes zig-zag.

(Sway from side to side.)
He goes, flip-flop,

(Flap hands as ears.)
Wig wag,

(Shake hips.)
Zig-zag

(Sway side to side.)
He goes flip-flop, wig-wag, zig-zag,
He goes flip-flop, wig-wag, zig-zag.
I love Rags and he loves me!

(Give child a hug.)

89

Six Little Dogs

(Tune: Six Little Ducks)
(Suit actions to words.)

Six little dogs that I once knew,
Small ones, skinny ones, fair ones too.
But the one little dog with the brown
   and curly fur,
He led the others with a grr, grr, grr.
Grr, grr, grr.
Grr, grr, grr.
He led the others with a grr, grr, GRR!

Out to the doghouse they would go,
Wig-wagging their tails to and fro,
But the one little dog with the brown
   and curly fur,
He led the other with a grr, grr, grr.
Grr, grr, grr.
Grr, grr, grr.
He led the others with a grr, grr, GRR!
Back in for suppertime they would run,
Gobble, gobble, gobble, gobble, gulp!
   They were done.
But the one little dog with the brown
   and curly fur,
He led the others with a grr, grr, grr.
Grr, grr, grr.
Grr, grr, grr.

Here Is a Puppy

(Use your fingers to represent the puppies in this rhyme.)

Here is a little puppy,

(Hold up thumb on right hand.)
Here is a kitty cat.

(Hold up thumb on left hand.)
Puppy goes to sleep,

(Pretend to sleep.)
Curled up on his mat.
Kitty creeps up softly,

(Move left thumb slowly towards the right thumb.)
Tickles puppy's chin.

(Tickle child under chin.)
Puppy wakes up quickly,

(Pop up right thumb.)
See the chase begin.

Mrs. Kitty

 (Do as the actions indicate.)
  Mrs. Kitty, sleek and fat,

(Hold up thumb on right hand.)
  With her kittens four,

(Hold up four fingers on same hand.)
  Went to sleep upon the mat,

(Pretend to sleep.)
  By the kitchen door.
  Mrs. Kitty heard a noise,
  Up she jumped with glee,

(Pop up thumb.)
  Kittens, maybe that's a mouse?

(Put up all five fingers.)
  Let's all go and see!

  Creeping, creeping, creeping on,

(Slowly sneak five fingers across the floor.)
  Silently they stole.
  But the little mouse had gone,

(Mouse is thumb on left hand.)
  Back into his hole.

(Tuck thumb into fist.)

5 Little Kittens

 (Use your fingers to represent the kittens in this rhyme.)
  5 little kittens standing in a row,

(Hold up 5 fingers.)
  They nod their heads to the children so.

(Bend fingers.)
  They run to the left; they run to the right,

(Move fingers left, then right.)
  They stand up and stretch in the bright sunlight.

(Stretch fingers out.)
  Along comes a dog who's in for some fun,

(Hold up one finger from opposite hand.)
  ME-OW!
  See those little kittens run!

(Move fingers quickly.)

Counting Cats

 (Pretend to be the cats in this rhyme by suiting your actions to the words.)

  One cat napping in the sun.
  Two cats playing pounce and run,
  Three cats eating from one dish.
  Four cats fishing for a fish,
  Five cats lazing on a fence.
  Six cats peeking under paper tents.
  Seven cats blinking crossed blue eyes,
  Eight cats chasing butterflies.
  Nine cats cuddled tail to head,
  Ten cats bouncing on my bed.

Perfect Puppy Headband

Make a puppy ear headband and let your child have fun using his or her imagination pretending to be a puppy.

Materials

2 puppy ear shapes per person

1 strip of poster board (2-by-20-inch or 5 cm-by-50 cm) per person

1 sheet black construction paper per person

1 sheet brown construction paper per person

Adhesive tape

Instructions

1. Enlarge the dog ear pattern on the photocopier (to fit on the sides of a child's head).
2. Trace and cut out two long dog ears from construction paper.
3. Tape the ears one-third of the way in from either end of the strip of poster board.
4. Paste spots onto the ears (or provide bingo dabbers at craft time for children to add spots).
5. Measure the ears to child's head for a perfect fit and tape accordingly.

Extra: With washable face paints, you can add a black button nose, and children will make perfect puppies.

Dog ear pattern

Program 7

Fun with Ones: Jingle Jollies

Here it is—the first of our holiday celebration themes to be introduced! Your ears may be ringing after this session, but what a great time you'll have! This is a program where children and caregivers will *want* to get rowdy to wear off some of that holiday excitement and anticipation. You might want to let your caregivers know, a week in advance, that the bells will be coming out in the following program (if you don't use them on a regular basis). This will allow the caregivers to be a little better prepared for what is sure to follow. A group of one year olds, bells, and the Christmas season all wrapped up into one exciting session. Ho! Ho! Ho!

Plan Ahead Note

As a programmer, it is important to stay flexible in your programming. This is one program where flexibility will be needed. If you have children from other countries in your program, their caregivers may wish to tell you about their culture. Give them the opportunity to share and take the opportunity to learn something new yourself. If they are willing, they could even teach you and your group a song or two.

Books to Share

Three Little Teddy Bears, by Nicola Smee

Baby's Christmas, by Susan Baum

Where Is Snowy's Nose, by Kelly Asbury

More books to share with one year olds can be found in the bibliography at the end of this chapter.

Fun with Ones: Jingle Jollies

Rhymes and Songs

Ring Those Bells

(Tune: Jimmy Crack Corn)
(Break out the bells!)

Ring those bells and turn around,
Ring those bells and turn around,
Ring those bells and turn around,
Christmas time is here.

Additional verses:

Ring those bells and stamp your feet
Ring those bells and clap your hands
Ring those bells and jump up high
Ring those bells and touch the floor.

Little Bell

(Break out the bells!)

Five little bells hanging in a row,

(Fingers hanging down.)

The first one said, "Ring me slow."

(Wiggle thumb.)

The second one said, "Ring me fast."

(Wiggle index finger.)

The third one said, "Ring me last."

(Wiggle second finger.)

The fourth one said, "I'm like a chime."

(Wiggle third finger.)

The fifth one said, "Ring me at Christmas time."

(Wiggle fourth finger.)

The Lights on the Tree

(Tune: The Wheels on the Bus)
(Suit actions to words.)

The lights on the tree go blink, blink, blink,
Blink, blink, blink. Blink, blink, blink.
The lights on the tree go blink, blink, blink.
All Christmas Day.

Additional verses:

The presents at the house go rattle, rattle, rattle.
The mommy at the house goes bake, bake, bake.
The daddy at the house goes snore, snore, snore.
The grandma at the house gives hugs, hugs, hugs.
The grandpa at the house gives kisses, kisses, kisses

Ring Your Bells

(Suit actions to words.)
(Bring out the bells!)

Ring, ring, ring your bells,
Ring them loud and clear.
Tell everybody everywhere
That Christmas time is here!

Stamp, stamp, stamp your feet,
Stamp them loud and clear.
Tell everybody everywhere
That Christmas time is here!

Clap, clap, clap, your hands,
Clap them loud and clear.
Tell everybody everywhere,
That Christmas time is here!

95

Toys on the Tree

(Tune: This Old Man)
(Suit actions to words.)

This little drum, on the tree,
Santa put it there for me,
With a boom-boom, rat-a-tat,
Rummy-tummy-tum,
Christmas day is so much fun!

This little train, on the tree,
Santa put it there for me,
With a chug-chug, choo-choo,
Rummy-tummy-tum,
Christmas Day is so much fun!

This little doll, on the tree,
Santa put it there for me,
With a Ma-ma, Ma-ma,
Rummy-tummy-tum,
Christmas Day is so much fun!

5 Little Reindeer

(Use your fingers to represent the reindeer in this rhyme.)

5 little reindeer, standing by the gate,
The first one said, "Hurry, don't be late!"
The second one said, "Did I hear Santa call?"
The third one said, "Careful now, don't fall."
The fourth one said, "It's time to load the toys!"
The fifth one said, "Merry Christmas girls and boys!"

Reindeer Pokey

(Tune: Hokey Pokey)
(Stand and do as the actions indicate.)

You put your antlers *(head)* in, you take your antlers out,
You put your antlers in and you shake them all about.
You do the reindeer pokey and you turn yourself about
That's what it's all about. CLAP!

Additional verses:
Put your front legs *(hands)* in
Put your back legs *(feet)* in
Put your reindeer tail *(backside)* in
Put your whole self in

When Santa Got Stuck in the Chimney

(This song is so much fun that the children will want you to sing it again and again.)

When Santa got stuck in the chimney,
He began to shout,
"You girls and boys won't get any toys,
If you don't pull me out!
My beard is black,
There's soot in my sack,
My nose is tickly too."
When Santa got stuck in the chimney,
ACHOO! ACHOO! ACHOO!
Was on the eve before Christmas Day,
When Santa arrived in his sleigh.
Into the chimney he climbed with his sack,
But he was so fat—he couldn't get back
Oh, what a terrible plight,
    GANGWAY!
He stayed up there all night.

When Santa got stuck in the chimney,
He began to yell,
"Oh hurry, please,
It's all such a squeeze,
The reindeer's stuck as well!
His head's up there in the cold night air,
Now Rudolph's nose is BLUE!"
When Santa got stuck in the chimney,
ACHOO! ACHOO! ACHOO!

Oh, Christmas Tree!

Young children enjoy dropping sparkling "decorations" onto the sticky Christmas tree.

Materials

1 sheet of green construction paper per person

Sticky-backed clear plastic paper/mac tac (enough for your group)

Cardstock or construction paper

Instructions

1. Photocopy and cut out the Christmas tree illustration.

2. Glue onto cardstock or construction paper to make your tracer a little more sturdy.

3. Place the sheet of green construction paper in front of you lengthwise, trace the Christmas tree onto the middle of the paper, and cut it out (using an Exacto knife).

4. Cut a piece of sticky-backed paper 4-by-4-inches or 10 cm-by-10 cm. Peel the waxy back of the sticky paper off and place it over the Christmas tree cut-out. Put the waxy back of the sticky paper over top of the sticky part (to prevent all the paper from sticking together).

5. At craft time, peel off the waxy-back paper and have children decorate the tree by dropping chunky glitter, ripped paper, or confetti onto the sticky paper centre.

Sticky paper

98

Program 8

Fun with Ones: Anything Goes

Why not close out your session with a general theme like "Anything Goes?" Stomping, singing, and especially clapping will be great fun with the help of our storytime souvenir, "Clickety-Clack Clappers." This easy-to-make and fun-to-use craft is sure to be a hit once children hear the unique clicking sound of the buttons. What could be more perfect for a group of pot-banging one year olds than a craft that allows them to do what they do best, make noise? Clapping the hands together is sure to keep their busy hands just that . . . busy!

Plan Ahead Note

This craft requires the programmer to do all of the preparation and assembly ahead of time. Children can use these clappers in the program and then decorate them at craft time. You may want to collect them after you have sung a few songs with them. If you don't, you may be finding them crumpled on the floor, leaving you with no craft!

Books to Share

Peek-a-Boo, Lizzy Lou!, by Lauren Attinello

Peek-a-Boo!, by Janet Ahlberg

Peek-a-Boo, by Jan Ormerod

More books to share with one year olds can be found in the bibliography at the end of this chapter.

Fun with Ones: Anything Goes

Rhymes and Songs

Reach for the Ceiling

 (Suit actions to words.)

Reach for the ceiling,
Touch the floor,
Stand up again,
Let's do some more.
Touch your head,
Then your knees,
Up to your shoulders,
Like this you see.
Reach for the ceiling,
Touch the floor,
That's all now,
There isn't any more.

You Can Clap

 (Tune: If You're Happy and You Know It)
(Do as the actions indicate.)

You can clap your hands . . . clap, clap,
    clap.
You can clap your hands . . . clap, clap,
    clap.
When the day is done and you want to
    have some fun,
You can clap your hands . . . clap, clap,
    clap.

Additional verses

You can stamp your feet . . . stamp,
    stamp, stamp.
You can shake your head . . . shake,
    shake, shake.

Kookaburra

 (Clap hands throughout this song.)

Kookaburra sits in the old gum tree,
Merry, merry king of the bushes he,
Laugh kookaburra, laugh kookaburra,
Happy your life must be.

Kookaburra sits in the old gum tree,
Eating all the gumdrops he can see,
Stop kookaburra, stop kookaburra,
Leave some there for me.
Kookaburra sits in the old gum tree,
Counting all the monkeys he can see,
Stop kookaburra, stop kookaburra,
That's not a monkey, that's me!

Boom Boom

 (Suit actions to words.)

Boom, boom ain't it great to be crazy,
Boom, boom ain't it great to be nuts?
Silly and foolish all day long,
Boom, boom ain't it great to be crazy?

A horse and a flea and three blind
    mice,
Sat on a corner shooting dice.
The horsie slipped and he fell on the
    flea,
"Whoops!" said the flea, "there's a
    horsie on me!"

Boom, boom ain't it great to be crazy?
Boo, boom ain't it great to be nuts?
Silly and foolish all day long,
Boom, boom ain't it great to be crazy?

100

The Bubble Song

(Pretend to be blowing and popping bubbles in this song.)

1 little, 2 little, 3 little bubbles,
4 little, 5 little, 6 little bubbles,
7 little, 8 little, 9 little bubbles,
10 little bubbles go POP! POP! POP!
Pop those, pop those, pop those
    bubbles,
Pop those, pop those, pop those
    bubbles,
Pop those, pop those, pop those
    bubbles,
10 little bubbles go POP! POP! POP!

Good-Bye

(Suit actions to words.)

Two little hands go clap, clap, clap.
Two little arms lie in my lap.
Two little feet go bump, bump, bump.
Two little legs give one big jump.
Two little hands reach oh so high.
Two little hands wave bye, bye, bye.

Good Morning

(Having pictures of the animals mentioned in this rhyme would be a great extension.)

One day I saw a downy duck with
    feathers on his back,
I said, "Good morning downy duck,"
    and he said, "Quack, quack, quack."
One day I saw a timid mouse, he was
    so shy and meek,
I said, "Good morning timid mouse,"
    and he said, "Squeak, squeak,
    squeak."
One day I saw a scruffy dog, I met him
    with a bow,
 I said, "Good morning scruffy dog,"
    and he said, "Bow-wow-wow."
One day I saw a scarlet bird, he woke
    me from my sleep,
I said, "Good morning scarlet bird,"
    and he said, "Cheep, cheep, cheep."

Here's a Ball

(Suit actions to words.)

Here's a ball for baby, big and fat and
    round.

(Make a large circle with arms.)

Here is baby's hammer, see how it can
    pound.

(Making a fist, pound one hand on the other.)

Here are baby's soldiers, standing in a
    row.

(Make a saluting motion.)

Here is baby's music, clapping,
    clapping so.

(Clap hands.)

Here is baby's trumpet,
    tootle-tootle-oo.

(Pretend to play a trumpet.)

Here's the way the baby plays
    peek-a-boo.

(Play peek-a-boo.)

Here's a big umbrella to keep baby
    dry.

(Hold hands over your head.)

Here is baby's cradle, rock-a-bye

(Rock child back and forth.)

Clickety-Clack Clappers

Craft clappers that toddlers will enjoy for the interesting sounds they make.

Materials

2 photocopied hands (the size of a child's hand) per person

2 large craft buttons per person

2 Popsicle sticks per person

Cardstock or construction paper

Glue sticks or white glue

Tape

Scissors

Instructions

1. Photocopy the hand template (to the size of a child's hand) and cut out two hands. Glue them onto cardstock or construction paper to reinforce.

2. Cut the hands out and tape a Popsicle stick on the back of each hand to make the handles.

3. Glue a large bright button in the centre of each hand.

4. Clap the hands together to hear the clapping sound.

5. Let the children colour the hands using markers, crayons, etc.

6. Bibliography of Books to Share

Ahlberg, Janet. 1997. *Peek-a-Boo!*. New York: Viking Children's Books.

Asbury, Kelly. 2000. *Where Is Snowy's Nose?* New York: Price Stern Sloan.

Attinello, Lauren. 1997. *Peek-a-Boo! Lizzy Lou: A Playtime Book and Muppet Puppet.* New York: Workman.

Bampton, Bob. 2001. *Bouncing Bunnies.* New York: Cartwheel Books.

Barton, Byron. 1997. *Little Red Hen.* New York: HarperCollins Juvenile Books.

Barton, Byron. 2001. *My Car.* New York: Greenwillow.

Baum, Susan. 1998. *Baby's Christmas.* New York: Little Simon.

Cousins, Lucy. 1996. *Humpty Dumpty and Other Nursery Rhymes.* New York: Dutton Books.

Crossley, David. 2000. *Hide-and-Seek Puppy.* New York: Little Simon.

Ehlert, Lois. 1997. *Color Zoo.* New York: HarperCollins.

Geddes, Anne. 2000. *Ten in the Bed.* Kansas City, MO: Andrew McMeel.

Harter, Debbie. 2001. *Walking Through the Jungle.* New York: Orchard Books.

Hood, Susan. 1999. *Peekaboo Zoo.* New York: Friedman/Fairfax.

Litzinger, Rosanne. 1999. *Wheels on the Bus: A Pop-Up Book.* Brookfield, CT: Millbrook Press Trade.

Matthews, Derek, et al. 2000. *Jolly Jungle.* Brookfield, CT: Millbrook Press Trade.

Matthews, Derek. 2000. *Zany Zoo: A Happy Snappy Book.* Brookfield, CT: Millbrook Press Trade.

McCue, Dick. 2000. *Kitty's Colours.* New York: Little Simon.

McCue, Lisa. 2000. *Busy Bunnies Touch-Me-Book.* Pleasantville, NY: Reader's Digest.

Miranda, Anne. 2000. *Beep! Beep!* New York: Turtle Books.

Ormerod, Jan. 1998. *Peek-A-Boo.* New York: Dutton Books.

Raffi. 1990. *Shake My Sillies Out.* New York: Crown.

Simon, Francesca. 1994. *But What Does the Hippopotamus Say?* New York: Gulliver Books.

Smee, Nicola. 1995. *Three Little Teddy Bears/With 3 Finger Puppets.* New York: Cartwheel Books.

Spowart, Robin. 2001. *Ten Little Bunnies.* New York: Cartwheel Books.

Steer, Dug. 2000. *Happy Snappy Pet Parade.* Brookfield, CT: Millbrook Press Trade.

Wood, Audrey. 1998. *Quick As A Cricket.* Swindon, England: Childs Play International Limited.

Wood, Audrey. 1999. *Silly Sally.* Lake Worth, FL: Red Wagon.

Chapter 4
Terrific Twos

   Children in their second year of life are often labelled "Terrible Twos" by society. At this age children are testing their independence and are likely to have tantrums and mood swings. For a programmer, however, two year olds are terrific; they are just beginning to *independently* appreciate the literate world—the oral tradition in story, rhyme, and song. Two year olds enjoy stories that contain humour, suspense, and characterisation. They continue to grow and flourish in an environment where a caregiver is present; they enjoy tickle rhymes and manipulative action songs. But they are also ready for exposure to activities usually contained in a traditional storytime: listening to a story surrounded by a group of their peers, taking part in participatory activities such as fingerplays and follow-the-leader style games, and mastering the functional parts of the program on their own (e.g., choosing their own bell and returning it after the song).

The predictability of a routine and the addition of independent activities for the two year olds will create a new wrinkle in your storytime: idle caregivers. Adults will quickly grow accustomed to their two year old toddling away, and left to their own devices, grown-ups have a natural tendency to chat amongst themselves or grow restless. The challenge is to keep the adults involved but still encourage the twos to participate independently.

A program for two year olds will not usually be as fast paced as a program for one year olds. Instead of trying to entertain with a variety of adult-led activities, the focus in a two year old program is on the process. A song that requires children to use a prop, for example, will take much longer than the same song would have with a group of one year olds. The twos will toddle up on their own and choose their own prop carefully (even if the props are all identical). Holding it proudly, they will then toddle back to their spot and enjoy the song. After all the participatory elements of the song are complete, it will be time to return the prop, and the twos will do this with the same deliberation they used for the original choosing. Do not rush this process; twos become easily frustrated if an adult tries to take away their new-found independence. It will seem to take a long time to begin and end these types of activities, but for the two year olds, the beginning and endings are just as important, developmentally, as the activity itself.

Do not force a group to fit into a structure or routine that does not work for them; instead, adapt or develop a routine that works for everyone. It is simply a matter of trial and error as well as lots of listening and experimentation. A registered program for this age group, with a predictable group of attendees, will likely prove to be the most beneficial format and, in fact, will be easier on both the programmer and the participants.

1. What Can Twos Do?: Child Development at Twenty-four to Thirty-six Months

There are many things you can do with twos because they have mastered new skills and love using and showing off their acquired talents. Two year olds should be given challenges and activities that will help them learn about the world around them, as well as group dynamics. Also, the bond between adult and child should not be forgotten. Although twos enjoy their independence, they also need love and nurturing. The reassurance they receive from a touch and a tickle will help to boost them for the next challenge.

To create a program that enhances their skills, you should focus on the milestones that many two year olds will have accomplished or be approaching. Developmental markers for thirty month olds include

- turning pages of a book;

- walking up and down stairs;

- feeding themselves;

- pushing, pulling, filling, and dumping;

- stacking objects;

- tossing or rolling a ball;

- playing make-believe;

- dressing up in costumes or hats;

- speaking in two- or three-word sentences;

- pointing to parts of the body or common objects; and

- learning how to use common household items.

Because children at this age have begun to appreciate themselves within the context of the world around them, they are also learning about others and how to interact. This inevitably leads to some frustration and difficulties, socially, for two year olds. Some examples of social challenges two year olds face are

- shyness around unfamiliar children and adults,

- insistence on accomplishing tasks without help,

- possessiveness with toys and objects,

- demanding attention and focus of the caregiver,

- showing aggression or frustration,

- feelings of jealousy and possessiveness for loved ones, and

- an inability to sit still for more than a few minutes.

Many twos will be shy in the beginning weeks of the program. Programmers should be sensitive to this and keep their body language relaxed and welcoming. A gentle approach works better with a new group of two year olds: coax with a soft voice, allow children to approach you and always meet them at their level, never loom above them looking down. Once the two year olds get over a little initial intimidation, they will become your best friends and biggest fans.

To successfully integrate a group of two year olds into a program, the parents and caregivers should be familiar with the structure of the program and what is considered acceptable behaviour. On the first week of the program, explain to the adults that children should be allowed to enjoy the program at their own pace, and therefore it may seem that transitions are slow, but the deliberate pace will be more in tune with the two year olds' style. Also, encourage adult participation and remind adults that children take cues for behaviour from them and that they must participate if they expect their two year old to participate.

2. Two Year Old Programming Guidelines

2.1 Starting a Program for Two Year Olds

The best two year old program will be offered as a preregistered series that runs for at least six consecutive weeks. Children need this length of time, and ideally even longer, to be comfortable in the routine. More than with any other age group, it is important to have a consistent group of attendees so children know what and who to expect. The programmer should be the same person each week, for the same reason.

If your facility is unable to support a registered program, it is still possible to run a drop-in program. In this case the routine must be well-established and flow easily from one element to the next. The group of attendees will not be consistent, but the expectations for repeat participants will be established. In a drop-in program for two year olds, a maximum number of participants, based on the available space, should be established. Keep a record of the number of attendees, especially if you often approach your maximum. The statistical evidence of the success of your program may be exactly what is needed to make a case for a regular preregistered program to run instead of, or in addition to, the drop-in program. The quality of a preregistered program for two year olds is undeniable, so an effort to try and achieve that status is recommended.

2.2 Getting Ready

Once you have decided to run a series of programs for two year olds, you will need to set the stage for your eager participants. Two year olds have a special ability to sense mood; they pick up on positive energy and are more likely to be happy if the people around them are lighthearted and optimistic. This is true for children of all ages, but two year olds are particularly sensitive to mood and atmosphere. To make the entire experience enjoyable, be sure to choose program elements that you enjoy and share those with the two year olds. Maintain an upbeat, positive approach to situations and your programs will be enjoyable for everyone.

2.2a Books to Share

Sharing books with two year olds is a gratifying experience. Children will participate in and experience the story; they can appreciate humour and will laugh at silly antics and comical visuals. Books should be short and grab their attention. Pictures should be colourful, clean, and uncluttered. Stories should have a simple plot and a minimal number of characters. Two year olds begin to identify with characters and will appreciate stories about experiences similar to their own: exploring the world around them, simple adventures, and everyday occurrences with a silly twist are all popular themes. Children enjoy a repeated phrase or sound they can imitate. Two year olds are especially good at repeating animal sounds and identifying body parts. One interesting aspect of reading to two year olds is the concept of flaps, or novelty books. Two year olds love to lift flaps and see what is underneath. There are quality books available in this format, even in the oversized style that is perfect for sharing with a group. If you are using a lift-the-flap book as a read-aloud with the group, be prepared to give every child a chance to come and lift the flaps; it can take quite a long time to read a book in this format, but children will delight in the experience.

2.2b Books to Display

Adults will be choosing most of the books to take home from your display table, so be sure to include books on parenting topics that are of interest to them, such as toilet training, tantrums, and nightmares. General parenting resources that focus on two year olds are also good choices. Find out, on an individual basis, a little more about the people in your group so you can tailor future book displays to their needs (e.g., books on expecting a new sibling, moving, or special family relationships may be appropriate).

For the two year old, your supply of books will be virtually limitless: board books, simple picture books, and nonfiction picture titles that focus on popular themes (trains, pets, and farm animals, for example) are reliable choices. Any titles you choose to display should have limited text and exceptional pictures. The two year olds should be able to experience the books independently and with an adult reading aloud.

3. Programs for Two Year Olds: Format and Routine

Twos respond to gentle leaders and energetic entertainers. They enjoy any program as long as it includes lots of participation and chances for them to show off their new-found independence. The following sections discuss some successful methods for programming with two year olds, but as programmers you should be aware that finding the rhythm and dynamic that best suits the group is the most important first step that you can take. Work with your group to come up with the best routine, even if it takes two or three weeks to get it right.

3.1 Format

Any format that establishes a routine is a good jumping-off point for a program for two year olds. Keep in mind that transitions should be predictable, so always begin and end the same way. Memorable ingredients that will be repeated from week to week should be included at the same time each week. For example, if you always begin your program with free play that includes painting, sensory stations, toys on the floor, etc., it would be difficult to begin your program any other way. Change would undoubtedly be met with confusion and frustration. If you usually include a craft in your program, it would be difficult to replace that time with something else unless the process were very similar. For example, one week you could blow bubbles instead of creating a craft, if you did it in the craft area with a similar set-up and adult assistance. Keeping the main elements consistent for the program will benefit everyone involved. In addition, specific key ingredients should be exactly the same each week; these ingredients will provide cues for the transitions. A consistent opening and closing, a song to move the group from one area to another, and a visual trigger such as a puppet or prop are all useful elements and should be included in the program's format.

To illustrate the model we have been discussing, a sample program format follows. Each week the stories, activities, rhymes, and songs will change, but the order and type of activities will remain consistent.

Two Year Old Program: Sample Format

1. Opening: greet with puppet

2. Five minutes of free play

3. Song to gather group to circle

4. Give out name tags

5. Bonding rhymes for adult and child together

6. Story

7. Song

8. Action rhyme

9. Fingerplay

10. Group activity: include one prop for each child

11. Story

12. Song

13. Action rhyme

14. Fingerplay

15. Group activity: creative movement to music

16. Craft

17. Goodbye song

18. Closing: use puppet to say goodbye

EXPERT ADVICE

Keep the order of program elements consistent from week to week. Two year olds learn the routine in the first few weeks and will be upset if things aren't completed in the appropriate sequence. For example, if you do a craft at the end of the program for the first three weeks, but in the fourth week you choose do the craft in the middle of the program, the two year olds will think the program is over at the midway point and it will be difficult to regain their attention.

The running time for the program will be approximately thirty to forty minutes. Caregivers should be encouraged to come on time because being late will disrupt and change the experience for the children.

3.2 Opening Routine

At this age, some children can be quite shy, while others are gregarious and outgoing. To encourage children with all sorts of different personality traits to come into the program and feel welcome, a puppet works very well. Children respond quickly to a friendly animal or character that you wear on your hand. The size is closer to their own, and they use their imaginations to bring the puppet to life; they will quickly learn the puppet's name, and many children will interact with the puppet. For the programmer, learning to use a puppet can be difficult and intimidating. Although the process can take a little while, there is a simple method to animate a puppet that anyone can use to make a hand-held friend come to life:

1. *Choose a puppet.* You may have puppets at your facility that you can choose from, or you may have to go out and purchase one. Or you can make a puppet from an old sock, a small paper bag, or other inexpensive materials. Be sure to choose a puppet that looks friendly and appeals to you. Try it on and make sure it feels comfortable for the size of your hand and that you can use your fingers to make it talk and to move its arms, if it is designed that way. A good choice for a puppet to use with two year olds is one that stands upright in a traditional hand puppet stance.

2. *Bring your puppet to life.* Give your puppet a name and a personality. You can have your puppet act in a way that is a little different from you, if you are comfortable with that, or you can give your puppet personality traits that are similar to your own. Having your puppet act shy or immature is a good way to bring timid children out. Once you have decided on a name and personality, put on your puppet and practice. Will you feel silly? Of course, you are talking and playing with your hand! However, you know the power you have in stories to bring characters to life and give them voice and the power to inspire. Draw on that same part of you to animate your puppet. It will feel silly at first, but practice for a few minutes every day and you will soon become accustomed to your puppet friend.

3. *Look at your puppet when you talk to it and when it talks to you.* To make your puppet believable, when it talks you should be looking at it. In the same way that you look at anyone during a conversation, you must look at your puppet while it is talking. There is no need to disguise the fact that the voice is coming from your mouth; you do not need to be a ventriloquist. Instead, when your puppet talks, focus on it and react in natural ways to what it is saying. If your focus is on your puppet, your group's focus will be on your puppet. Although this sounds simple, this aspect of puppetry takes practice. We are conditioned in a program to speak to the group, and speaking away from the group will seem foreign and unnatural at first. Speak in a slightly elevated voice because you are facing away from the group and it will be more difficult for them to hear what you are saying to your puppet.

4. Put your puppet away and out of sight when it is not speaking. To create the illusion of another character in storytime, it is necessary to physically put the puppet out of sight, or at the very least, out of reach. Otherwise children will play with the puppet when it is not animated, and the illusion and characterisation will be lost. You can have a selection of puppets for children to play with, but keep the illusion and personality of your special puppet alive by having it leave or nap while not in use during storytime.

Your puppet should be an active part of the opening of storytime, so have it greet the children and hand out the name tags (see the appendix for sample name tags). Be sure to introduce your puppet in a very gentle way. Never use loud noises or wild gestures as you introduce your puppet to the group because some children may be frightened. Begin with your puppet having a shy and quiet nature. As a novice puppeteer, you could have the puppet only speak to you while you translate for the group. The children will understand and relate to the puppet's reluctance to speak out loud, and this will make them feel more comfortable. Allow children to touch it, if they choose to, *while it is on your arm*. Never force a child to touch or interact with the puppet, but most of the children will warm up to it quite quickly. Children will take their cues on how to behave from the puppet. You can use it to regain control of a distracted group or to help a shy group warm up and have fun.

3.3 Group Dynamics

Two year olds are at a suitable age to encourage them to leave the lap of their accompanying adult and move together as a group to enjoy a story or activity. Programmers should be gentle in their encouragement and should never force a child away from a parent or caregiver. Parents and caregivers should be encouraged to allow children to move to sit with their peers, if they are comfortable and ready to take that social leap.

One way to help children become more comfortable is to give every child a prop or object to hold or use for an activity, but instead of moving around the circle handing out the props, encourage the children to come up and retrieve the objects from a container you are holding. Most children will come, and you will likely only have to give out a few after the majority of the children have come forward. Even a child who was reluctant to come and pick up a prop might feel comfortable coming forward to put the prop away. If you do have to go the child to retrieve the prop, bring the container with you; even shy children may like to drop their props into the box or basket.

> ### EXPERT ADVICE
>
> Two year olds find it difficult to take turns, and they find it especially difficult to wait any length of time for a chance to participate. If you are using props in a program, be sure to have one for each child to hold and use while you complete the activity.

3.4 Closing Routine

Bring your puppet out again at the end of storytime. Have it sing a closing song along with the group. Following is an example of a simple closing song (children wave goodbye while singing) that might work well:

Goodbye, Goodbye, Goodbye

(Tune: Farmer in the Dell)
Goodbye, goodbye, goodbye
Goodbye, goodbye, goodbye
Goodbye-goodbye, goodbye-goodbye
Goodbye, goodbye, goodbye

4. Two Year Old Programming Techniques and Activities

One of the most satisfying aspects of a two year old program is that it combines the best activities enjoyed by the younger set with the first of the activities enjoyed by older children who attend storytime independently. While executing a program for two year olds, you can include activities for both the child alone and the child and adult together.

4.1 Special Activities

To enhance the stories chosen for a program, extras included in a successful program may be elements such as

- flannel or felt

- stories and rhymes

- props

- dancing

- puppets (hand puppets, stick puppets, glove puppets, etc.)

- crafts

- sensory stimulators

- action rhymes and songs

- gross motor activities

- sing-along songs

- games (circle games, one-on-one, and interactive games with the entire group).

The activities you can include in a program for two year olds are limited only by the programmer's imagination and comfort level and the dynamics of an individual group. Programmers should asses their group's inclinations and favourites in the first few weeks of the program and emphasise those activities to make the experience as positive as possible for everyone involved.

4.2 Activities Just for Twos

One of the most exciting aspects of a program for two year olds is the children's ability to take part in activities as a group of *children*. Although the adults remain in view, it is the perfect time to encourage children to gather as a group to listen to the stories, take part in an action rhyme, or come to the front of the circle to take part in an interactive game. For many of the rhymes and songs you will be expecting the two year old to move, bend, and stretch and, although the adults may not be actively assisting their two year olds, let them know participation on their part is also mandatory. The two year olds will frequently make a visual check to ensure their caregivers are participating as well.

4.3 Adult Participation

Ensure that adult caregivers take part in storytime, even when their child is not sitting next to them. Let adults know that they need to take part in rhymes and songs, even if their child is interacting with the group away from them. If adults choose instead to chat with other adults, or become uninterested, the two year olds will quickly retreat back to the adults, mistakenly sensing that they have done something wrong or inappropriate. Although the two year olds are growing independent, they still take their cues from trusted adults. However, it is a natural inclination for parents and caregivers to want to chat and share time with other adults. Therefore, it is important to include some time for free play, ideally after the program, when the adults can gather, chat, and interact, if they choose.

Program 1

Time for Twos: Teddy Tales

Welcome to the terrific world of two year olds! Whether you're a new recruit or a seasoned veteran, programming for an active group of two year olds can certainly be a challenge. Unlike babies and toddlers, two year olds can communicate their likes and dislikes and are pretty quick on their feet. Once you have your first program under your belt, however, you'll have a better sense of what makes your group tick. So let's get started! The first program in this chapter is "Teddy Tales" (any two year old's best friend). Why not include (in the brochure or at the time of registration) a special invitation for your group to bring along their favourite friends? This may also help make the children feel more comfortable in their new surroundings if this is their first program. Let participants know that any favourite stuffed animal will do, and you may want to have extras at the library for those without.

Plan Ahead Note

The storytime souvenir in this program is tons of fun and it really works! Other than tracing and cutting out enough bears for your group, the only other preparation is going to your local grocery store to purchase cinnamon sticks (again, enough for your group). As an extra, you could provide each child with two wiggle eyes and a glue stick to glue them on with.

Books to Share

Brown Bear, Brown Bear, What Do You See?, by Bill Martin Jr.

When You Grow Up, by Lennie Goodings

When Will It Be Spring?, By Catherine Walters

More books to share with two year olds can be found in the bibliography at the end of this chapter.

Time for Twos: Teddy Tales

Rhymes and Songs

Teddy Bear, Teddy Bear

 (Suit actions to words.)
Teddy Bear, Teddy Bear, turn around,
Teddy Bear, Teddy Bear, touch the
  ground.
Teddy Bear, Teddy Bear, reach up
  high,
Teddy Bear, Teddy Bear, touch the
  sky.
Teddy Bear, Teddy Bear, bend down
  low,
Teddy Bear, Teddy Bear, touch your
  toes.
Teddy Bear, Teddy Bear, show your
  shoe,
Teddy Bear, Teddy Bear, that will do.
Teddy Bear, Teddy Bear, turn around,
Teddy Bear, Teddy Bear, now sit
  down.

Five Little Bears

 (Hold fingers up one by one while counting.)
One little bear
Wondering what to do.
Along came another,
Then there were two.

Two little bears
Climbing up a tree.
Along came another,
Then there were three.

Three little bears
Ate an apple core.
Along came another,
Then there were four.

Four little bears
Found honey in a hive.
Along came another,
Then there were five!

Little Bear

(Tune: Frere Jacques)
(Suit actions to words.)
Are you sleepy, are you sleepy,

(Stretch and yawn.)
Little Bear? Little Bear?
Wintertime is coming,
Wintertime is coming,
Very soon, very soon.

Find a cave, find a cave,
Little Bear, Little bear.
Wintertime is here, wintertime is here,
Go to sleep, go to sleep.

(Pretend to sleep.)
Are you sleepy, are you sleepy,
Little Bear? Little Bear?
You will wake in springtime,
In the warm, warm springtime,
Little Bear, Little Bear.

(Start to wake up.)
Time to wake up!
Time to wake up!
Little Bear, Little Bear.
Springtime has come back around,
Flowers sprouting from the ground,
Wake up now! Wake up now!

(Wake up and stretch.)

Teddy Bear Bounce

(Follow along using your own teddy bear to do the actions.)

Pick your teddy bear up from the
   ground,
Then go dancing all around.
Hold him high and hold him low,
Round and round and round you go.

Pick your teddy bear up from the
   ground,
Then go dancing all around.
Hold him left and hold him right,
Hold him tight with all your might!
Pick your teddy bear up from the
   ground,
Then go dancing all around.
Hold him close and hold him far,
Pretend that he can drive a car.

Pick your teddy bear up from the
   ground,
Then go dancing all around.
Hold him in front and hold him back,
Sit down with him on your lap.

Teddy Bears Cold

(Suit actions to words.)
In this house there is a room,

(Make a circle using both hands.)
And in this room there is a bed,

(Hold hand flat, palm side up.)
And in this bed is a little teddy bear
With a very bad cold in his head.
ACHOO!
With a very bad cold in his head.
ACHOO!

Now if this little teddy bear,
Stays in bed and he takes care,
Soon he'll be out and running all about
And he'll have no more cold in his head.
ACHOO!
He'll have no more cold in his head.
ACHOO!

Put Your Teddy in the Air

(Follow along with the actions using your teddy bear.)

Put your teddy in the air, in the air.
Put your teddy in the air, in the air.
Sing hip hip hooray!
'Cause it's teddy, teddy day.
Put your teddy in the air, in the air.

Additional Verses:
Dance your teddy on the floor
Sit your teddy on your lap

Cinnamon Bear

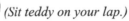
(Don't forget to use teddy!)
Cinnamon, cinnamon, cinnamon bear,
Sitting on a kitchen chair.

(Sit teddy on your lap.)
Cinnamon sugar in a shaker,
Shake, shake, shake it like a baker.

(Make teddy dance.)
Sprinkle it on buttered toast,
It's the treat you'll love the most.

(Rub your tummy.)
Cinnamon, cinnamon, cinnamon bear,
Do you think that we may share?

(Hug teddy.)

Bear Song

(Tune: Row, Row, Row Your Boat) (A great song to sing using a teddy bear!)
Hug, hug, hug your bear,
Squeeze him very tight.
Hold him high,
Help him fly,
Then hug with all your might.

115

Cinnamon Bear

This is a great sensory prop to use with any of the "Teddy Bear" rhymes or songs.

Materials

1 sheet of sandpaper, medium or fine grain (enough for your group)

1 cinnamon stick (enough for 1 per child)

1 sheet of cardstock per person

Medium wiggle eyes, 2 per person (optional)

Glue sticks (optional)

Scissors

Instructions

1. Enlarge the bear template (below) on the photocopier to desired size.

2. Using the bear template, trace the bear shape onto the sandpaper and cut the shape out.

3. Glue the sandpaper bears onto the cardstock to make them more sturdy.

4. Holding the cinnamon stick like a crayon, colour the bear; when you're finished, it will look, feel, and smell like a cinnamon cookie!

116

Program 2
Time for Twos: Fun in the Sun

What summer means to you or me is not necessarily what it means to a two year old. To adults, summer means hot not cold, shorts not sweaters, and lawn mowers not shovels. To a two year old, summer means one thing: F-U-N! Just like winter, spring, and fall. This program is fun, and the craft is one that every child knows something about: ice cream! At what other time would a child be able to create his or her own ice cream cone with as many scoops as he or she wants piled on top? Don't forget your sunscreen as we jump into this program!

Plan Ahead Note

The storytime souvenir for this program requires that the programmer do very little preparation. Since the craft is similar to the *Ice Cream* rhyme used in the program, it would be easy to make a cone and ice cream scoops (of construction paper or felt) to use along with it. Tape or place the cone on a felt or magnet board where your entire group can see it, and then if you have time, have the children in your group take turns putting the ice cream scoops on top of the cone.

Books to Share

It Looked Like Spilt Milk, by Charles G. Shaw

The Carrot Seed, by Ruth Krauss

In Wibbly's Garden, by Mike Inkpen

More books to share with two year olds can be found in the bibliography at the end of this chapter.

Time for Twos: Fun in the Sun

Rhymes and Songs

Summer

 (Suit actions to words.)
    These are my sunglasses,

(Circle eyes with fingers.)
    This is my great sun hat.

(Hands over head.)
    This is the way I fold my hands,

(Fold hands.)
    And rest them, just like that.

(Rest hands in your lap.)
    Pack the paper plates and napkins,

(Pretend to pack.)
    Don't forget the food and drink.

(Shake your head no.)
    Hot dogs, potato salad,
    Cake and lemonade pink.

    It's fun to go on a picnic,
    I simply cannot wait.
    To east and play, have fun all day,

(Rub your tummy.)
    And get home very late.

(Stretch and yawn.)

Waves at the Beach

 (Tune: Wheels on the Bus)
    (Suit actions to words.)
        The waves at the beach go up and
            down,
        Up and down, up and down.
        The waves at the beach go up and
            down,
        All day long.

Additional verses:
        Crabs at the beach—crawl back and
            forth
        Lobsters at the beach go—snap! snap!
            snap!
        Clams at the beach will—open and
            shut

Everybody Knows I Love My Toes

(Point to each body part as it is mentioned.)
    Everybody knows I love my toes,
    Everybody knows I love my toes.
    I love my nail, my knees,
    My neck and my nose,
    And everybody knows I love my toes!

    Everybody knows I love my eyes,
    Everybody knows I love my eyes.
    I love my legs, my lips,
    My neck and my nose,
    And everybody knows I love my toes!

    Everybody knows I love my feet,
    Everybody knows I love my feet.
    I love my skin, my chin,
    My knees and my nose,
    And everybody knows I love my toes.

To the Beach

(Tune: London Bridge)
(Suit actions to words.)

We are going to the beach,
To the beach, to the beach.
We are going to the beach
In our bathing suits.

We will find some rocks and shells,

(Pretend to sift sand.)

Rocks and shells, rocks and shells.
We will find some rocks and shells
To gather by the water.

We will build a sand castle,

(Pretend to build a sandcastle.)

Sand castle, sand castle.
We will build a sand castle
With bridges and a tower.

Home we'll go with sunburned cheeks,

(Rub your cheeks with your fingertips.)

Sunburned cheeks, sunburned cheeks.
Home we'll go with sunburned cheeks
And treasure from our visit.

I Went Swimming in the Ocean

(Tune: I've Been Working on the Railroad)
(Pretend you're at the beach as you follow along with the actions below.)

I went swimming in the ocean

(Pretend to swim.)

On a summer day.
I went swimming in the ocean
And kicked and splashed and played.
After lunch we looked for seashells,

(Hold one hand above your eye and pretend to look.)

I found three or four.
You can hold up next to your ear
And hear the ocean roar.

(Place your hand by your ear and pretend to listen.)

Hear the ocean roar,
Hear the ocean roar,
You can hear the ocean roar and roar.

Hear the ocean roar,
Hear the ocean roar,
You can hear the ocean roar!

My Feet

(Tune: Three Blind Mice)
(Alternate picking up the child's feet, left and right.)

My feet have toes,
My feet have toes,
My feet have toes,
My feet have toes.

Whenever my feet are tickled,

(Tickle your child's feet.)

My toes start to wiggle,

(Wiggle your child's toes.)

And then I begin to giggle,

(Tickle your child's tummy.)

My feet have toes.
My feet have toes.

Ice Cream

 (This is a great rhyme to use with a flannel board. Simply make ice cream scoops and cone shapes out of coloured felt.)

First we need a cone,
Nice and crunchy.

(Place cone felt piece on the flannel board.)

Then we need some ice cream,
Sweet and yummy.
Scoop 'em, on,
Stack 'em on,
Up to the sky.
We love ice cream, my oh my!

First comes vanilla,

(Place white felt on the cone.)

Cold and sweet.
Then comes chocolate,

(Place brown felt on top of white.)

A delicious treat.
Here's some strawberry,

(Place pink on top of brown.)

Orange sherbet too.

(Place orange on top of pink.)

A super-duper ice cream cone
Just for you!

One scoop, two scoops,
Three scoops, four.
We love ice cream,
Who wants more?

Let's Go to the Beach

  (Tune: A Hunting We Will Go)
(Suit actions to words.)

Let's go to the beach,
To swim and play and run.
Building castles in the sand,

(Pretend to build a castle.)

Is ever so much fun.

We'll fix a picnic lunch,
And eat it when we like.
And when we are all nice and full,

(Rub your tummy.)

We'll take a nature hike.

Be sure to wear your suit,
And bring along your float.
We'll ride so far out in the surf,
Pretending it's a boat.

(Sway back and forth.)

We'll find some pretty shells,
And throw the gulls some bread.
Put on lots of suntan oil,

(Pretend to put on lotion.)

So that we don't turn red.

We'll never want to leave,
Such fun this has all been.
But we'll come back another day,
And do it all again.
Yay!

(Clap your hands.)

Build Your Own Cone

Materials

1 sheet of brown construction paper for the cone (enough for your group)

Various colours of construction paper for the scoops of ice cream

Scissors

Glue

Decorating stuff: glitter, buttons, confetti, tissue paper squares

Instructions

1. Trace the template of the cone onto the brown construction paper and cut it out.

2. Trace the template of the ice cream scoops onto the various colours of construction paper and cut them out.

3. Let the children glue as many scoops onto their cones as they like.

4 Use glitter sprinkles, buttons, or markers or crayons to decorate the souvenirs.

Program 3
Time for Twos: All About Me

One of the first things a child learns to recognise is his or her name. "All About Me" focuses on the children in your group and their uniqueness. The storytime souvenir "That's My Name" allows each child in your group a sense of individuality. Although it is common for some children to share the same name, we as programmers can help to ensure that each craft is different by cutting the name plates out with different designs, coloured paper, or edges (pinking shears give a nice effect). Suggest to your group of caregivers that these be hung on their child's bedroom door. It will give the children a sense of pride and accomplishment to see something they did displayed for their entire family to admire.

Plan Ahead Note

The songs and rhymes in this program require a lot of movement. Make sure that you have enough room for all the children and caregivers to move around comfortably without bumping into others.

The storytime souvenir in this program requires little effort on the part of the programmer. As an added extra for this craft, have a pair of scissors, some yarn, and a hole punch handy and give the caregivers and children the option of making their name plates into signs that they can hang anywhere.

Books to Share

Clap Your Hands, by David Ellwand

Horns to Toes (and in Between), by Sandra Boynton

Eyes, Nose, Fingers, Toes, by Judy Hindley

More books to share with two year olds can be found in the bibliography at the end of this chapter.

Time for Twos: All About Me

Rhymes and Songs

Wink, Wink

 (Suit actions to words.)

Make one eye go wink, wink, wink.
Make two eyes go blink, blink, blink.
Make two fingers stand just so,
Then ten fingers all in a row.
Front and back your head will rock,
Then your knees will knock, knock,
   knock.
Stretch and make a yawn so wide,
Drop your arms down to the sides.
Close your eyes and help me say,
Our very quiet sound today.
Sh . . . Sh . . . Shhhhhhhhhhhh!

Me

 (Point to each body part as it is mentioned.)

Here are my fingers and here is my nose,
Here are my ears and here are my toes.
Here are my eyes that can open wide,
Here is my mouth with my white teeth
   inside.
Here is my pink tongue that helps me
   speak,
Here are my shoulders and here is my
   cheek.
Here are my hands that let me play,
Here are my feet that go walking each
   day.

The Shape-Up Song

 (Tune: The Farmer in the Dell)
*(Start this song standing with the caregivers
and children facing each other
so that they can do the movements together.)*

We're jumping up and down,
We're jumping up and down,
We're getting lots of exercise,
We're jumping up and down.

Additional verses:

Let's bend and touch our toes
Let's kick our legs up high
Let's reach and touch the sky

We sit down on the floor,
We sit down on the floor,
When our exercise is done,
We sit down on the floor.

Stretch, Stretch, Stretch

 (Tune: Row, Row, Row Your Boat)
(Suit actions to words.)

 Stretch, stretch, stretch your arms,
High above your head.
Stretch so high,
Reach the sky,
And then we'll stretch again.

Stretch, stretch, stretch your arms,
High above your head.
Stretch so high,
Reach the sky,
And bring them down again.

Active You

(Suit actions to words.)

You wiggle your fingers and clap your
    hands,
And then you stamp your feet.
You turn to the left, you turn to the
    right,
And make your fingers meet.
You raise them high and let them
    down,
You give a little clap.
You wave your hands then fold your
    hands,
And put them in your lap.

The Finger Song

(Tune: ABC's)
(Suit actions to words.)

1, 2, 3, 4, 5 fingertips,
I can touch them to my lips.
I can cover up my eyes,
I can clap them on my thighs.
I can make them touch the sky,
I can make them wave bye-bye!

All About Me

(Point to the body parts as they are mentioned.)

In my mirror I can see,
Two little eyes that look like me.

Two little ears and one little nose,
Ten little fingers and ten little toes.

One little mouth I open wide,
Two little rows of teeth inside.

A tongue that pops both in and out,
Lots of joints that bend about.

Muscles and bones that do most things,
All held together with my skin.

Hickory Dickory Dock

*(This song should be done with the caregivers
and children sitting face to face.)*

Hickory Dickory Dock,

(Clap each word.)

The mouse ran up the clock.

(Run your fingers up the child's arm.)

The clock struck 1,
The mouse ran down,

(Run your fingers back down the child's arm.)

Hickory Dickory Dock.
Hickory Dickory Dock,

(Clap each word.)

The mouse ran up the clock.

(Run your fingers up the child's arm.)

The clock struck 2,
The mouse said "BOO!"
Hickory Dickory Dock.

Hickory Dickory Dock,

(Clap each word.)

The mouse ran up the clock.

(Run your fingers up the child's arm.)

The clock struck 3,
The mouse said "WHEEEEE!"

*(Slide your fingers down the child's arm
and tickle their tummy.)*

Hickory Dickory Dock,
TICK! TOCK!

That's My Name!

Materials

1 sheet of construction paper, various colours (enough for your group)

1 sheet of photocopy paper, various colours (enough for your group)

Cardstock

Glue

Scissors

Decorating supplies: glitter glue, bingo dabbers, markers or crayons

Hole punch (optional)

Yarn, various colours (optional)

Instructions

1. Using a computer or a thick black marker, write or print each child's name on a coloured piece of paper.

2. Cut out each name, being careful to leave a small border around the outside.

3. Glue each name onto cardstock to make it more sturdy.

4. The names can either be cut out again (leaving a small border) or left on a full sheet of cardstock.

5. Display the names on your craft table; each child can then find and decorate his or her own name.

Program 4
Time for Twos: Tea for Twos

C is for cookie, and that's good enough for all of us! Children are not alone in their love of cookies, and this program just may stir up the baker in everyone! The storytime souvenir "Crazy Cookies" gives the crafty chef inside your group a chance to get cooking. By providing them with the materials they need, your twos will have a blast creating their very own cookie concoctions. Don't forget the glitter sprinkles!

Plan Ahead Note

Many of the songs and rhymes in this chapter work well if they have the props or pictures to accompany them. We recommend that you go through and pick the songs or rhymes that you will be using ahead of time so that you are prepared in your program. It will be more exciting for the children if they can see what they are talking and singing about.

Books to Share

Who Stole the Cookies from the Cookie Jar?, by Jane Manning

Miss Spider's Tea Party, by David Kirk

My Very 1st Tea Party, by Michal Sparks

More books to share with two year olds can be found in the bibliography at the end of this chapter.

Time for Twos: Tea for Twos

Homemade Gingerbread

 (Suit actions to words.)
> Stir a bowl of gingerbread,

 (Pretend to be stirring a bowl.)
> Smooth and spicy and brown.
> Roll it with a rolling pin,

(Pretend to be rolling out the dough.)
> Up and up and down.
> With a cookie cutter,

(Hold up a cookie cutter.)
> Make some little men.
> Put them in the oven,

(Pretend to put them in the oven.)
> 'Til half past ten.

(Pretend to check your watch.)

Gingerbread Man Song

 (Tune: Do You Know the Muffin Man?)
(Have a paper gingerbread man, decorated, to use as a prop for this song.)
> Oh, do you know the Gingerbread
>   Man?
> The Gingerbread Man?
> The Gingerbread Man?
> Do you know the Gingerbread Man,
> Who ran and ran and ran?
>
> He said "Catch me if you can,
> If you can,
> If you can.".
> He said "Catch me if you can,"
> Then he ran and ran and ran.
> Oh, do you know the Gingerbread
>   Man?
> The Gingerbread Man?
> The Gingerbread Man?
> Do you know the Gingerbread Man
> Who ran and ran and ran?

Gingerkids

 (Use your fingers to represent the gingerkids.)
> 1 little, 2 little, 3 little gingerkids,
> 4 little, 5 little, 6 little gingerkids,
> 7 little, 8 little, 9 little gingerkids,
> 10 little gingerbread kids!

Cookie Jar, Cookie Jar

 (This rhyme is simple and fun! Draw and cut out a cookie jar from construction paper. Colour and decorate the front and on the back attach an envelope. Make different kinds of cookies out of construction paper, label them, and put them in the envelope. Pull the cookies out as they are mentioned in the rhyme. Also, for the final verse, you could have a small mirror on your lap to hold up so that the children in front of you can be the children in the rhyme!)
> Cookie jar, cookie jar, what do you see?
> I see a chocolate chip cookie inside of
>   me!

(Replace chocolate chip with oatmeal, peanut butter, Oreo, Christmas etc.)

Last verse:
> Cookie jar, cookie jar, what do you
>   see?
> I see children wanting to eat those
>   cookies,
> That's what I see!

(Hold up a mirror if you have one.)

Cookie Cutters

 (Make construction paper cookies to use for counting down this rhyme.)

5 yummy cookies with frosting galore,
Mother ate the white one,
Then there were 4.

4 yummy cookies, two and two you
    see,
Father ate the green one,
Then there were 3.
3 yummy cookies, but before I knew,
Sister ate the yellow one,
Then there were 2.

2 yummy cookies, oh what fun!
Brother ate the brown one,
Then there was 1.

1 yummy cookie, watch me run.
I ate the last one,
Now there are none.

Ice Cream Rhyme

 (Suit actions to words.)

There's something soft and fluffy,
And icy, icy cold.
It's very nice to look at,
But much to cold to hold.
Whether you're on an outing,
Or spending time at home,
You cannot eat this with your hands,
So we'll put it on a cone!

Gingerbread Boy

 (Tune: Six Little Ducks)
(Suit actions to words.)

1 gingerbread boy popped out one day,
Over the hill he ran away.
When the man called, "Come back
    little man!"
He only answered "Catch me if you
    can,
If you can,
If you can."
He only answered, "Catch me if you can."

(Repeat the verse, each time replacing the "man" with a different character from the story, e.g., woman, cow, horse.)

Last verse:

One gingerbread boy popped out one
    day,
Over the hill he ran away.
When the fox called, "Hop on my nose
    little man
I'll gobble you up just as fast as I can,
As fast as I can,
As fast as I can,
I'll gobble you up as fast as I can!"

129

5 Ice Cream Cones

(Make construction paper ice cream cones of different "flavours" to show the children as you say this rhyme.)

> 5 ice cream cones at the ice cream
>   shop,
> No one wanted to buy them with
>   vanilla on top.
> 1 little ice cream cone took some time
>   to think,
> He mixed in some bubble gum and
>   turned himself pink.
> Then little _____ came along,
> And took that yummy ice cream home.
>
> 4 ice cream cones at the ice cream
>   shop,
> No one wanted to buy them with
>   vanilla on top.
> 1 little ice cream cone knew what to
>   do,
> He mixed in some blueberries and
>   turned himself blue.
> Then little _____ came along,
> And took that yummy ice cream home.
> 3 ice cream cones at the ice cream
>   shop,

> No one wanted to buy them with
>   vanilla on top.
> 1 ice cream cone was a smart little
>   fellow,
> He mixed in some lemonade and
>   turned himself yellow.
> Then little _____ came along,
> And took that yummy ice cream home.
>
> 2 ice cream cones at the ice cream
>   shop,
> No one wanted to buy them with
>   vanilla on top.
> 1 ice cream cone got an idea in his
>   head,
> He mixed in some strawberries and
>   turned himself red.
> Then little _____ came along,
> And took that yummy ice cream home.
>
> 1 little ice cream cone at the ice cream
>   shop,
> But no one would buy it with vanilla
>   on top.
> Alone and sad, he really wanted to go,
> So he mixed in all the Colors
> And made his shade—RAINBOW!

130

Crazy Cookies

Materials

1 sheet of grey construction paper per person

1 sheet of brown construction paper per person

Scissors

Glue sticks (enough for your group)

Decorating supplies: glitter sprinkles, markers or crayons

Instructions

1. Using a plastic cup or any round object the size of a cookie, trace and cut out six brown circles per person. These are your cookies.

2. Cut a small slit diagonally in each corner of the grey construction paper, fold the edges up, and tape them in place. This is your cookie sheet.

3. Glue the six circles (evenly spaced) on the sheet of grey construction paper

4. Let the children decorate the cookies.

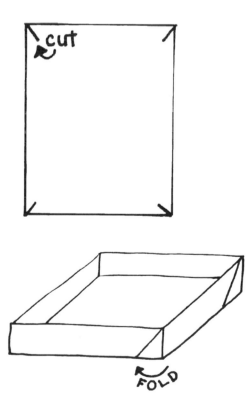

Program 5
Time for Twos: Fuzzytail Friends

Welcome to the green forest, where the stories you've read about all come to life. This program introduces a new set of animals to your group. Although your format and your routine will be consistent, it is important to introduce the new and different in small doses. Children at this age thrive on routine but do possess the tools they need to accept change easily. In this program, none of the core songs will be familiar to your group, only your openers. If you don't feel comfortable or if you notice that your group isn't participating as they have in previous weeks, try including some of your group's favourites from other programs or even using the traditional standbys such as *If You're Happy and You Know It.*

Plan Ahead Note

In this program the storytime souvenir is very fitting. While you're photocopying one squirrel for every child in your group, photocopy an extra for yourself and decorate it. Since there are a lot of squirrel rhymes in this program, the squirrel you make could accompany them and give the children some ideas on how they can decorate their own squirrels.

Books to Share

Owl Babies, by Martin Waddell

Raccoon on His Own, by Jim Arnosky

Fuzzytail Friends Lift-and-Look Animal Book, by Lisa McCue

More books to share with two year olds can be found in the bibliography at the end of this chapter.

Time for Twos: Fuzzytail Friends

Rhymes and Songs

5 Little Squirrels

 (Use your fingers to represent the squirrels in this rhyme or photocopy and colour the squirrel template.)

> 5 little squirrels with acorn to store,
> 1 went to sleep, then there were 4.
> 4 little squirrels hunting acorns in a
>   tree,
> 1 fell down, then there were 3.
> 3 little squirrels wondering what to do,
> 1 got lost, now there are 2.
> 2 little squirrels tossing acorns for fun,
> 1 got tired, now there is 1.
> 1 little squirrel, playing in the sun,
> He ran away, now there are none.

Mr. Bear

 (Tune: If You're Happy and You Know It)
> Mr. Bear says all he wants to do is
>   sleep.

(Clap, clap.)
> When the winter comes and snow is
>   very deep.

(Clap, clap.)
> He will curl up in his den,
> And we probably won't see him,
> 'Til the spring and that's when all he'll
>   do is eat!
> Yum! Yum!

(Rub your tummy.)

5 Little Owls

 (Use your fingers to represent the owls in this rhyme.)

> 5 little owls on a moonlit night,
> 5 little owls are quite a sight.
> 5 little owls, are you keeping score?
> 1 flew away and that left 4.

> 4 little owls, happy as could be,
> 1 flew away, now there are 3.

> 3 owls calling out "Toowit, Toowoo."
> 1 flew away and now there are 2.

> 2 little owls having lots of fun,
> 1 more flew away and now there is 1.

> 1 little owl, this story is almost done,
> He flew away, now there are none.

Frisky Squirrel

 (Tune: The Grand Old Duke of York)
(Suit actions to words.)

> Oh, the frisky little squirrel,
> He gather nuts and seeds.
> He hides them for the winter months,
> So he'll have all he needs.

> Oh, up-up-up he goes,

(Stand up.)
> And down-down-down he comes.

(Sit down.)
> He runs around, goes up and down,

(Stand quickly and sit down again.)
> His work is never done.

(This song can be repeated over and over again, going a little faster each time.)

133

The Owl Song

(Tune: I'm a Little Teapot)
(Suit actions to words.)

I'm a great big owl as you can see,
I live high up in a tree.
All the other birds wake me up when
    they play,
Because I like to sleep in the day.

Racoon

(Tune: Kookaburra)
(Suit actions to words.)

Racoon sleeps in a hollow tree,
While the sun shines on you and me.
Sleep, racoon,

(Pretend to sleep.)

Sleep, racoon,
Warm and cosily.

In the very darkest part of night,
Racoons have the best eyesight.
Look, racoon.

*(Shade your eyes with one hand and pretend to
be searching.)*

Look, racoon.
My your eyes are bright.

Racoon hardly makes a sound,
When he prowls all around.
Hunt, racoon,

*(Have children walk like they think a racoon
would walk.)*

Hunt, racoon,
Find food on the ground.

Hibernation

(Tune: Alouette)

Hibernation, time for hibernation.
Hibernation, time to go to sleep.

In the winter where's the bear?
Sleeping in his log or lair.
Where's the bear? Log or lair?
Ohhhhhhhhhh . . .

Hibernation, time for hibernation.
Hibernation, time to go to sleep.

Additional verses:

In the winter where's the frog?
Sleeping by a pond or log.

In the winter where's the snake?
In the mud beneath the lake.

In the winter where's the bat?
In the cave is where it's at.

A Squirrel Song

(Tune: She'll Be Coming 'Round the Mountain)
(Suit actions to words.)

I'll be gathering all the acorns 'til
    they're gone.
I'll be gathering all the acorns 'til
    they're gone.
I'll be gathering all the acorns,
Gathering all the acorns,
Gathering all the acorns 'til they're
    gone.

Additional verses:

And I'll put them all inside my little
    home.
And I'll eat the nuts until the winter's
    gone.
Then I'll do it again come next fall.

"Nuts" the Squirrel

Materials

1 sheet of brown or grey photocopy paper per squirrel

Cardstock

Cotton balls (enough for your group)

Glue

Instructions

1. Photocopy one squirrel (to fit on an 8½-by-11-inch sheet of paper) per person.

2. Glue each squirrel onto cardstock to make it more sturdy.

3. Have the children glue cotton balls onto the squirrel's tail or colour it to create their own "fuzzytail" friend.

Program 6

Time for Twos: Rainbow Connection

Take a ride on the reading rainbow. We waited until this part of the book to introduce a colour theme because two years of age is when children start to recognise and enjoy the different colours they see. The storytime souvenir "Over the Rainbow" lets your group take home a piece of the sky. Children will enjoy gluing cotton ball clouds on their creations to create a three-dimensional effect. Of course they won't know that's what the cotton balls do, they'll just think they're soft or fluffy. What a great sensory experience!

Plan Ahead Note

This program focuses on colours, from the songs and rhymes to the storytime souvenir. Making props to accompany them will probably be easier here then in any other program. Simply gather sheets of construction paper in some or all of the colours mentioned throughout the program. You can cut the paper into shapes or anything you choose without having to worry about doing any colouring or decorating yourself.

Books to Share

    Ten Little Ladybugs, by Melanie Gerth   Storytime

    White Rabbit's Color Book, by Alan Baker   Jp Bak

    What Makes a Rainbow?, by Betty Ann Schwartz

More books to share with two year olds can be found in the bibliography at the end of this chapter.

Time for Twos: Rainbow Connection

Rhymes and Songs

Rainbow Colours

(Tune: Hush Little Baby)
(Make a construction paper rainbow to use as a visual aid.)

Rainbow purple, rainbow blue,
Rainbow green and yellow too.
Rainbow orange, rainbow red,
Rainbow smiling overhead.
Come and count the colours with me,
How many colours do you see?
One, two, three colours down to green,
Four, five, six colours can be seen.
Rainbow purple, rainbow blue,
Rainbow green and yellow too.
Rainbow orange, rainbow red,
Rainbow smiling overhead.

Rainbows

(Tune: Mary had a Little Lamb)
(Draw or find pictures of the things mentioned in this song to use as visual aids.)

Rainbow over the waterfall, waterfall,
    waterfall,
Rainbow over the waterfall, rainbow
    over a tree.

Rainbow over the mountain, mountain,
    mountain,
Rainbow over the mountain, rainbow
    over the sea.

Rainbow over the flowers, flowers,
    flowers,
Rainbow over the flowers, rainbow
    over the bee.

Rainbow over the dancers, dancers,
    dancers,
Rainbow over the dancers, rainbow
    over me!

Rainbow Train

(Tune: Mary Had a Little Lamb)
(As an extension, the children could take turns naming things that could be in the rainbow train.)

The rainbow train is coming to town,
Coming to town, coming to town.
The rainbow train is coming to town
It's moving very fast.

The rainbow train is full of toys,
Full of toys, full of toys.
The rainbow train is full of toys,
For all the girls and boys.

Red and orange, yellow and green,
Blue and purple cars I see.
The rainbow train is here at last,
I'm glad it came so fast.

Spaghetti Sauce Is Red

(Tune: The Farmer in the Dell)
Spaghetti sauce is red,
Spaghetti sauce is red.
I can think of lots of things,
That are the colour red.

(Substitute other items for "spaghetti sauce," such as "The grass outside is green;" after singing each verse, have the children name things of that colour.)

If You're Wearing Red

(Tune: If You're Happy and You Know It)
(Suit actions to words.)

If you are wearing red, shake your
head,
If you are wearing red, shake your
head.
If you are wearing red,
Then please shake your head.
If you wearing red, shake your head.

Additional verses:

Blue, touch your shoe
Green, bow like a queen
Yellow, Shake like Jell-O
Brown, turn around
Black, take two steps back

Have You Ever Seen a Lizard?

(Tune: Have You Ever Seen a Lassie?)
(Point to each body part as it is mentioned.)

Have you ever seen a lizard, a lizard, a
lizard?
Have you ever seen a lizard all dressed
in pink?
With pink eyes, a pink nose,
And pink legs and pink toes?
Have you ever seen a lizard all dressed
up in pink?

(Substitute other colours for pink.)

Colours and Shapes

*(Prepare a class set of shapes out of construc-
tion paper. Hold up a different shape and colour each time.)*

I have a red square, so do you.
Red and yellow and green and blue.
If your colour is the same as mine,
Come and have a happy time.

*(All children with a red square go into the circle
to dance, clap and sing .)*

Tra-la-la-la-la-la-la
Tra-la-la-la-la-la-la
Tra-la-la-la-la-la-la
Tra-la-la-la-la-la-la

Painting Fun

(Tune: Twinkle, Twinkle Little Star)
*(As an extension, have the children name things
that are the colours in the song.)*

I know the colours for painting fun,
Green like the grass and yellow like
the sun.
Orange like a pumpkin, white like the
snow,
A ruby red rose and a jet black crow.
Blue like a mailbox, brown like an ape,
A little pink pig and some purple
grapes.

Over the Rainbow

Materials

1 photocopied rainbow per person (enlarged to fit two horizontally on an 8½-by-11-inch sheet of paper.)

Cardstock

1 Popsicle stick per craft

Cotton balls (enough for your group)

Masking tape

Glue sticks or white glue (enough for your group)

Decorating supplies: glitter, markers and crayons

Instructions

1. Photocopy one rainbow per person and glue it onto cardstock to make it more sturdy.

2. Tape a Popsicle stick onto the back of the rainbow using masking tape.

3. Let the children colour the rainbow and glue cotton balls on either end to make the clouds.

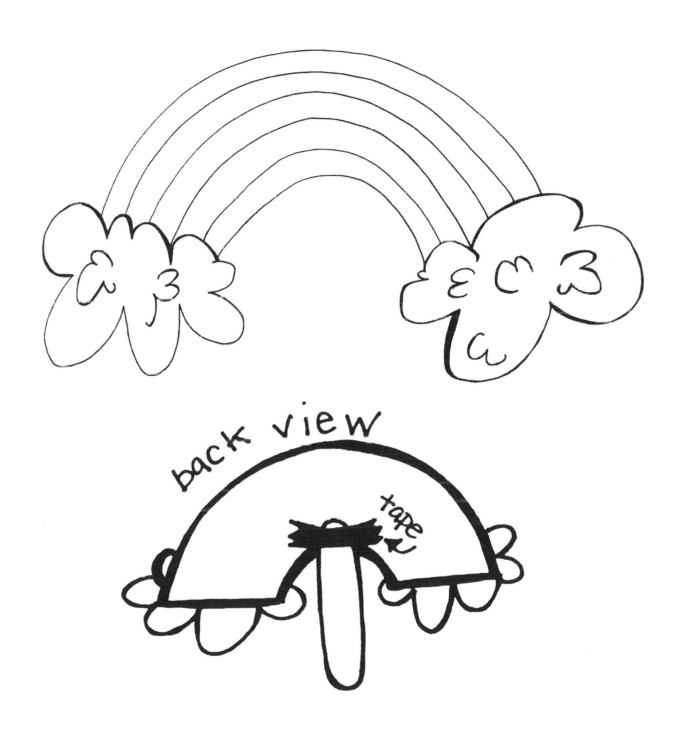

back view

tape

Program 7

Time for Twos: Winter Wonderland

Your group will welcome the winter once they have participated in this program. We've taken the best part of winter (according to the kids) and built a program around it. Snowmen come to life as the children in your group ride on a sled, stand in a row, and melt away just like Frosty!

Plan Ahead Note

Snowmen are the focus of most of the songs and rhymes in this next program, so it would be a good idea to draw or photocopy pictures of some to accompany them. Also, the storytime souvenir requires that the programmer do the painting ahead of time. This is to speed up the craft process. Although the painting would be fun for the children, it would be extremely time consuming, and before you know it, your program would be over. Besides, those busy little hands will have plenty to do gluing on buttons and decorating their snowmen.

Books to Share

The Snowy Day, by Ezra Jack Keats

Bunny's First Snowflake, by Monica Wellington

Little Fern's First Winter, by Jane Simmons

More books to share with two year olds can be found in the bibliography at the end of this chapter.

Time for Twos: Winter Wonderland

Rhymes and Songs

Disappearing Snowman Cookies

 (Use your fingers to represent the snowmen in this rhyme.)

> Five cookie snowmen sitting on a tray,
> Five cookie snowmen smiling all day.
> Along came a little boy/girl rubbing
>   his/her tummy,
> One cookie disappeared,
> Yum, yum, yummy!

(Repeat with 4, 3, and 2.)

> One cookie snowman sitting on a tray,
> One cookie snowman smiling all day.
> Along came a little boy/girl rubbing
>   his her tummy,
> The last cookie disappeared,
> Yum, yum, yummy!

5 Snowmen

(Tune: 5 Little Monkeys)
(Use your fingers, or draw or photocopy five snowmen to accompany this rhyme.)

> 5 happy snowmen riding on a sled,
> 1 fell off and bumped his head.
> Frosty called the doctor and the doctor
>   said,
> "No more snowmen riding on that
>   sled!"

(Repeat with 4, 3, 2, and 1.)

Snowflake, Snowflake

 (Tune: Twinkle, Twinkle Little Star)
(Suit actions to words.)

> Snowflake, snowflake fancy free,
> Snowflake, snowflake dance with me.
> Touch my head, then my toes,
> Land on my nose where the cold wind
>   blows.
> Snowflake, snowflake turn around,
> Snowflake, snowflake touch the
>   ground.

> Snowflake, snowflake fancy free,
> Snowflake, snowflake dance with me.
> Touch my elbow, then my shoulder,
> Land on my chin where it's a bit colder.
> Snowflake, snowflake turn around,
> Snowflake, snowflake touch the ground.

> Snowflake, snowflake fancy free,
> Snowflake, snowflake dance with me.
> Touch my ears, then my knees,
> Snowflake, I'm about to freeze!
> Snowflake, snowflake turn around,
> Snowflake, snowflake please sit down.

Snowmen in a Row

 (Tune: 6 Little Ducks)
(Use your fingers to accompany this song.)

> 5 little snowmen standing in a row,
> Each had a hat and a big red bow.
> Out came the sun and it shone all day,
> And 1 little snowman melted away.

Repeat with 4, 3, and 2.

> 1 little snowman standing all alone,
> He wore a hat and a big red bow.
> Out came the sun and it shone all day,
> And the last little snowman melted away.

143

Chubby Little Snowman

 (Suit actions to words.)
> A chubby little snowman
> Had a carrot nose.
> Along came a bunny
> And what do you suppose?
> That hungry little bunny
> Looking for his lunch,
> Ate that snowman's nose with a
> Nibble, Nibble, CRUNCH!

Snowflake Song

 (Tune: Teddy Bear, Teddy Bear)
(Suit actions to words.)
> Snowflake, snowflake falling down,

(Flutter hands down.)
> Twirling, whirling to the ground.
> Softly, lightly on my nose,

(Touch your nose.)
> Snowflake, snowflake icy cold.

(Fold arms and shiver.)
> Snowflake, snowflake falling down

(Flutter hands down.)
> Twirling, whirling to the ground.

I'm a Friendly Snowman

 (Tune: I'm a Little Teapot)
(Suit actions to words.)
> I'm a friendly snowman big and fat,

(Stretch arms out to sides.)
> Here is my tummy and here is my hat.

(Point to your tummy and the top of your head.)
> I'm happy fellow, here is my nose,

(Smile and point to your nose.)
> I'm all snow from my head to my toes.

(Point to your head and then your toes.)
> I have two bright eyes so I can see,

(Point to your eyes.)
> All the snow falling down on me.

(Flutter your fingers down to the floor.)
> When the weather's cold I'm strong
> and tall,

(Stand up tall.)
> But when the weather's warm I get
> very small.

(Crouch down low.)

5 Melting Snowmen

 (Use your fingers to represent the snowmen.)
> 5 little snowmen
> On a winter's day,
> The first one said,
> "Wake up so we can play!"
>
> The second one said,
> "Let's stomp on the ground."
> The third one said,
> "Let's roll around."
>
> The fourth one said,
> "Let's run and run and run,"
> The fifth one said,
> "I'm afraid I feel the sun."
>
> "Oh dear!" cried the snowmen,
> As they looked toward the sky,
> And the five melting snowmen
> Waved a fond goodbye.

(Wave goodbye.)

Paint Stick Snowmen

Materials

1 paint stick per person

1 bamboo stick (approx. 10 inches or 25 cm) or long twig per person

Felt, various colours

Buttons, 2 or 3 per child

White washable tempera paint

Black construction paper

2 small wiggle eyes

Decorating supplies: markers, crayons, decorating snow, tissue paper

Glue sticks (enough for your group)

Instructions

1. Paint the stick white on both sides.

2. Glue the wiggle eyes in place.

3. Trace and cut out two mittens and one scarf from felt.

4. Tape the mittens on the bamboo stick or twig.

5. Cut a small strip of black construction paper and glue it near the top of the paint stick. This is the rim of the snowman's hat. Be careful to leave enough room for the top of the hat.

6. Provide the buttons, scarves, and other materials for the children to decorate their snowmen with.

145

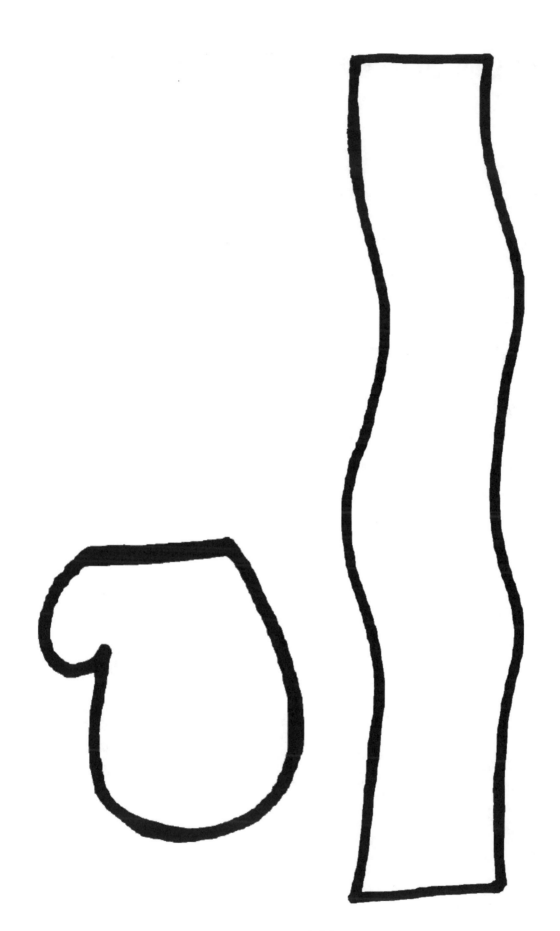

146

Program 8

Time for Twos: Oink, Cluck, Moo

Put on your straw hat and hitch up your pants, it's time to do the barnyard dance! You're sure to have a cluckin' good time in this session. Most two year olds can tell you what a cow or a pig says, so you're sure to have plenty of group participation. That's the great thing about doing a well-known theme; it won't really matter what you sing. Most barnyard or farm songs will have you singing about the noises animals make, and once you start, your group of little ones will just follow along. They may even add some lyrics or sounds of their own. Get ready to have some fun as you just never know what sounds you'll hear on the farm!

Plan Ahead Note

In this program having pictures to accompany the songs and rhymes will come in very handy. You can photocopy the ones in this book or go through various books and magazines you may have lying around. The children will identify easily with this theme, but visual aids are always beneficial for the children and the programmer and to ensure the program's success.

Books to Share

Barnyard Dance!, by Sandra Boynton

Big Red Barn, by Margaret Wise Brown

Who Said Moo? (Lift-the Flap Barnyard Mystery), by Harriet Ziefert

More books to share with two year olds can be found in the bibliography at the end of this chapter.

Time for Twos: Oink, Cluck, Moo

Rhymes and Songs

Five Little Pigs

(Tune: Five Little Ducks)
(Use your fingers or a child's toes to represent the piggies in this song.)
(Suit actions to words.)

5 little pigs rolled in the mud,
Squishy, squashy, squishy, squashy,
  felt so good.
The farmer took one little piggy out,
"Oink, oink, oink," the piggy did
  shout!

(Repeat with 4, 3, 2, and 1.)

No little piggies rolled in the mud,
They all stayed clean and oh so good,
The farmer turned his back and then,
Those piggies rolled in the mud again!

Take Me Out to the Barnyard

(Tune: Take Me Out to the Ballgame)
(Photocopy or find pictures of the barnyard animals mentioned in this song.)

Take me out to the barnyard,
Take me out there right now.
Show me the cows, pigs and horses too,
I hear an oink, a neigh and a moo.
There are chickens laying their eggs,
If they don't lay it's a shame.
Oh it's one, two, three eggs today,
And I'm glad I came.

The Tail of a Pig

(Tune: The Wheels on the Bus)
(Suit actions to words.)

The tail of a pig curls round and round,
Round and round, round and round.
The tail of a pig curls round and round,
All through the mud.

Additional verses:

Mouth of a pig goes oink, oink, oink
Snout of a pig goes root, root, root
Feet on the pig go run, run, run
Ears on the pig go twitch, twitch,
  twitch

Over in the Barnyard

(Tune: Down by the Station)
(Suit actions to words.)

Out in the barnyard,
Early in the morning,
See the yellow chickies

(Pretend to see chickies.)

Standing in a row.
See the busy farmer,
Giving them their breakfast.

(Pretend to feed the chickies.)

Cheep, cheep, cheep, cheep,
Off they go.

(Substitute other barnyard animals for the yellow chickies.)

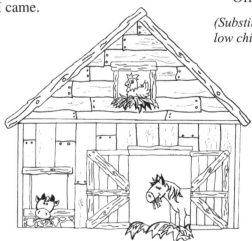

Barnyard Dance

(Suit actions to words.)

The barnyard dance is about to begin,
So hitch up your pants and jump right
in!
Pick the apples! Husk the corn!
Crow with the rooster in the early
morn.
Bow to your partner. Wave hello.
Clap your hands and tap your toe.
Feed the chickens! Milk the cow!
Hoe the weeds and push the plow.
This barnyard dance has come to an
end,
So sit on the floor and rest my friends!

Moving Around

(Suit actions to words.)

Wiggle your fingers and clap your
hands,
Quickly turn around,
Hop to your left,
Hop to your right,
Bend low and touch the ground.

Wiggle your fingers and clap your
hands,
Quietly sit down.
Bend to your left,
Bend to your right,
Now don't make a sound.
Shhhhhhhhh!

Cows in the Meadow

(Do as actions indicate.)

Cows in the meadow,
Take a little nap.

(Pretend to sleep.)

Thunder!

(Stamp your feet on the floor.)

Lightning!

(Clap your hands.)

Jump up and clap!

(Jump to your feet and clap.)

Visiting the Farm

*(Have children chime in with noises that they
think the animals make.)*

I went to visit the farm one day.
I saw a cow across the way.
And what do you think I heard it say?
Moo, moo, moo.

I went to visit the farm one day,
I saw a duck across the way.
And what do you think I heard it say?
Quack, quack, quack.

*(Repeat this rhyme, substituting other barnyard
animals, such as chickens, pigs, roosters, or
horses, and the noises they make.)*

149

Hand Print Sheep

Materials

1 sheet black construction paper (should make 4 sheep)

1 construction paper hand per person

Cotton balls (any colour)

1 wiggle eye per child

Yarn (any colour)

Glue sticks (enough for your group)

Scissors

Chalk (any colour)

Instructions

1. Photocopy and cut out the hand template to the size of a child's hand.

2. Fold the black construction paper in half lengthwise and then in half again. Trace the hand onto the black construction paper and cut it out.

3. Place the hand (fingers pointing downward) on the table in front of you.

4. Glue on enough cotton balls to cover the body of the sheep (the palm of the hand) except for the bottom of the fingers and the tip of the thumb; these are the sheep's legs and face.

5. Glue the wiggle eye onto the thumb. (This is the sheep's face.)

6. The yarn can be used to make a bow for each sheep and be glued on at the neck(or any- where).

7. Children can colour the sheep with c

6. Bibliography of Books to Share

Arnosky, Jim. 2001. *Raccoon On His Own*. New York: Putnam.

Baker, Alan. 1994. *White Rabbit's Color Book*. Sutton in Ashfield, United Kingdom: Kingfisher Books.

Boynton, Sandra. 1993. *Barnyard Dance!* New York: Workman.

Boynton, Sandra. 1995. *Horns to Toes (and in Between)*. New York: Little Simon.

Brown, Margaret Wise. 1995. *Big Red Barn*. New York: HarperFestival.

Ellwand, David. 2002. *Clap Your Hands*. New York: Handprint Books.

Gerth, Melanie. 2001. *Ten Little Ladybugs*. Santa Monica, CA: Piggy Toes Press.

Gooding, Lennie. 2001. *When You Grow Up*. New York: Phyllis Fogelman Books.

Hindley, Judy. 1999. *Eyes, Nose, Fingers, Toes*. Cambridge, MA: Candlewick Press.

Inkpen, Mike. 2000. *In Wibbly's Garden*. New York: Viking Children's Books.

Keats, Ezra Jack. 1996. *The Snowy Day*. New York: Viking Children's Books.

Kirk, David. 1997. *Miss Spider's Tea Party: The Counting Book*. New York: Scholastic Trade.

Krauss, Ruth. 1993. *The Carrot Seed*. New York: HarperFestival.

Manning, Jane. 2001. *Who Stole the Cookies from the Cookie Jar? (Playtime Rhymes)*. New York: HarperFestival.

Martin, Bill, Jr. 1996. *Brown Bear, Brown Bear, What Do You See?* New York: Henry Holt.

McCue, Lisa. 1997. *Fuzzytail Friends Lift-and-Look Animal Book*. New York: Random House.

Schwartz, Betty Ann. 2000. *What Makes a Rainbow?* Santa Monica, CA: Intervisual Books Inc.

Shaw, Charles G. 1993. *It Looked Like Spilt Milk*. New York: HarperCollins Juvenile Books.

Simmons, Jane. 2001. *Little Fern's First Winter*. New York: Little Brown.

Sparks, Michael. 2000. *My Very 1st Tea Party*. Eugene, OR: Harvest House.

Waddle, Martin. 2000. *Owl Babies*. Cambridge, MA: Candlewick Press.

Walters, Catherine. 2001. *When Will It Be Spring?* New York: Button Books.

Wellington, Monica. 2000. *Bunny's First Snowflake*. New York: Button Books.

Ziefert, Harriet. 2002. *Who Said Moo? (Lift-the-Flap Barnyard Mystery)*. New York: Handprint Books.

Chapter 5

Just Threes

Three year olds are at an age of discovery and rapid growth. Physically, intellectually, and socially, the time between thirty-six and forty-eight months encompasses rapid change for children as they become independent and more cerebral. Three year olds, as they mature, are ready for an independent storytime setting. This milestone is achieved by threes at different times, as is the case for all developmental hurdles. Generally speaking, however, three year olds younger than forty months of age are more comfortable having a parent or caregiver in sight.

Preschool storytime, in many library settings, is a program for children three to five years of age. However, some of these three year olds are not ready for storytime with older children who have more accomplished social skills in a group setting. A negative library experience may be the result if children are forced to attend storytime on their own before they are ready. One option to help children embrace their new-found independence is to offer a transitional program giving children and adults the flexibility to decide whether the child will attend independently or with an adult in sight. As three year olds gain confidence and grow comfortable with the routine, they are more likely to be able to participate without an adult present.

1. What Can Threes Do?: Child Development for Three Year Olds

As children grow into their preschool years, the range of abilities and accomplishments that they achieve as milestones also grows. It is more difficult to define a "typical" three year old because during their toddler development these children experience very different worlds in their family life, and these experiences influence who they are becoming as people. However, there are some general trends that can be identified in the development of most three-year-old children, and many of these trends relate directly to literacy and the child's ability to participate in and enjoy an independent storytime.

The following list includes many of the things you can expect three year olds to accomplish before their fourth birthdays:

- Developing a three-minute attention span

- Appreciating stories with a developed plot and characters

- Drawing simple shapes

- Putting together a puzzle (five pieces)

- Following uncomplicated directions

- Playing spontaneously with other children

- Identifying objects, colours, and sounds

- Counting, often up to five

- Pretending

- Speaking in full sentences

- Singing simple songs

- Repeating simple rhymes

- Developing an individual sense of humour

- Walking on tiptoes

- Throwing a ball

Because they are developing into little people who can appreciate a joke and listen to a story, three year olds can fool us into thinking they are much more mature than they really are. For example, some three-year-old children will recognise that moving cars are dangerous, but they won't realise that it might hurt another child if they crash into him or her with their tricycle. It is important for programmers to keep in mind that three year olds are still developing all the skills that older children take for granted. Another example is their ability to sit and listen. Some of them may be able to sit for as long as five minutes, but these children are not typical of all three year olds. Many threes will only be able to sit for two minutes at a time, and some younger threes will last less than a minute. Therefore, if you choose to engage and challenge the children in your storytime with a longer story, expect some children to stand and move around while the story is being read. Accept this as a normal part of storytime with three year olds. As the weeks go on and children grow more confident, you may find you have fewer wanderers as you read aloud.

2. Three Year Old Programming Guidelines

2.1 Starting a Program for Three Year Olds

Many libraries include three year olds in their programming line-up. However, having three year olds in a program to *themselves* is the most advantageous way to share a literacy experience with this group. This approach has advantages for the children, the programmer, and the institution. The children enjoy a setting of their peers, where caregivers can attend if a child is timid or uncomfortable. The rhymes, songs, stories, and activities are simple and easy for them to follow and participate in. There is no expectation of children sitting quietly; longer stories are followed by gross motor activities to match the children's short attention span. Programmers benefit by having the youngest children together in one group. In programs with three year olds and five year olds in the same group, there can be problems with developmental discrepancies. Although the three year old may be occupied and entertained, the five year old will not always be challenged intellectually. Three year olds who are allowed the comfort of a parent but the independence of peer participation will have a positive experience in the program. These positive, independent experiences are priceless for children and their families and will cast the institution in a positive light.

2.2 Getting Ready

One of the insider hints to working with a group of three year olds is to keep the set-up simple and safe. Choose elements that are not only developmentally appropriate but also uncluttered and secure for children to explore and examine on their own. Children at this age are natural explorers looking for external stimulation. If you are confident that all the program elements you have brought in and set up in the room are safe, you will be confident allowing children to explore and move around the room.

2.2a Books to Share

Books read aloud to three year olds should include a number of key features:

CONFIDENCE BOOSTER

Create a friendly space for three year olds by bringing props and toys that are safe for the children to play with on their own. Three year olds tend to wander and are curious about everything they can reach or touch. If the programming space is safe for the children, the programmer will be able to continue the program even while curious or restless children are wandering.

Essential Elements in Read-Aloud Picture Story Books for Three Years Olds

- Text and pictures that complement each another (e.g., *The Napping House,* by Audrey Wood)

- Concepts that are familiar or presented in a visually appealing way by the pictures (e.g., *Red Is Best,* by Kathy Stinson)

- A simple, singular plot (e.g., *Peter's Chair,* by Ezra Jack Keats)

- Characters with childlike characteristics (e.g., *Owl Babies,* by Martin Waddell)

- Predictable plots and endings, even in the realm of fantasy (e.g., *Where the Wild Things Are,* by Maurice Sendak)

Of course, even if a book has achieved excellence in all the required elements, if the reader does not enjoy the story, the listener will not enjoy the story. No matter what age group you are reading to, choose books that you really like and are excited about sharing.

2.2b Books to Display

There is no limit to the choices available for books to display; in fact, there is almost no limit to the number of books appropriate for children at this age, and borrowing books should be an integral part of any lending library's program. Use the lower shelves of a library cart or keep the books in a covered container and move it over at the appropriate time to allow children access to the books. This will minimise distractions during the program but will give children access to books chosen especially for them to take home.

BRIGHT IDEA

Use a puppet to introduce a selection of books for children to take home. Select one book for each child and use masking tape to label it with the child's name. Have the puppet call the child by name, and he or she can come forward and take the special book the puppet has chosen for him or her.

2.2c Extra Preparation

One of the best ways to get ready for a program with three year olds is to spend a little extra preparation time. Practice rhymes and songs a number of times so that you are comfortable with the tune or beat. The more time you can spend concentrating on your group, the smoother your program will run. Also, be prepared with extra materials. Because three year olds have short attention spans, you may find it necessary to change a plan you had for a program if it is not going well. Have extra games, rhymes, and songs ready to swap in, in case one of your scheduled program elements is not succeeding.

3. Programs for Three Year Olds: Format and Routine

When designing the routine for your three year old program, the key to success is the routine itself. Combine elements in small groups and give them names children will remember. The names should be simple and obvious, for example stories, songs, rhymes, games, or crafts. This may seem like an obvious tip, but the use of repetitive, memorable language is very important to three year olds. If you follow the opening routine with a story and announce "it is time for a story," after a few weeks children will understand the routine that goes along with that element of the program. They will move to the story area and sit on their mats, anticipating the routine that allows them to concentrate on listening.

3.1 Format

The format of your three year old program should be quite simple. Keep grouped activities in approximately three-minute segments. Although you don't need to spend time with a stop watch, you should get a sense of the three-minute time span. You may be amazed at how much you can accomplish in three minutes. By using the "three-minute rule" your program will be fast paced and developmentally appropriate.

When you are singing simple rhymes and songs, complete them once and then repeat them again with the children. The average rhyme or short song can be completed twice in one minute. You can group two or three of these similar activities together in a single section of the program. For example, children will enjoy doing several fingerplays in a row, or if you hand out musical instruments, they will have fun doing a few songs.

> **BRIGHT IDEA**
>
> To help three year olds, and older children, prepare for a story (during which they will be expected to listen quietly), use a listening routine:
> ✔ Have the children pantomime picking up their listening ears from the ground and snapping them into place to show they are ready to listen.
> ✔ Use a quieting fingerplay or action rhyme (one that ends with the children in a sitting position, ready to listen).
> ✔ Use a feather duster and pantomime dusting children with listening dust.

A sample format for a three year old program follows. It is not important for you to use a routine exactly like this one, but it is important to design a routine that works and use it *every* week. Each section detailed below is approximately a "three-minute" group. The entire program, including transitions from one activity to another, takes about half an hour.

Three Year Old Program Routine

1. Opening (includes name tags and song)

2. Story (includes listening routine and read-aloud story)

3. Fingerplays

4. Movement rhymes

5. Story (includes listening routine and read-aloud story)

6. Action songs

7. Group activity or game

8. Craft

9. Closing routine (includes handing back name tags and song)

3.2 Opening Routine

Children in a three year old program, especially if they are attending without their parents, should have some sort of individual identifier. This identifier, usually a name tag, allows the children to feel special and belong to the group but also allows the programmer to quickly identify the children by name, a very useful tool for managing a group. Sample name tags appear in the appendix. You can use one of these samples or design one of your own. The tags should be large, with clear printing that is easy to read from a distance. They should be made from (or backed onto) sturdy cardboard and then laminated for durability. Lamination does not require a machine like the one used to give a clear plastic

> **BRIGHT IDEA**
>
> Put the program name, the institution's name, and the date on the back of each child's name tag. This transforms each name tag into a keepsake for parents. Long after the child has graduated from storytime, parents will have a reminder of what great fun the program was for their child, and what a great place your facility was to visit.

coating to identification cards. Sticky-backed clear plastic paper is available from most craft stores. Affix the laminating paper to both sides of the name tag. Although this paper can be expensive, it is worth the extra cost and effort to make name tags durable for the duration of the program. Otherwise, minor repairs to name tags for individual children who chew on the edges or fold them while they listen will take quite a bit of time each week.

You can display the name tags on hooks, and the children and their caregivers can begin the program by picking up the appropriate tags. After all have their identifiers in place, begin storytime in a way that might be familiar to the children—with a song or rhyme. Use a song you have used in a previous program, or try this one:

Hello My Friends

 (Tune: Farmer in the Dell)
Hello my friends hello,
Hello my friends hello,
Hello my friends,
Hello my friends,
Hello my friends hello!

This song has the advantage of being very simple and easy for three year olds to remember.

3.3 Group Activities and Games

There are some wonderful activities for a group of three-year-old children to play with a leader. For this portion of your program, you may decide to hand out musical instruments and have children play and sing. Another activity that works well with this age group is to have them march in a circle to the beat of a drum. Other traditional circle games and activities also work well with three year olds, such as *Ring Around the Rosy* or *The Hokey Pokey*. You may decide to use this time for dancing or a follow-the-leader style game. Whatever activity or game you choose, it should involve all the children and enable them to do some gross motor activity.

If children are reluctant to take part in the activity, don't force them to participate. Instead, encourage them to watch everyone and join in when they feel comfortable. Keep your tone positive, light, and encouraging. The children should not feel that you are scolding them; some may prefer to watch. As long as they are not distressed, this should not become a problem. If a child continues for several weeks to "sit out" of the group activities and his or her parent is not present, you may want to mention it to the parent after the program in a friendly, conversational manner.

3.4 Predictability and Comfort Elements

Predictability plays an important role in storytime for three year olds. To make the transitions easy and comfortable, you may want to use a rhyme or song. *The Farmer in the Dell* has a predictable tune that children can learn quickly, and you can add your own words for the transitions. For example, before each read-aloud story you could sing:

 It's time to read a story.
It's time to read a story.
It's time to read,
It's time to read,
It's time to read a story.

The same tune can be used to introduce each program element: "It's time to play a game," or "It's time to do a craft," or "It's time to use the instruments" can be used to signal a move to the next section of the program. A familiar tune will help children who have become distracted refocus on the program.

Another element of predictability comes from using popular elements over and over. For example, children love to act out the rhyme *Five Little Monkeys Jumping on the Bed*. If your program begins to get disrupted, gather your group and have them act out this rhyme. After the first week or two, change the characters that jump on the bed, but keep all the other words and actions the same. If you have a theme-related program you can have a character from your theme do the jumping for that week. All sorts of animals and characters can jump on the bed; cows, ladybugs, and bunnies are just a few examples. You can use the flannel board to immortalise this program element quite easily. Use the template in figure 5.1 to make a flannel board bed. Then simply create five theme-related characters to jump on it each week.

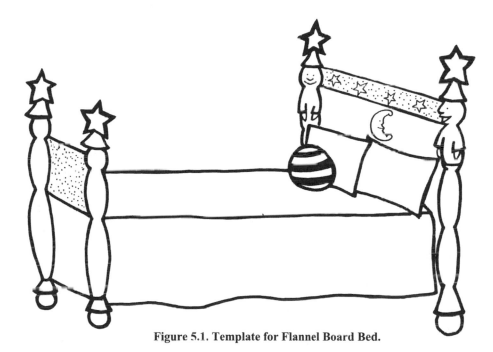

Figure 5.1. Template for Flannel Board Bed.

3.5 Print Materials

Although three year olds cannot read on their own, it is important to have print materials to accompany the program. These can be given to parents and caregivers to explain what they should expect in storytime. You can design a brochure (see figure 5.2), draft a letter, or compile a calendar. Whichever format you decide to use, your objective should be to help the adults understand what will happen during storytime so that they can share this information with their children. Include information about upcoming themes and your contact information so an adult can get in touch with you if necessary to explain an absence or discuss a problem his or her child is having in the program. And finally, include a little information on what children will experience to reassure parents about what to expect.

Books for Three Year Olds

<u>Ten, Nine, Eight</u> by Molly Bang   JP Bang

<u>Freight Train</u> by Donald Crews   JP Crews

<u>The Very Hungry Caterpillar</u> by Eric Carle
    JP Carle

<u>Sheep in a Jeep</u> by Nancy Shaw   JP Shaw

<u>Red is Best</u> by Kathy Stinson   JP Stins

<u>Jamberry</u> by Bruce Degen   JP Degen

<u>If You Give a Mouse a Cookie</u>
    by Laura Joffe Numeroff   JP Numer

<u>I Went Walking</u> by Sue Williams   JP Willi

<u>Silly Sally</u> by Audrey Wood   JP Wood

<u>Polar Bear, Polar Bear, What do you Hear?</u>
    by Bill Martin Jr.   JP Marti

Just Threes

Wednesdays, April 3 to May 22 2:00 to 2:30 pm.

Welcome to Just Threes

Just Threes is a special program designed specifically to introduce your child to storytime as an independent group activity while fostering a lifelong love of books and reading. Each week this thirty minute program will expose your child to stories, songs, rhymes and activities that are fun and educational. This is a great time to get your child their own library card and to begin encouraging them to select stories that they love or would like to share with you. A library card is the key to a world of resources and its use will develop your child's language skills as well as their sense of responsibility and independence.

During the course of the program your child may need to leave the room to find you. Please wait near the program room to greet your child, but feel free to quietly help your child reenter the program if time permits. We also invite you to use this time to browse through our wonderful selection of parenting books and magazines or choose some picture books and fairytales to take home. Please feel free to browse the book display in the program room with your child before leaving so that you can continue the fun at home and share in some of their special experiences.

Please do not hesitate to ask me, or any other Children's Staff member for suggestions on good books for you and your child. If you have any questions, or if your child is unable to attend a session, please call me at 658-4412.

Kim Sachs
Children's Services
Hespeler Library

Your child will explore the exciting world of books and reading with the following themes.

Week 1	Old MacDonald...
Week 2	Fun with Mother Goose
Week 3	Buzz, Buzz, Buzz
Week 4	Just Ducky
Week 5	Spring Fling
Week 6	Beautiful Butterflies
Week 7	Gone Fishing
Week 8	Rainbow of Colours

Figure 5.2. Sample Brochure for Three Year Old Program.

3.6 Closing Routine

End the program each week the same way it began, with name tags and a song. Collect the name tags by having children place them back on the designated hooks, or have the children hand them directly to you. Finish out the program by singing a song to say goodbye. If you use the welcome song *Hello My Friends*, it makes sense to use the closing song *Goodbye My Friends*.

Goodbye My Friends

(Tune: Farmer in the Dell)

Goodbye my friends goodbye,
Goodbye my friends goodbye,
Goodbye my friends,
Goodbye my friends,
Goodbye my friends goodbye!

4. Three Year Old Programming Techniques

4.1 Connecting with Adults

The adults who accompany their children to the program are very important to the successful implementation of the program. You should let them know what is expected of them and their children for the duration. Before the program begins, decide what to do about children who are not comfortable staying on their own. These children need to have access to their parents or caregivers. Following are some techniques you can use to help make the transition to independent storytime easier for three year olds and their families:

- *Option 1.* Have all adults and children attend the first week of the program together and explain to the adults that there will be seating available for them near the door if they choose to remain in the program room. Encourage adults to take their cues from their children; if they are anxious about attending alone, encourage the adults to remain inside.

- *Option 2.* Invite adults in for the beginning of the first class and give them the option of leaving at any time during the first three weeks. At the end of three weeks, ask anyone who remains to attempt to leave their children on their own, unless a child is genuinely uncomfortable.

- *Option 3.* Announce before the first program that this is a very exciting time for three year olds because they get to attend storytime all by themselves. Encourage adults to come into the program only if necessary for their children.

Finally, all adults should be asked to remain outside the door of the program room, in case their children need them. Parents and caregivers can use this time to socialise or catch up on their own reading. If your facility has the appropriate set-up, they may be able to use this time to choose books to take home to read with their three year olds. Programmers will not be able to leave the program room to accompany individual children to the washroom or to find parents if the children become distressed. Adult caregivers should keep an eye on the program room door in case their children need them. It is important to reinforce this information, as some adults will use their free half hour to run errands, and this could be detrimental to the safety of their children. If possible, it is good to have an assistant or a volunteer on hand to assist children who need to leave the room to find their caregivers. If the program is not disrupted each time a child needs to leave it will be easier to maintain the program's pace and focus.

4.2 Controlling a Group

To maintain a positive atmosphere and upbeat attitude, it is important to be able to manage the entire group of children. One way to accomplish this is to limit the number of children allowed to attend the program. Twelve to fifteen is a comfortable maximum for most programmers. You need to have enough children to make circles, games, and group activities enjoyable, but you also need a limit so that it is possible to keep an eye on all of them at all times.

Once you have fifteen three year olds assembled, it may be necessary to refocus the group from time to time if children have begun to wander or do their own thing. One technique you may wish to use to refocus your group is to have children actively participate in a repetitive task until all are repeating the task and focused. Clapping your hands, tapping your feet, snapping your fingers, or some rhythmic combination of these is a good method. Explain to the children that when you clap your hands, it means everyone should return to their spots and clap along. Continue clapping until everyone follows suit. Ignore all distractions while clapping (except emergencies, of course) and continue to clap until all the children are clapping with you. This could take as long as three minutes on your first couple of attempts. Once you have refocused the group, praise them for a job well done and move on to the next program element.

Finally, whichever techniques you decide to use to help the children understand that they are part of a group, never raise your voice or speak in an angry manner. Three year olds are controlled by their growing brains, and while it may seem like bad behaviour when they move around or become disruptive, most of them are simply learning how to become part of a group and, through experience, to increase their attention span and ability to sit for extended periods of time.

Program 1

Just Threes: Hallowe'en Howl

Bright. Bold. Energetic. Enthusiastic. Any of these words can be used to accurately describe one or a group of three year olds. The most noticeable change that you're likely to see in this age group is their openness and independence. Whereas some two year olds tend to err on the side of shyness, most three year olds gain confidence with people, surroundings, and themselves as they get older (especially if they have been regular members of interactive programs like the ones we have laid out here). This group will be ready for whatever you have in store for them—so let's explore the endlessly energetic world of the three year old!

We waited until we reached three year olds before introducing a Hallowe'en theme. Why? Let's face it . . . Hallowe'en does deal with more than just pumpkins. Ghosts, goblins, and ghouls can be scary, and even though the songs and rhymes are meant to be fun, it's amazing what a year can do when you're talking about the cognitive development of a child. Whereas a two year old may be afraid of a bat or a witch, a three year old may be better equipped mentally to understand play and pretend things. So let's jump in and join the fun. This program is filled with interactive songs and rhymes for the whole group to enjoy. Happy howling!

Plan Ahead Note

The songs and rhymes in this program are very interactive. Make sure that your space is large enough and that you have enough room to move with the whole group without anyone bumping into anyone else. You may not have time to get through all of the songs and rhymes we have listed here. We have found these to be the favourites of many children, so don't be surprised if you find yourself singing some of these songs over and over again.

Books to Share

Zoom Broom, by Margie Palatini

Pumpkin Eye, by Denise Fleming

Seen on Hallowe'en—Wacky Flaps, by Pat Binder

More books to share with three year olds can be found in the bibliography at the end of this chapter.

┌─ Rhyme and Song Legend ─┐
♪ Song
Clapping   Bouncing
Actions   Fingerplay

Just Threes: Hallowe'en Howl

Rhymes and Songs

The Goblin in the Dark

(Tune: The Farmer in the Dell)
(Have the children sit in a circle to play this game.)

The goblin in the dark,
The goblin in the dark,
Heigh-ho on Hallowe'en,
The goblin in the dark.

Additional verses:

The goblin picks a witch
The witch picks a cat
The cat picks a bat
The bat picks a ghost
The ghost says BOO!

Five Little Ghosts

(Use your fingers to represent the ghosts and hold up one finger at a time.)

Five little ghosts all dressed in white,
Were scaring each other on
Hallowe'en night.
"Boo!" said the first one, "I'll catch you!"
"Woooo" said the second, "I don't care
if you do!"
The third ghost said, 'You can't run
away from me."
And the fourth one said, "I'll scare
everyone I see."
Then the last one said, "It's time to
disappear."
"See you all at Hallowe'en time next
year!"

Hallowe'en

(Suit actions to words.)
Here is a witch with a tall, tall hat,

(Make a hat using your hands over your head.)
Two big eyes on a black, black cat.

(Put your hands in circles around your eyes.)
Jack o'lanterns in a row,

(Draw circles in front of you.)
Funny clowns laughing ho, ho, ho.

(Hold your stomach.)
Bunny ears flopping up and down,

(Use your hand to make bunny ears above your head.)
Fairy Queen wears a fairy crown.

(Pretend to place a crown on your head.)
Gypsy plays a tambourine,

(Clap your hands.)
Cowboy twirls a rope.

(Pretend to twirl a lasso above your head.)
It's Hallowe'en!
HOORAY!

Hooky Spooky

(Tune: Hokey Pokey)
(Gather the children into a circle so everyone can see everyone else to start this song.)

Put your right arm in,
Take your right arm out
Put your right arm in
And you shake it all about.
You do the Hooky Spooky
And everybody shout,
"That's what it's all about. BOO!"

(Substitute your right arm for other body parts, e.g., left leg, left arm.)

Five Little Goblins

 (Use your fingers to represent the goblins or say the rhyme once and then have the children be the goblins the second time.)

> 5 little goblins on Hallowe'en night,
> Made a very, very, spooky site.
> The first one danced on his tippy toes,
> The next one tumbled and bumped his nose.
> The next one jumped up high I the air,
> The next one said "We have no cares!"
> The last one sang a Hallowe'en song,
> Five little goblins played the whole night long.

8 Giggling Ghosts

 (Use your fingers to represent the ghosts.)

> 8 giggling ghosts
> Like to give you a fright.
> When they come out to play
> On Hallowe'en night.
> 1 ghost laughs,
> And 1 ghost giggles.
> 1 ghost ha-ha's,
> And 1 ghosts wiggles.
> 1 ghost cackles,
> And 1 ghost roars.
> 1 ghost howls,
> And 1 rolls on the floor.
> 8 giggling ghosts,
> Aren't much of a fright.
> When they come out to play,
> On Hallowe'en Night.

Hallowe'en Ghost

 (Do as the actions indicate.)
> There once was a ghost,

 (Extend hand and wiggle fingers.)
> Who lived in a cave.

(Form an "O" shape with your hands by touching thumb to thumb, and fingertips to fingertips.)
> She scared all the people away.

(Point to the children.)
> She said "Boo" to a fox,
> She said "Boo" to a bee,
> She said "Boo" to a bear,
> She said "Boo" to me!

(Point to yourself.)
> Well, she scared that fox,

(Nod head yes.)
> And she scared that bee,

(Nod head yes.)
> She scared that bear,

(Nod head yes.)
> But she didn't scare me!

(Shake head no.)

Hallowe'en Hallowe'en

 (Tune: Jingle Bells)
(Have the children pretend to be the ghosts, etc., in this fun song.)

> Hallowe'en, hallowe'en,
> Hallowe'en is here.
> Ghosts and goblins, spooks and bats
> Are flying through the air, Boo!
> Hallowe'en, Hallowe'en,
> Hallowe'en is here.
> Ghost and goblins, spooks and bats
> Are flying through the air, Boo!

"Spook" the Bat

Materials

1 photocopied bat per person

1 paint stick per person

1 sheet of black construction paper per person

4 black tissue paper strips (approx. 10 inches or 25 cm in length)

Glue

Scissors

Decorating supplies: markers and/or crayons, glitter

Instructions

1. Photocopy the bat template (to fit an 8½-by-11-inch sheet) on white paper and cut it out.

2. Glue the bat onto the black construction paper and cut it out, leaving a black outline.

3. Tape the bat onto the paint stick.

4. Cut out four 6-inch strips of black tissue paper and tape them onto the bat's wings.

5. Let the children decorate with crayons, glitter, and markers.

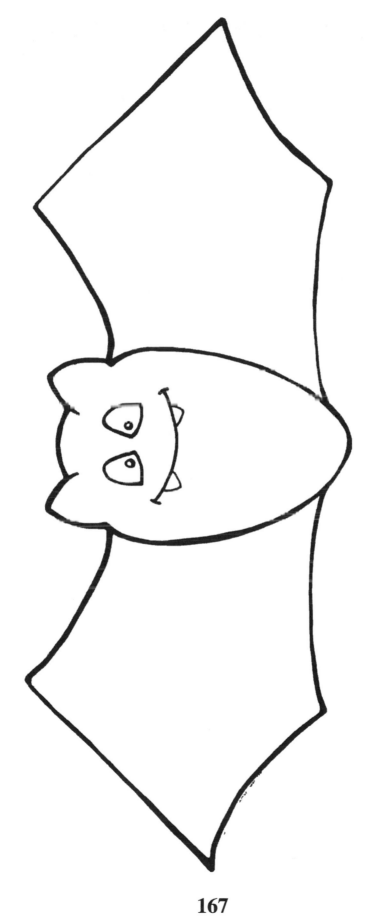

Program 2

Just Threes: Spring Fling

Pull on your rubber boots and dust off your umbrellas. Spring has arrived! The "Awesome Umbrellas" storytime souvenir is sure to complete the experience and remind your group that just because it's grey outside doesn't mean that they should feel blue. This is a great time to encourage group participation. Talk about what the children like to do in the rain. Make a list and post it where the children can see it the next time they come for a program. This program is bound to put that happy feeling in your heart, and your entire group will feel like singing in the rain afterwards.

Plan Ahead Note

Although there are recommended sizes for photocopying the storytime souvenirs, it is important to remember that these are only guidelines. As the programmer, you should use your own judgement about how large to make the umbrellas or any other craft. Only you know what is best for your group, so keep that in mind as you prepare for your programs.

Books to Share

Spring Song, by Barbara Seuling

When Will It Be Spring?, by Catherine Walters

Spring Fever, by Sarah Albee

More books to share with three year olds can be found in the bibliography at the end if this chapter.

Just Threes: Spring Fling

Rhymes and Songs

I See the Wind

 (Suit actions to words.)
I see the wind when the leaves dance by,

(Dance hands around.)
I see the wind when the clothes wave "Hi."

(Wave hello.)
I see the wind when the trees bend low,

(Bend arms over and down.)
I see the wind when the flags all blow.

(Wave arms high.)
I see the wind when the kites fly high,

(Raise arms high.)
I see the wind when the clouds float by.

(Wave hands gently.)
I see the wind when it blows my hair,

(Lift hair with hands.)
I see the wind most everywhere.

(Hold hands out, palms up.)

What the Robin Told

 (Do as the actions indicate.)
The wind told the grasses,

(Shape your hand like a cloud and then flutter your fingers to look like grass.)
And the grasses told the trees.

(Stand your arm up straight to look like a tree.)
The trees told the bushes,

(Form your hands into fists to look like a bush.)
And the bushes told the bees.
The bees told the robin,

(Flap like a bird.)
And the robin sang out clear,
"Wake up! Wake up!
Spring is here."

Kite Flying

 (Suit actions to words.)
On many spring days I wish that I,
Could be a kite flying in the sky.
I would climb high toward the sun,
And chase the clouds. Oh, what fun!
Whichever way the wind chanced to blow,
Is the way that I would go.
I'd fly up, up, up.
I'd fly down, down, down.
Then I'd spin round and round and round.
And finally float softly to the ground.

Relaxing Flowers

 (Use your fingers to represent the flowers.)
5 little flowers standing in the sun,

(Hold up five fingers.)
See their heads nodding, bowing one by one?

(Bend fingers several times.)
Down, down, down comes the gentle rain,

(Flutter fingers downward to look like rain.)
And the 5 little flowers lift their heads again.

(Hold up five fingers again.)

Umbrellas

 (Use your fingers to represent the umbrellas or photocopy and colour five umbrellas.)

5 umbrellas stood by the back door,
The red one went outside, then there
were four.
4 umbrellas pretty as can be,
The blue one went outside, then there
were three.
3 umbrellas with nothing to do,
The green one went outside and that
left two.
2 umbrellas not having much fun,
The pink one went outside and that left
one.
1 umbrella blue and all alone,
Decided to go join his friends and that
left none.

Farmer Plants the Seeds

 (Tune: The Farmer in the Dell)
(Suit actions to words.)

The farmer plants the seeds,

(Pretend to plant a seed.)

The farmer plants the seeds.
Heigh Ho and Cherry O
The farmer plants the seeds.

Additional verses:

The rain begins to fall
The sun begins to shine
The plants begin to grow
The buds all open up
The flowers smile at me

Blow, Blow, Blow the Wind

 (Tune: Row, Row, Row, Your Boat)
(Suit actions to words.)

Blow, blow, blow the wind
Gently through the trees.
Blow and blow and blow and blow,
How I like the breeze!

Blow, blow, blow the clouds,
Blow them through the sky.
Blow and blow and blow and blow,
Watch the clouds roll by!

The Wind

 (Suit actions to words.)

The wind came out to play one day.
He blew the clouds out of his way.

(Make sweeping motion with hands.)

He blew the leaves and away they flew.

(Make fluttering motions with fingers.)

The trees bent low and their branches
did too!

(Lift arms high and lower them.)

The wind blew the great big ships at
sea.

(Repeat sweeping motion.)

The wind blew my kite away from me!

170

Awesome Umbrellas

Materials

1 photocopied umbrella per person

1 sheet construction paper (any colour) per person

1 bendable straw per person

Scissors

Glue sticks (enough for your group)

Tape

Decorating supplies: crayons, markers, glitter, lickable stickers, bingo dabbers

Instructions

1. Photocopy the umbrella template (approx. 5½ inches long by 5 inches high or 14 cm long by 12 cm high) and cut it out.

2. Glue the umbrella onto the construction paper and cut it out, leaving a small border.

3. Tape the straw onto the back of the umbrella and curl the "bendy" part up. (This is the handle.)

4. Let the children decorate the umbrellas.

Program 3

Just Threes:
Crunch, Munch, and Slurp

What do three year olds love to do other than sleep and play? Eat! This session will be as easy as pie, and you'll almost have the kids eating out of the palm of your hands (or at the craft table). The songs and rhymes in this program were included not only because of their relevance but also because of their likeability. The children in your program can relate to this theme because it's all about food. Some three year olds are well known for their pickiness when it comes to eating, but not many can resist the temptation to sing along or join in when they know the subject very well. So roll up your sleeves and let's get eating. . . . I mean singing!

Plan Ahead Note

It is a good idea to keep any resources you may make along the way at your fingertips. Some of the songs and rhymes that we have provided can use the same props from chapter to chapter (as is the case with the *Ice Cream* rhyme in this program as well as in chapter 4). Although the props are the same, the rhymes and songs are different, so the props will still be just as effective as they were the first time you used them.

Books to Share

Crunch Munch, by Jonathan London

If You Give a Moose a Muffin, by Laura Joffe Numeroff

Maisy Goes Shopping, by Lucy Cousins

More books to share with three year olds can be found in the bibliography at the end of this chapter.

Just Threes:
Crunch, Munch, and Slurp

Rhymes and Songs

Guess the Veggie

 (Have pictures of each of the following vegetables to accompany this rhyme. Read the clue for each one and have the children "guess the veggie.")

I'm round and red and juicy too.
Chop me for a salad
Or dump me in your stew.
I'm a Tomato.

Chop me and slice me,
But keep a tissue near.
I sometimes get juicy
And can bring on a tear!
I'm an Onion.

Orange is my colour,
I stand long and lean.
In the garden you'll see
Just my bright leaves of green.
I'm a carrot.

I live in a pod
With so many others.
I think I was born
With one hundred brothers.
I'm peas in a pod.

I have eyes for perfection
To give you the best.
Baked, mashed or fried,
I'll pass the test.
I'm a potato

My friends call me trees,
Now that's a funny name.
Though I am a dark green,
With stalks just the same.
I'm broccoli.

Picnic Basket

 (Tune: A-Tisket, a-Tasket)
(Sing this verse and let each child in your group have a turn to say what he or she would like to have in the picnic basket.)

A-tisket, a-tasket,
Let's pack a picnic basket.
We'll fill it up with food to munch,
What's in our picnic lunch?

Way Up High

 (Tune: This Old Man)
(Do as the actions indicate.)

Way up high in a tree,
Two little apples smiled at me.
So I shook that tree as hard as I could,

(Pretend to shake a tree.)

Down came the apples,
Mmmm, they were good!

(Rub your tummy.)

173

5 Red Apples

 (Use your fingers to represent the apples.)
    5 red apples hanging in a tree,

(Hold up five fingers.)
    The juiciest apples you ever did see.
    The wind came by and gave an angry
        frown,

(Flutter fingers downward.)
    And 1 little apple came tumbling
        down.

(One finger falls.)
    4, 3, 2, 1

Ice Cream Cones

 (Make felt ice cream cones or use the ones you made in chapter 4. Place them on the board as you say the rhyme.)
        5 little ice cream cones so good to eat.
        The first one said, "I'm a summer time
            treat."
        The second one said, "It's such a hot
            day,"
        The third one said, "I'm melting
            away."
        The fourth one said, "Don't lose your
            top!"
        The fifth one said, "Oh dear,"
            KERPLOP!

(Place the last cone upside down.)

I Eat

 (Suit actions to words.)
        I eat apples,
        Crunch, crunch, crunch.
        I eat sandwiches
        Munch, munch, munch.
        I eat lollipops
        Lick, lick, lick.
        But I eat ice cream
        Quick, quick, quick!

The Food Chant

(Suit actions to words.)

Apples on a tree,
Apples on a tree,
Pick them off!
Eat them up!
Apples on a tree.

Carrots in the ground,
Carrots in the ground,
Pull them up,
Wash them off,
Carrots in the ground.

Sausage in a pan,
Sausage in a pan,
Sizzle, Sizzle,
Bam! Bam!
Sausage in a pan.

Milk in a glass,
Milk in a glass,
Lift it up,
Drink it all,
Milk in a glass.
Jelly in a bowl,
Jelly in a bowl,
Wibble, Wobble,
Wibble, Wobble,
Jelly in a bowl.

Food in your tummy,
Food in your tummy,
Lick your lips,
Mmmmm, Mmmmm,
Yum, yum, yummy!

Crackers and Crumbs

(Point to each body part as it is mentioned.)

Crackers and crumbs,
Crackers and crumbs.
These are my fingers,
These are my thumbs.

These are my eyes,
This is my nose.
These are my feet,
And here are my toes.

These are my elbows,
These are my ears.
They'll all grow big like me,
In the next ten years!

Fruit Loopy Jewelry

Materials

Colourful round cereal (suitable for lacing)

Yarn or plastic lace (any colour)

Instructions

1. Cut an arm's length of yarn or plastic lace. (approx. 20 inches or 50 cm)

2. Provide the children with two handfuls of cereal each.

3. Let the children lace the cereal onto the string to create their own Fruit Loopy Jewelry.

Children may need assistance with this craft, so once you have them set up you can open the door and announce to the caregivers that the children are doing their craft and that the caregivers should feel free to come in.

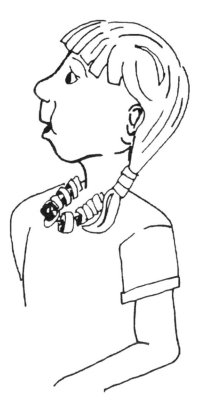

Program 4

Just Threes:
Splish-Splash! Who's in the Bath?

Run the water. Get the toys. Bath time fun for girls and boys! Welcome to bath time with three year olds! Would a bath ever really be complete without a rubber ducky? Well, we didn't think so. So we've provided a bathtub and rubber ducky of their very own for the children to decorate and take home with them. By including ducks in your bath time program you enhance your resources and have two ways to expand on your songs, rhymes and books.

Plan Ahead Note

As another extender of this program, you could encourage caregivers to send a "washable something" along to the program. If your time and space allow, provide a tub, a small amount of water, or even some wet paper towels, and let the children in the group wash their dolls or toys. This would encourage discussion on a variety of topics such as bath time, soap, and bubbles, and the children would enjoy getting to do something a little different.

Books to Share

Jack—It's Bathtime, by Rebecca Elgar

Baby's Bathtime, by Fiona Watt

Have You Seen My Duckling?, by Nancy Tafuri

More books to share with three year olds can be found in the bibliography at the end of this chapter.

Just Threes:
Splish-Splash! Who's in the Bath?

Rhymes and Songs

5 Little Ducklings

 (Use your fingers to represent the ducks in this rhyme or photocopy the duck template to use as a prop.)

5 Little Ducklings sitting in the bath,
One jumped out and said with a laugh,
"There's not enough room for me to splash!"
Four little ducklings sitting in the bath.

4, 3, 2, 1

Yellow Ducky

 (Suit actions to words.)

When a yellow ducky,
Walks down the street,

(Walk in place.)

Quack! Goes his bill,

(Open and close your hand like a duck bill.)

Waddle go his feet.

(Waddle in place.)

He comes to a puddle and with a bound,
In goes the ducky and he swims around.

(Pretend to jump into a puddle and swim.)

Quack, Quack

 (Suit actions to words.)

Now I'm up,

(Stand up.)

Now I'm down.

(Squat down.)

See me waddle all around.

(Waddle like a duck.)

Put my hands behind my back,
Like a duck I'll say,
"Quack, quack, quack."

Little Ducklings

 (Suit actions to words.)

All the little ducklings line up in a row,

(Stand up straight.)

Quack, quack, quack! And off they go.
They jump in the bathtub and bob up and down,

(Jump in place and bob from side to side.)

"Quack, quack, quack!" They swim all around.

Little Yellow Duck

 (Suit actions to words.)

If I were a yellow duck,
Yellow duck, yellow duck.
If I were a yellow duck,
This is what I'd do.

I'd give a little "Quack, quack, quack,
Quack, quack, quack.
Quack, quack, quack."
I'd give a little "Quack, quack, quack."
That is what I'd do.

I'd flap my wings with a flap, flap,
    flap,
Flap, flap, flap. Flap, flap, flap.
I'd flap my wings with a flap, flap,
    flap.
And say good-bye to you.

The Duck Song

 (Photocopy the duck template and colour the ducks in a variety of shades to accompany this song.)

I see a duck,
The duck sees me.
I like the ducks,
The ducks like me.
Big yellow ducks,
One, Two, Three.
I like the ducks,
And the ducks like me.

(Substitute yellow for other colours.)

Ducks in the Water

(Suit actions to words.)

Ducks in the water, quack, quack, quack!
Soft, white feathers on your back,
    back, back!
Duck in the water, splash and splish!
Dip in your bill and catch those fish!

Duck out of water, walk on land.
Your webbed feet make it hard to
    stand!
Waddle with your family, waddle in a
    pack.
Duck out of water, quack, quack,
    quack!

Miss Lucy Had a Baby

 (Suit actions to words.)

Miss Lucy had a baby,
His name was Tiny Tim.
She put him in the bathtub,
To see if he could swim.
He drank all the water,
He ate all the soap.
He tried to eat the bathtub
But it wouldn't go down his throat!

So . . .

Miss Lucy called the doctor,
The doctor called the nurse,
The nurse called the lady with the
    alligator purse.

In walked the doctor,
In walked the nurse,
In walked the lady with the alligator
    purse.

"Mumps!" said the doctor.
"Measles!" said the nurse.
"PIZZA!" said the lady with
the alligator purse.

"Quackers" the Duck

Materials

1 photocopied bathtub (to fit an 8½-by-11-inch piece of paper) per person

1 photocopied duck per person

1 sheet yellow Wonderfoam or foam sheet

1 medium wiggle eye

Blue cellophane/basket wrap (optional)

Decorating supplies: glue, marker, crayons

Scissors

Glue

Instructions

1. Photocopy the bathtub template.

2. Photocopy the duck template (approx. 4 inches high by 3 inches wide or 10 cm high by 8 cm wide) and cut it out.

3. Trace the duck onto the yellow foam and cut it out.

4. Glue the wiggle eye onto the duck.

5. Cut out the blue cellophane and glue it on the bathtub or let the children colour the water themselves.

6. Let the children decorate using markers or crayons.

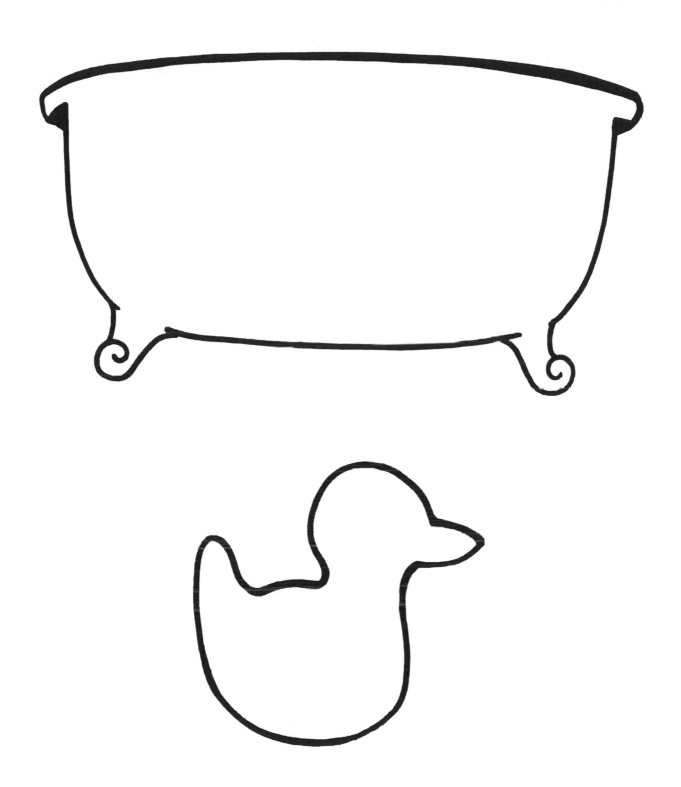

Program 5
Just Threes: Frogs, Fish, and Fun

We start each of these programs with the idea that we want to provide you with a stable base from which to start your programming. That's why there are so many familiar songs and rhymes found throughout this book. But it is also our goal to encourage you, the programmer, to try something different along with your group(s). In this program you have three elements to choose from: frogs, fish, or fun. Choose one or combine all three. The more elements in a program, the greater the number of ideas to use with it. The song *Gang Goo* is one of our favourites, and surprisingly we have found that not a lot of children know it. Perhaps this is because some programmers may feel silly doing the actions that accompany the song. Try not to let looking silly get in the way of what you are trying to accomplish with your group. In our experience, once the children see you, the adult, do something a little kooky or funny, they are more willing to try whatever it is you're doing. Come on now, you can do it. Put a little wiggle to it!

Plan Ahead Note

This program contains one of the easier storytime souvenirs (for the programmer to prepare). Visit your local dollar or discount store to purchase the paper bags needed for this craft. Sometimes you can even find them in a variety of colours. Pick up a few to give your group some variety.

Books to Share

Froggy Plays in the Band, by Jonathan London

Jumping Frog, by Amanda Leslie

Mommy, May I Hug the Fishes?, By Crystal Boroman

More books to share with three year olds can be found in the bibliography at the end of this chapter.

Just Threes: Frogs, Fish, and Fun

Rhymes and Songs

5 Little Froggies

 (Use your fingers to represent the frogs, or have the children stand up and act out this rhyme.)

1 little froggy goes—HOP!
Along comes another and they just
    can't stop,
So . . .

Two little froggies go—HOP! HOP!
Along comes another and they just
    can't stop,
So . . .

Three little froggies go—HOP! HOP!
    HOP!
Along comes another and they just
    can't stop,
So . . .

Four little froggies go —HOP! HOP!
    HOP! HOP!
Along comes another and they just
    can't stop,
So . . .

Five little froggies go—HOP! HOP!
    HOP! HOP! HOP!
DROP!

(Fall to the floor.)
Time to stop!

Froggy Dance

 (Suit actions to words.)
5 little froggies sitting by the well,

(Hold up one hand and wiggle your fingers.)
1 fell off and down she fell.

(Bend one finger down.)
Froggies dance high,

(Wiggle fingers high.)
Froggies dance low,

(Wiggle fingers low.)
4 little froggies sitting in a row.

4, 3, 2,

1 little froggy sits alone by the well,

(Hold up one finger.)
She fell off and down she fell.

(Bend one finger down.)
Froggies dance high,

(Wiggle fingers high.)
Froggies dance low,

(Wiggle fingers low.)
No little froggies sitting in a row.

Tired Turtle

 (Tune: I've Been Working on the Railroad)
(Suit actions to words.)

I've been crawling through the mud,
All the whole day long.
I've been crawling through the mud,
Just listen to my song.

Oh, my house is getting heavy,
My legs are tired and sore.

(Start singing slowly and quietly.)
I am moving very slowly now,
I can't sing anymore.

I Had a Little Turtle

(Suit actions to words.)
 I had a little turtle,
 He lived in a box.

(Put hands together to make a box.)
 He swam in the puddles

(Make swimming movements.)
 And he climbed on the rocks.

(Make climbing motions.)
 He snapped at a minnow,

(Snap your fingers.)
 He snapped at a flea.

(Snap your fingers.)
 He snapped at a mosquito

(Snap your fingers.)
 And he snapped at me.

(Snap your fingers.)
 He caught the minnow,

(Clap.)
 He caught the flea.

(Clap.)
 He caught the mosquito

(Clap.)
 But he didn't catch me!

(Shake your head "no.")

Baby Frogs

 (Use your fingers to represent the frogs.)
 "Ribbit, ribbit," said mama frog,
 Sitting on a great big log.
 "Where are my babies? Where can
  they be?"
 Then out of the pond jumped 1, 2, 3.

(Hold up three fingers.)
 She was happy as can be,
 But where were the others? She
  couldn't see.
 So, "Ribbit, ribbit," she called out again.
 Then out jumped 4, 5, 6, 7, 8, 9, and 10.

(Hold up remaining fingers.)

Little Froggy

 (Tune: I'm a Little Teapot)
(Do as the actions indicate.)
 See the little froggy
 Swimming in the pool.
 The water is great,
 It's nice and cool.
 When he gets all cleaned up,
 Out he'll hop.
 Squeaky clean from bottom to top.

(Point to your head and toes.)
 See the little froggy
 On the lily pad.
 Trying to catch flies,
 She's getting sad.
 When she catches one
 She'll gobble it up.
 Back in the water she'll go
 KERPLOP!

Gone Fishin'

(Suit actions to words.)

Have you ever gone a fishin' on a
warm summers day?

(Pretend to cast a fishing pole.)

Have you ever seen the fishies just a
playin' in the bay?
With their hands in their pockets and
their pockets in their pants,

(Pat your pockets, pat your pants.)

Have you ever seen the fishies do the
Hootchie-Kootchie dance?

*(Put your hands on your hips and wiggle back
and forth.)*

Have you ever gone a fishin' on a cold
winter's day?

(Pretend to cast a fishing pole.)

Have you ever seen the fishies just a
frozen in the bay?
With their hands in their pockets and
their pockets in their pants,

(Pat your pockets, pat your pants.)

Have you ever seen the fishies do the
Hootchie-Kootchie dance?

*(Put your hands on your hips and wiggle back
and forth.)*

Have you ever gone a fishin' on a
warm spring day?

(Pretend to cast a fishing pole.)

Have you ever seen the fishies just a
swimmin' in the bay?
With their hands in their pockets and
their pockets in their pants,

(Pat your pockets, pat your pants.)

Have you ever seen the fishies do the
Hootchie-Kootchie dance?

*(Put your hands on your
hips and wiggle back
and forth.)*

Gang Goo

*(This one will take some practice. Simply follow
the directions and you'll have it down in no
time!)*

"Gang Goo" went the little green frog
one day.

*(Touch your shoulders each time you say "Gang";
touch your knees each time you say "Goo.")*

"Gang Goo" went the little green frog.
"Gang Goo" went the little green frog
one day.
And they all went "Ging, Gang, Goo."

*(Touch your head when you say "Ging"; touch
your shoulders when you say "Gang"; touch
your knees when you say "Goo.")*

But we know frogs go

(Clap.)

La Di Da Di Da,

(Wave your hands at your side.) (Clap.)

La Di Da Di Da,

(Wave your hands at your side.)

(Clap.)

La Di Da Di Da

(Wave your hands at your side.)

But we know frogs go

(Clap.)

La Di Da Di Da
They don't go
"Ging, Gang, Goo."

(Touch your head, shoulders, and knees.)

185

Fred E. Fish

Materials

1 medium brown paper lunch bag per person

Tissue paper (various colours)

Yarn (any colour)

2 large wiggle eyes per person

Glue sticks (enough for your group)

Decorating supplies: markers and/or crayons

Newspaper

Instructions

1. Crumple a few pieces of newspaper and stuff the sealed end of the paper bag (this is the body of the fish), leaving enough room so that you can tie the open end closed to form the tail of the fish.

2. Tie the open end closed using yarn.

3. Rip the tissue paper into pieces and glue them onto the body of the fish. (These will be the gills of the fish.)

4. Glue one wiggle eye onto each side of the fish.

5. Let the children finish decorating their fish with crayons and markers.

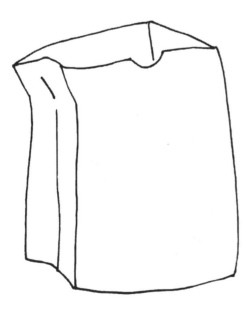
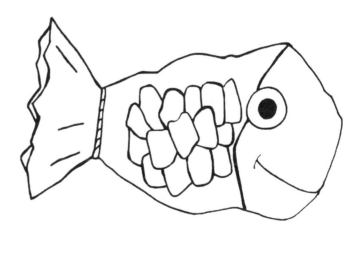

Program 6

Just Threes: Roses Are Red

Ahhhh. Valentine's Day. This is when the children in your group get to explore a different side of themselves. We've talked about the silly side, the fun side, and even the outside. But this is where we discover their inside. The feelings and emotions they have, along with their friends and friendships. At three years of age, while some are still amazed by spiders and birds, some children have begun to form lasting friendships. Talk to your group about their friends: what makes them happy, what makes them sad, and what they most like to do with them. Understand that some of the three year olds in your group are starting to feel things that they've never felt before and may need help expressing those feelings in a positive way. So on Valentine's Day take the time to celebrate friendships, feelings, and just being three!

Plan Ahead Note

The storytime souvenir for this program requires that the programmer do a lot of preparation, but the end result is worth it. Children enjoy being able to make their puppet pals dance. This is a nice variation from traditional paper bag puppets and is interactive in a fun and silly sort of way. The tracing and cutting is time consuming, so if you are planning to use this souvenir, you may wish to enlist the help of a volunteer or start your preparation a week or two in advance.

Books to Share

Counting Kisses, by Karen Katz

Guess How Much I Love You, by Sam McBratney

Would You Love Me?, by Andrea Wayne von Konigslow

More books to share with three year olds can be found in the bibliography at the end of this chapter.

Just Threes: Roses Are Red

Rhymes and Songs

Down on the Corner

 (Fill in the blank using a child's name or the name of a storybook or movie character.)

Down on the corner at the candy shop,
There were 5 little valentines waiting
to be bought.
Along came _____ all alone,
And she [or he] picked up a valentine
and took it home.

(Repeat with 4, 3, 2, and 1.)

Counting Valentines

 (Make hearts out of construction paper to accompany this rhyme.)

Valentines, valentines, how many do I
see?
Valentines, valentines, say their
colours with me.

(Point to the different colours as you say them.)

I see red ones, orange ones, yellow
ones too.
I see green ones, purple ones and some
that are blue.
Valentines, valentines, how many do I
see?
Valentines, valentine, count them all
with me.
"1, 2, 3 . . ."

Look Who's Coming

 (Tune: This Old Man)
(This is a great song to use if you hand out your own valentines to your group.)

Look who's coming down the walk,
Mr. Mailman won't you stop?
With a knock, knock, knock, knock,
Anyone at home?
A valentine for you has come!

The Love Bug

 (Suit actions to words.)

It begins with a grin,

(Smile broadly.)

It turns to a giggle.

(Put both hands over your mouth and giggle.)

Then you start to laugh,

(Throw your head back and laugh out loud.)

And your legs start to wiggle.

(Put your feet in the air and shake.)

You look all around for someone to
hug,

(Move your eyes back and forth.)

UH-OH! You've caught the love bug!
ACHOO!

I'm a Little Valentine

(Tune: I'm a Little Teapot)
(Make a valentine and decorate an envelope to use as props for this rhyme.)

I'm a little valentine,
Red and white.
With ribbons and lace,
I'm a beautiful sight.
I can say "I love you"
On Valentines Day,
Just put me in an envelope
And give me away.

Valentines for You

(Tune: She'll Be Comin' Round the Mountain)
(Give each child a small, medium, and large heart. Have them lay them in front of them and hold up the different sizes for each verse.)

I'm a teeny, tiny valentine for you,
I'm a teeny, tiny valentine for you.
I'll be yours, will you be mine?
A teeny, tiny valentine.
I'm a teeny, tiny valentine for you.

I'm a medium size valentine for you,
I'm a medium size valentine for you.
I'm not big and that's just fine,
I'll be yours, will you be mine?
I'm a medium size valentine for you.

I'm a great big valentine just for you,
I'm a great big valentine just for you.
I'll be yours will you be mine,
I will love you all the time.
I'm a great big valentine just for you.

5 Big Valentines

(Make construction paper hearts in various colours to use as props to accompany this rhyme.)

5 big valentines from the corner store,
I mailed one to my friend and then
   there were 4.
4 big valentines, lovely ones to see,
I mailed one to mommy, then there
   were 3.
3 big valentines, red, shiny and new,
I mailed one to my daddy, then there
   were 2.
2 big valentines, the best is yet to
   come,
I mailed one to Grandma, then there
   was 1.
1 big valentine, the giving is almost
   done,
I mailed one to Grandpa, now there are
   none.

Valentine's Day

(Give the children construction paper hearts that they can throw in the air when you get to the part in the rhyme when the postman scatters happiness.)

If I could be the postman
For just one single time,
I'd choose to carry Valentines
So lovely and so fine.
I would not mind the heavy load,
Or mind my tired feet.
If I could scatter happiness

(Throw hearts in the air.)

All up and down the street.

189

Puppet Pal

Materials

1 sheet red or pink Bristol board (enough for your group)

Yarn (any colour)

Masking tape

Decorating supplies: stickers, glitter

Glue sticks (enough for your group)

Scissors

Instructions

1. Cut one large heart, two medium hearts, and two small hearts out of the Bristol board.

2. Cut four 1-inch wide strips from the Bristol board and taking one at a time, fold an end to form a small square. Fold it again, this time in the opposite direction. Keep folding the strip until you reach the end. (It should resemble an accordion when you're finished.) Continue with the rest of the strips. (These are the arms and legs of your puppet.)

3. Tape the arms and legs onto the back of the large heart.

4. Tape or glue the medium hearts onto the bottom of the legs. (These are your feet.)

5. Tape the small hearts onto the ends of the arms. (These are your hands.)

6. Attach the string onto either side of the back of the heart. (This is how you can make your puppet dance.)

7. Let the children decorate the heart—add eyes, a nose, etc.

Program 7

Just Threes: 1, 2, 3, Count with Me

Three is the magic number when you're thinking of introducing this program. With kindergarten just around the corner, it's a good time to start including themes with a concept base (letters, numbers, shapes, sizes). At three years of age, some children can begin to recognise basic letters and numbers. By starting off slowly and using repetitive rhymes and songs, the children in your group will start to remember a number of things such as number and letter sequencing (2 comes after 1, B comes after A). Also, by including this program with three year olds, you may give parents and caregivers the jump start they need to start focusing on these things at home.

Plan Ahead Note

The storytime souvenir for this program requires a moderate amount of preparation for the programmer. Size and photocopy your frogs and lily pads however you like them and make a contact sheet (this should be one sheet with one or two frogs and a lily pad that you can photocopy instead of fiddling with one picture or template at a time). Once you have done this, photocopy as many contact sheets as you will need. To streamline the cutting process, staple five or six of the sheets together (one staple in each corner and one on each side, being careful not to staple to close to the pictures) and cut them out. This process saves the programmer quite a bit of time.

Books to Share

Catnap, by Dawn Bentley

Ten Little Ladybugs, by Melanie Gerth

How Many Bugs in a Box?, by David A. Carter

More books to share with three year olds can be found in the bibliography at the end of this chapter.

Just Threes: 1, 2, 3, Count with Me

Rhymes and Songs

Number Poem

(Have large numbers cut out and move finger, tracing over the number, to show the children as you say each rhyme, or use a dry erase board and dry erase markers to draw the numbers as you say them.)

Number 1 is like a stick,
A straight line down,
That's very quick.

For number 2 go right around,
Then make a line,
Across the ground.

Go right around what will it be?
Go around again,
It's number 3.

Down and over
And down some more.
That's the way to make a 4.

Go down and around,
Then you stop.
Finish the 5 with a line on top.

1, 2, 3, 4, 5

(Hold up your fingers as you say this rhyme.)

1, 2, 3, 4, 5,
Once I caught a fish alive!
6, 7, 8, 9, 10,
Then I let him go again.

Why did you let it go?
Because it bit my finger so.
Which finger did it bite?
This little finger on my right!

(Hold up right pinky finger.)

The Garden

(Pretend to be tending a garden. Have a picture of a carrot and a flower to show the children at the end of the rhyme.)

One, two, three,
The garden is growing.
Four, five, six,
Now it needs hoeing.
Seven, eight, nine,
Down go the weeds.
Ten, eleven, twelve,
Water it needs.
Thirteen, fourteen,
Here comes a shower.
Look at what has grown,
A carrot and a flower.

193

One Little Duck

 (Snap your fingers or clap your hands in time as you say this rhyme.)

One little duck went splish, splash . . . hooray!
Over in the water on a bright and sunny day.
Another duck saw him and knew just what to do,
He waddled on over and one became two.

Two little ducks went splish, splash . . . hooray!
Over in the water on a bright and sunny day.
Another duck saw them as he walked by a tree,
He waddled on over and two became three.

Three little ducks went splish, splash . . . hooray!
Over in the water on a bright and sunny day.
Another duck saw them as he came through the door,
He waddled on over and three became four.

Four little ducks went splish, splash . . . hooray!
Over in the water on a bright and sunny day.
Another duck saw them as he danced the jive,
He waddled on over and four became five.

Five little ducks went splish, splash . . . hooray!
Over in the water on a bright and sunny day.
They played in the water and they basked in the sun,
Never had 5 ducks had so much fun.

The Ants Go Marching

 (Suit actions to words.)

The ants go marching one by one, hurrah, hurrah.
The ants go marching one by one, hurrah, hurrah,
The ants go marching one by one,
The little one stopped play his drum—clap, clap, clap
And they all went marching down, to the ground,
To get out, of the rain.
Boom, boom, boom, boom.

Two by two—tie his shoe
Three by three—climb a tree
Four by four—slam the door
Five by five—dance the jive

One Is a Giant

 (Suit actions to words.)

One is a giant who stomps his feet,
Two is a fairy so light and neat.
Three is a mouse who crouches small,
Four is a great big bouncing ball.

5 Green Speckled Frogs

 (Use your fingers to represent the frogs or have the children form a circle, then choose five children at a time to take turns being the frogs.)

5 green and speckled frogs,

(Hold up five fingers.)

Sat on a speckled log,
Eating some most delicious bugs
YUM! YUM!

(Rub your tummy.)

1 jumped into the pool,
Where it was nice and cool,
Now there are 4 green speckled frogs,
GLUB! GLUB!
4, 3, 2, 1

Ten Little Clothespins

 (To accompany this rhyme, have ten clothespins hanging on a string taped to the back of a chair or other sturdy surface.)

Ten little clothespins hanging on a line,
One lost his grip, then there were nine.
Nine little clothespins standing up so
    straight,
One broke his string, then there were
    eight.
Eight little clothespins on a line so
    even,
One went snip-snap, then there were
    seven.
Seven little clothespins, are you
    keeping score?
Three took flip-flops, then there were
    four.
Four little clothespins, as joyful as can
    be,
One opened his mouth, fell off, then
    there were three.
Three little clothespins with nothing
    left to do.
One turned a somersault, then there
    were two.
Two little clothespins smiling at the
    sun,
They felt pitter-patter raindrops
    starting,
Now there are none.

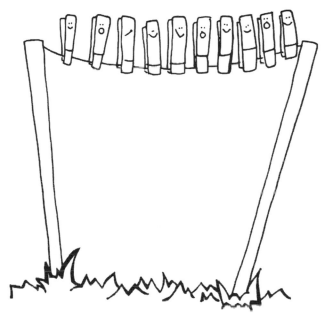

195

Leapin' Lilypads

Materials

1 sheet blue construction paper per person

1 photocopied frog per person

1 photocopied lily pad per person

Glue sticks (enough for your group)

Scissors

Decorating supplies: glitter, stickers, bingo dabbers

Instructions

1. Photocopy the frog to fit a 4-by-4-inch or 5.3 cm-by-5.3 cm piece of paper and cut it out.

2. Photocopy the lily pad templates to fit a 8½-inch long by 5½-inch wide or 21.5 cm long by 14 cm wide piece of paper and cut it out.

3. Provide each child with one sheet of blue construction paper.

4. Let the children glue as many frog and lily pad pictures on their paper as they like.

5. Let the children decorate their pictures.

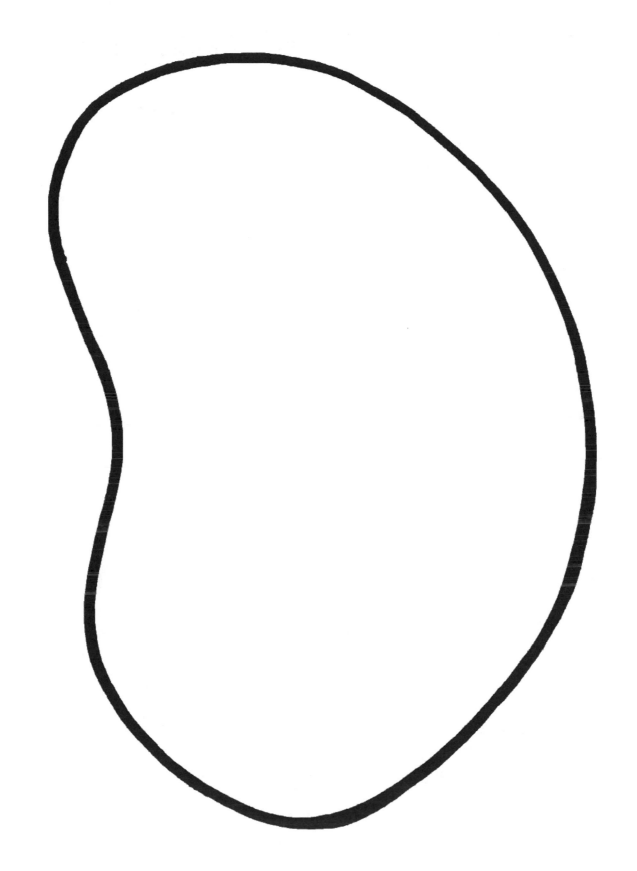

197

Program 8

Just Threes: Monkeying Around

Monkey see, monkey do. Children need little encouragement to act like monkeys, so this program just fits right in! Silly songs and rhymes are just the beginning here, and our "Clownin' Around" storytime souvenir triples the fun. It's a clown, it's a puppet, and the pom-pom nose will keep the kids laughing long after they've left your program! Get ready! Get set! Get silly!

Plan Ahead Note

Caution: The following program is filled with active songs for you and your group! This is another of those programs where you'll need to check your room space and plan ahead. Choose your songs and rhymes ahead of time and become familiar with them before you sing them with your group. The more comfortable you are . . . the more comfortable the kids will be. Don't forget to visit your local dollar to discount store to purchase your paper bags and pom-poms before you go "Clownin' Around" with the storytime souvenir!

Books to Share

5 Little Monkeys Wash the Car, by Eileen Christelow

5 Little Monkeys Jumping on the Bed, by Eileen Christelow

Silly Sally, by Audrey Wood

More books to share with three year olds can be found in the bibliography at the end of this chapter.

Just Threes: Monkeying Around

Rhymes and Songs

Fast ABC's

(Start this song by slapping your hands on your thighs and sing quickly.)

ABCDEFGHIJKLM,

(Clap, clap.)

NOPQRSTUVWXYZ.

Jack and Jill went up the hill
To fetch a pail of water . . . .
Jack fell down and broke his crown
And Jill came tumbling after!
Oh!
ABCDEFGHIJKLM,

(Clap, clap.)

NOPQRSTUVWXYZ.

(Replace Jack and Jill with other nursery rhyme characters as suggested by the children in your group, e.g., Little Miss Muffet, Little Bo Peep . . .)

Rig-a-Jig-Jig

(Choose one child or ask for a volunteer to start this game and have the other children sit in a circle around him or her.)

As I was walking down the street,
Down the street, down the street.
As I walking down the street,
A friend of mine I chance to meet.

(Child picks a friend to bring into the circle to dance.)

With a Rig-a-jig-jig and away they go,
Away they go, away they go.
Rig-a-jig-jig and away they go,
Hi-ho, hi-ho, hi-ho.

(The child chosen to dance now gets to choose someone to dance with.)

Going to Kentucky

(Suit actions to words.)
(Have children choose partners or do this as a group.)

We're going to Kentucky,
We're going to the fair,
To see the señoritas
with roses in their hair.
So . . . shake it baby, shake it,
Shake it all you can.
Shake it like a milkshake,
Shake it in a can.
Rumba to the bottom,
Rumba to the top,
Turn around and turn around
Until we holler STOP!

(Everybody freeze.)

Good Morning

(Suit actions to words.)

Good morning, it's time to rise,
Stand up and wipe your sleepy eyes.
Reach and stretch up to the sky,
Hold your hands way up high.
Bend your body and touch the ground,
Stand up straight, now turn around.
Point to your eyes, point to your nose,
Jump up and down and touch your
     toes.
Clap your hands, stomp your feet,
Let's get started so take a seat.

Bump and Bop and Boogie

(Ask for a volunteer to get this song and the fun started.)
(Suit actions to words.)

You meet a good friend on a sunny
day,
You do the bump and bop and boogie
In your own special way.

You bump and boogie high,

(Wave your hands high in the air.)
You bump and boogie low.

(Wave your hands low to the ground.)
You do the bump and bop and boogie
And you don't do it slow!

Elephants Have Wrinkles

(Point to each body part as it is mentioned.)
Elephants have wrinkles, wrinkles,
wrinkles,
Elephants have wrinkles, wrinkles
everywhere.
On their nose? On their nose!
No one knows? No one knows!
Why-y-y-y
Elephants have wrinkles, wrinkles,
wrinkles,
Elephants have wrinkles, wrinkles
everywhere.

On their knees? On their knees!
On their toes? On their toes!
No one knows . . . why-y-y-y
Elephants have wrinkles, wrinkles,
wrinkles,
Elephants have wrinkles, wrinkles
everywhere.

(Substitute knees and toes for other body parts: ears, trunks, etc.)

5 Little Clowns

(Use your fingers to represent the clowns. Suit actions to words.)

5 little clowns, running through the
door,
1 fell down, then there were 4.
4 little clowns in an apple tree,
1 fell out, then there were 3.
3 little clowns stirring up some stew,
1 fell in, then there were 2.
2 little clowns having lots of fun,
1 ran away, then there was 1.
1 little clown left sitting in the sun,
He went home, now there are none.

I'm a Little Elephant

(Tune: I'm a Little Teapot)
I'm a little elephant short and stout,
Here is my tail and here is my snout.
(Point to your back and your nose.)
I'm a clever elephant can you see,
I can say the alphabet from A to Z.

(Programmer and children sing the alphabet.)
A, B, C, D, E, F, G . . .

Clownin' Around

Materials

1 photocopied clown per person

1 medium brown paper lunch bag per person

1 medium pom-pom

Glue sticks (enough for your group)

Scissors

Decorating supplies: glitter, bingo dabbers, sticky shapes

Instructions

1. Photocopy the clown template (to fit on the paper bag) and cut out all of the pieces.

2. Glue the clown face onto the folded flap of the paper bag.

3. Provide the children with the rest of the pieces and let them glue the clown together.

4. Give each child one pom-pom (this is the clown's nose) and let them all finish their clowns using the decorating materials you provide.

202

6. Bibliography of Books to Share

Albee, Sarah. 2001. *Spring Fever*. New York: Random House.

Bentley, Dawn. 1999. *Catnap*. Santa Monica, CA: Piggy Toes Press.

Binder, Pat. 2000. *Seen on Hallowe'en—Wacky Flaps*. Norwalk, CT: Innovative Kids Publishing

Boroman, Crystal. 2000. *Mommy, May I Hug the Fishes*? Grand Rapids, MI: Zondervan Publishing House

Carter, David A. 1988. *How Many Bugs in a Box*? New York: Little Simon

Christelow, Eileen. 1998. *5 Little Monkeys Jumping on the Bed*. Boston: Houghton Mifflin.

Christelow, Eileen. 2000. *5 Little Monkeys Wash the Car*. Boston: Houghton Mifflin.

Cousins, Lucy. 2001. *Maisy Goes Shopping*. Cambridge, MA: Candlewick Press.

Elgar, Rebecca. 1998. *Jack—It's Bathtime*. New York: Larousse Kingfisher Chambers

Fleming, Denise. 2001. *Pumpkin Eye*. New York: Henry Holt.

Gerth, Melanie. 2001. *Ten Little Ladybugs*. Santa Monica, CA: Piggy Toes Press.

Joffe Numeroff, Laura. 2001. *If You Give a Moose a Muffin*. Glenview, IL: Scott Foresman

Katz, Karen. 2001. *Counting Kisses*. New York: Margaret McElderry

Keats, Ezra Jack. 1967. *Peter's Chair*. New York: Harper & Row.

Leslie, Amanda. 2001. *Jumping Frog*. Alpharetta, GA: Tiger Tales

London, Jonathan. 2001. *Crunch, Munch*. San Diego: Silver Whistle

London, Jonathan. 2002. *Froggy Plays in the Band*. New York: Viking Children's Books

McBratney, Sam. 1995. *Guess How Much I Love You*? Cambridge, MA: Candlewick Press

Palatini, Margie. 2000. *Zoom Broom*. Concord, NH: Hyperion/Gibson Press

Sendak, Maurice. 1963. *Where the Wild Things Are*. New York: Harper & Row.

Seuling, Barbara. 2001. *Spring Song*. San Diego: Harcourt

Tafuri, Nancy. 1984. *Have You Seen My Duckling*? New York: Greenwillow Books

von Konigslow, Andrea Wayne. 1997. *Would You Love Me*? Toronto: Annick Press

Waddell, Martin. 1992. *Owl Babies*. Cambridge, MA: Candlewick Press.

Walters, Catherine. 2001. *When Will It Be Spring*? New York: Dutton Books

Watt, Fiona. 2001. *Baby's Bathtime*. London: Usborne Publishing.

Wood, Audrey. 1984. *The Napping House*. San Diego: Harcourt Brace Jovanovich.

Wood, Audrey. 1999. *Silly Sally*. Lake Worth, FL: Red Wagon.

Chapter 6
Family Fun

A child's journey towards personal potential is guided by his or her family. As a unit, families grow, change, and develop together. Positive experiences can be shared and enjoyed. If you add some stimulating ingredients for literacy and cultural growth, you also allow the family to share in a broadening educational experience. Family storytime is not a new concept, but it has grown in appeal as libraries explore the tenets of early literacy. Intellectual stimulation, early reading experiences, and modelled behaviour are important for emergent literacy in preschool children. Security, love, contentment, and a chance to play are also integral to a child's well-being and future development. By bringing the family into storytime as a unit you are giving people a chance to enjoy their siblings, parents, and grandparents in an environment devoted to recreational reading enhancement, access to information, and cultural stimulation. Program participants get a chance to meet new people while enjoying the comfort and security of having their family nearby.

Family storytime has a number of other benefits, in addition to its overall value to the community. Family programming accepts children of all ages and allows parents to bring several siblings to one program; therefore there are no problems related to child care or baby-sitting. Adults, caregivers, and parents stay with their children; therefore anxious preschoolers do not need to experience separation anxiety. The environment is one of inclusion and acceptance; everyone is welcome and there are few, if any, restrictions based on age or developmental achievement. It is a fun, welcoming experience through which members of the family enjoy, interact, and evolve in their own way.

1. Family Storytime: The Concept

Bringing the whole family into the library to read stories, sing songs, and play games is a wonderful idea. The practical implications of making it work for the programmer, however, can be a little intimidating. Luckily there are some tried and true key concepts that work well when you are entertaining a group of people ranging in age from birth to retirement. Instead of trying to entertain each individual in a way that stimulates him or her developmentally, you need to think of the family as a unit and consider the concept of family development. If a group of people have come together to enjoy storytime, they are considered a family for the purposes of the program. Programmers can entertain and engage them by considering what they might have in common and would enjoy as a unit. Some of the ways family members relate to one another are through

- Humour—people of all ages enjoy laughing and being amused. Even if some humorous elements are aimed at older children, if most of the participants are laughing and enjoying themselves, younger children will be happy in the pleasant atmosphere.

- Storytelling—traditional storytelling, without the use of written words or props, can engage an audience of all ages. By learning to tell stories without reading them aloud, you can learn to captivate a crowd with your voice and antics. You are able to make eye contact and connect with the entire audience.

- Music—songs, instruments, and recorded music appeal to all ages. We may not all have the same taste in music, but traditional, classical, and folk music each has wide appeal. Children's music is also fun and appeals to adults because the words and refrains are usually easy to remember and imitate. Popular songs that children have been singing since they were very young work well with this group because the participants will be able to sing along and feel comfortable. Use the popular songs in their original form, or vary the words and keep the original tune (many of the songs included in the program plans in this chapter are examples of this approach).

- Participation—involving the audience in any number of ways can be fun for the entire family. Movement, action rhymes, and songs can be enjoyed by the whole family, and adults should be encouraged to be silly and have fun alongside their children.

- Dramatic arts—entertaining a crowd with varying ages can be done effectively by using drama. Play different characters, use puppetry, or dazzle people with magic as a way of bringing drama into your program.

- Artistic expression and creativity—have family members use arts and crafts supplies to express themselves. Painting, drawing, sculpting, and collage are just a few suggestions that work well for the entire family. Young children may get their first exposure to a medium, and older children and adults may design works of art.

Elements such as these, when combined with carefully chosen read-aloud stories, make family storytime a successful, enjoyable event for the programmer and the participants.

2. Family Programming Guidelines

2.1 Starting a Program for the Entire Family

Some facilities will find the concept of storytime for the entire family unusual. As programmers, we are familiar with tailoring our programs to individual developmental milestones for children at a limited age. The key to understanding family storytime is to understand and embrace families as a single unit. Don't think of the program as a time to entertain a number of babies, pre-schoolers, elementary school children, parents, and grandparents. Instead, consider that some groups of people who know each other are together, prepared to have fun and to be entertained. This program is an excellent one to consider if your facility already offers a full range of programs for children, or if you are planning to start your very first program. People will come together for a positive library experience; they will take out books and enjoy what the facility has to offer. It is a program that includes all children and their respective adults, so it has wide appeal and great marketing potential. There is little need to require preregistration other than having a better sense of the number of participants to expect each week. Instead, this program is an ideal candidate to be offered as a drop-in program during an evening or weekend, when the entire family is together. It can run as a series of programs or as a single event. After the program is established, you are likely to find attendance will be high, perhaps running up to room capacity. However, with the inclusive, entertainment style this program usually adopts, maximum attendance is no problem.

> **BRIGHT IDEA**
>
> Instead of registering program participants for family storytime, give out tickets. The number of tickets you make available should be roughly equal to your room capacity. Tickets generate a sense of excitement and value for a program. They will serve as a visual reminder for the participants to return for the program. They will also be useful for you to anticipate the number of participants each week.

2.2 Getting Ready

Family programming does require some advance preparation. It is a very flexible and adaptable program, however, and can be run almost anywhere. To be prepared, programmers need to plan and anticipate what their programs will entail. Time your program for a weekday evening or on a Saturday morning or Sunday afternoon. Check to make sure your program will not conflict with other nearby family-style offerings such as swimming or skating. Your community's make-up will determine the age, cultural affiliations, and languages of participants. Take some time to get to know the participants, especially those who return week after week. Have your program reflect their experiences and cultural celebrations as well as your own. By fostering a relationship built on mutual respect, you are guaranteeing your program's success.

2.2a Whom to Expect

The crowd will vary from week to week in size and make-up. One week you may be entertaining a room full of babies and parents. The following week you may find that you have attracted a crowd of preteen sophisticates. Therefore, you need to expect the unexpected. Be prepared with lots of program ingredients, so you can choose the elements that you feel will best suit the group in front of you. Generally speaking, however, you will be entertaining families where one or more adults have brought several siblings to enjoy storytime together. The children are usually in the preschool range, with fewer preteens and tiny babies attending. A typical family storytime, in a reasonably large space, would host fifteen adults, five school-aged children, ten preschoolers, and five toddlers. The mix and interaction of these participants is fun and enjoyable. They are comfortable and relaxed because they feel the security of having their family nearby. This positive, open atmosphere is conducive to a great programming experience.

2.2b Books to Share

The books you choose to read aloud in family storytime must captivate and delight a wide range of listeners. There are two types of books you may choose to read aloud; those with universal appeal and those that appeal to individuals differently depending on their age. Books with universal appeal are those that are stimulating and enjoyable regardless of age. These can be classic titles such as *Snowy Day, Where the Wild Things Are,* or *Red Is Best* or other stories that parents remember from their own childhoods, such as *Curious George, Babar,* or popular folktales. These titles, and hundreds of others like them, stimulate the imagination of children. Adults will relate and remember the themes of these stories in a fond way. Some new titles also have the universal appeal you need for this type of program. Look for books with themes such as love, friendship, and family. Choose titles with strong characterisation and simple language. Rhythm and meter are also important so the stories sound pleasing when read aloud. The tone of the book is also a factor; humorous titles and lighthearted texts work very well.

Another type of book you may choose to read aloud is one that can appeal to people in different ways depending on their age. Stories with family themes are excellent choices because the adults will relate to the parent dilemmas and the children will enjoy the story itself and its younger characters. Examples of this type of book are *My Monster Mama Loves Me So* and *Guess How Much I Love You.* Other examples are books where the text may be directed at young children, but the illustrations are works of art, so everyone enjoys them. Examples of this type of book are *Time for Bed* and *The Midnight Farm.* Choose the oversized versions of these books, available from the publishers. The stories themselves are gentle and rhythmic, but the illustrations are beautiful and take the stories to another level.

2.2c Books to Display

The types of books you display are limitless for a group with a wide age span. If you are running theme-related programs, choose a variety of books that surround your theme. Include different types of books: board books, easy readers, nonfiction, picture books, and folktales. You can broaden your theme with your display books to improve the calibre and choice of books. For example, if your theme is trains, you could include books on other modes of transportation as well. You can also include a display of books that is not theme related. Titles that could assist with parenting, homework, and learning to read are good choices. Or include new materials and topical books based on the season and trends in parenting and family life.

3. Programs for Families: Format and Routine

The structure of a family-oriented program can be as loose and casual as you are comfortable with. Because the group is ready-made for security and openness, you need only supply a routine that will keep the pace moving and include something for everyone. Following are some useful suggestions for family programming based on past successes with large groups of diverse age ranges.

3.1 Format

The program's format is based on your individual style. Generally speaking, family storytime is a thirty- to forty-five-minute program that consists of a greeting; numerous group activities such as stories, music, rhymes and games; and a closing. There should also be an informal part of the program that includes time for the group to socialise and browse through the books displayed.

Included in this format will be routines and individual elements that work with your personal style; games, rhymes, activities, or songs that have been crowd-pleasers can be repeated from week to week. Participants who come each week should be able to anticipate certain elements and routines.

3.2 Opening Routine

To begin your family program you are going to want to get everyone's attention. One way of doing this is to open with the spotlight game. Turn on a flashlight and dim the lights in the room. Have participants sit in a circle and move the beam of the flashlight around and around while chanting this rhyme:

> Spotlight, spotlight is the name of the game.
> When the spotlight's on you, tell us your name.

Then focus the spotlight on two or three people (adults and children) at random and have them say their names aloud. Repeat the chant over and over until all have had the spotlight land on them. Adults will understand the game without the need for instruction, so it is often best to begin by shining the light on two or three adults in sequence. This dramatic introduction is a great way to set the stage for an exciting storytime. If the room you are presenting in doesn't have lights that dim, you may want to have a floor or table lamp in addition to the spotlight because complete darkness may be frightening for some children.

3.3 What to Include: Elements for Success

We have already discussed some elements that work well with a broad age range: humour, storytelling, music, etc. We discuss these in more detail in the following section. Along with these elements, there are other essential ingredients to make the most of your group's time together. These include a chance for the group to socialise and some form of creative expression.

Your group may have participants who know each other, or some of your participants may be interested in meeting and talking to new people. Enhance this experience by having some group activities that lend themselves to socialisation. Play music and have children dance, or set up sensory stimulators and pass them around to the group. Sensory stimulators work well with toddlers, preschool children, and their families, and you can include them for a variety of senses:

- Smell—Fill containers with smelly ingredients such as spices (e.g., cinnamon, cloves) or coffee. Cover the top of the jar with cheesecloth or any loosely woven fabric and fix it in place with a rubber band. Pass the jars around and have participants try to identify the ingredients by smelling them.

- Sight—use coloured mylar in frames to make looking glasses for everyone. Using a piece of construction paper or cardstock, cut out the centre to make a frame with a 2-inch border. Use mylar or coloured basket wrap inside the frame. Hold the frames up and show participants the world through a variety of colours.

- Hearing—play music, instruments, or sound effects and have the group identify the sounds.

- Taste—bring in some treats and have participants enjoy sweet and savoury tastes. This is a great celebratory event for the final program. Be sure to ask the group about allergies and sensitivities before handing out treats.

- Touch—put tactile materials such as cotton balls, fur, smooth stones, or feathers in closed shoe boxes with an arm-sized hole on one end. Have participants reach in and feel what's inside, then try to identify it.

These are examples of the type of activity that would allow members of your group to interact, talk to one another, and still remain focused on the group's activities.

Creative expression is also an important element of family programming. Participants can express their creativity through movement, crafts, and open discussion. Vary the type of activities from week to week, but keep in mind that artistic endeavours are especially popular with children.

3.4 Closing Routine

If you have opened your program with the spotlight game, it is a good idea to close it in a similar fashion. Use the following rhyme to end your program with the spotlight game:

> Spotlight, spotlight round 'n' round it flies
> When it stops on you, say goodbye.

Turn on the lights when the game is over and allow the group time to interact and, if possible, to choose books to take home.

4. Family Programming Techniques

4.1 Entertaining All Ages

Programming for babies and grandparents in one session is an exciting challenge. The task seems daunting, but in fact it is much simpler than it may at first appear. The secret is to include something for every participant and something for all:

- *Something for every participant*—Family storytime needs to include ingredients for every age. You may not make use of all your ingredients, but it is good to have them on hand. Rhymes, songs, fingerplays, and action games that appeal to children at every developmental stage should be included in your repertoire.

- *Something for all*—The program must also include elements that will appeal to all participants, regardless of their age or developmental achievements. These elements are usually drawn from the techniques discussed in the first section of this chapter: humour, storytelling, music, participation, dramatic arts, and artistic or creative expression. In a successful family program, artistic or creative expression should be emphasised in every program. The other techniques, discussed in the sections that follow, can be used frequently or infrequently depending on the programmer's personal style.

4.2 Humour

Laughter in the audience means the crowd is having a good time; this simple social standard is one that can be used to enhance your family programming. Use humour in a way that is natural for you to keep a group entertained. You may choose to read funny stories or sing funny songs. Children's poetry and rhyme is often based on humour. Begin or end a segment of your program with a joke. There are a wealth of simple jokes on virtually every theme, so you could choose to include theme-based puns or knock-knock jokes in every one of your programs. You don't need to be a stand-up comedian to make a group laugh; simply keep the tone of your program lighthearted and fun.

4.3 Storytelling Made Simple

Telling a story without the use of the written word, books, or props is an extremely effective way to entertain a group. The art of storytelling using the oral tradition has been around much longer than traditional library programming. Some programmers are intimidated by the thought of telling a story without the book in front of them. Storytelling is simple, however, once you learn to get inside a story. The secret to storytelling is not to memorise the words but to get a feel for the story and then practice it over and over and over. Unravel the mystery of successful storytelling by following these simple steps:

1. *Choose a story*—choose a story that you love. Read it out loud to someone unfamiliar with the story and make sure it stands alone, that is, that it is not dependant on the illustrations for its value. Stories that are easier to tell are those with repeated refrains or cumulative action.

2. *Get a feel for the story*—read it and examine it over and over. Visualise what happens. Think about the characters and why they do what they do. Imagine the situations as though they involved you and your family or friends.

3. *Read it aloud several times*—using the book exactly as it is written, read the story aloud word for word about fifteen times.

4. *Try telling the story without the book*—practice "reading" the story without the words until you are able to read the book without the book in front of you.

5. *Add the feeling to the words*—once you have a feel for the characters and situations and know all the words, put these two elements together. Add voices, emphasis, and hand gestures as appropriate.

6. *Tell the story to a friend*—practice telling the story to a friend, family member, or co-worker. Better yet, practice telling the story to all of those people!

4.4 Music

Music is a universal language, like art or dance. People don't need to speak the same language to enjoy the same music. Try leading your group in a sing-along. If you aren't a great singer, use sing-along CDs and videos to lead the group, but be sure to participate in the singing, even if you don't have the most melodic voice. Musical instruments are another popular way to bring music into a program. If your centre doesn't have a set of instruments, use homemade shakers or bells with the group. Dancing is another way to use music in a program. Play an action song, or contemporary music and have the group move in time. Popular action or dance songs for families include traditional favourites like *The Hokey Pokey* or *The Bunny Hop*. More current dances that work well with a group include the *Macarena* or the *Electric Slide*.

BRIGHT IDEA

If you don't play a musical instrument, you can still teach yourself to use a drum. Hand drumming is a beautiful art and even novices can captivate a group with the sound of a drum. Use the drum to help the group make a transition from one activity to another, or beat the tune of a marching song or rhyme and have the crowd move to the beat.

4.5 Participation

Participatory activities are popular with every age. There are a number of ways to involve your group in the elements of the program; for example, have participants take a part in appropriate rhymes, songs, stories, and games. Repeated refrains in stories and rhymes can be shouted in unison by the group. Fingerplays and action songs can be mimicked and then repeated back to you by the entire group. You can have attendees participate in other ways as well. Ask for volunteers to assist with elements of a story or song. The volunteers may hold up a sign or say a word or phrase at a designated time. You can divide your group into sections and have them "compete" during a song or rhyme. For example, you can have just the boys sing for a verse of a song, or just the children. Look at the elements you are considering for inclusion in your family program to see if they lend themselves to participation.

4.6 Dramatic Arts

Programmers do not have to be actors and actresses to include drama and dramatics in their programs. If you use voices when telling a story, or use a puppet to greet children on their way into a program, you are already using dramatic elements in your program's delivery. Drama enhances the value of a program for all ages because it brings the program to life and has great entertainment value. If you do not feel you have a flair for drama, test your skills by adding voices to stories. If that works, consider some live action storytelling, such as reading a popular folktale aloud and directing children in an ad hoc performance. If you feel you might want to attempt some drama in your program, consider starting with puppetry. Puppets are a wonderful way to bring another character into your program, and they are endearing and accessible to people of all ages. Flannel boards, costumes, and props are all dramatic elements that also work well in a group setting to bring characters and stories to life. Remember, no one expects you to be a professional actor; in fact the group will find it endearing and comforting if you make mistakes and can laugh at yourself.

CONFIDENCE BOOSTER

Creating a character or dramatic persona can be a simple way to add entertainment value to your program. Choose a performance art that you enjoy, such as singing, magic, rhyming, or voice manipulation and create a character. Ima Rhymer is a character developed by a programmer with a natural talent for poetry and rhyme. Suitcase Sally is another character developed to introduce storytime (by pulling a prop from her ever-present valise). Dress your character in a special hat, wig, or glasses and use a different voice or intonation to set your character apart from your natural identity.

Program 1

Family Fun: Pyjama Party

We made it! Welcome to the final chapter of programs, "Family Storytime." In this chapter you'll find the same great ideas as in previous chapters, but with one subtle difference. Here we are focusing on ideas meant for parents and caregivers to enjoy with children of all ages—together. If you've never tried throwing a family pyjama party, you're in for a pleasant surprise!

Plan Ahead Note

Let program participants know, starting two weeks in advance, that you're planning a pyjama party theme and ask if children could come dressed in pjs with their favourite sleeping buddies in tow. To get this program off to a great start, begin with a song like *Sleeping*. This song gets mommies, daddies, and kids involved. It's a great icebreaker!

Books to Share

The Big Yawn, by Keith Faulkner

Time for Bed, by Mem Fox

The Napping House, by Audrey Wood

More books to share with families can be found in the bibliography at the end of this chapter.

Family Fun: Pyjama Party

Rhymes and Songs

Pyjama Party

(Suit actions to words.)

Welcome to our pyjama party,
Come on, let's have some fun.
First we'll hop on slippered feet,
and then we'll run and run.

Now we'll stretch and stretch our arms,
and then we'll sigh and yawn.
Soon we'll all be fast asleep,
and we'll stay that way until dawn.

Good Night

(Suit actions to words.)

Two little hands go clap, clap, clap,
Two little arms lie in my lap.
Two little feet go bump, bump, bump,
Two little legs give one big jump.
Two little eyes are shut so tight,
One little voice whispers "Good Night!"

Twinkle, Twinkle Little Star

(As an added extra give each child a star taped to a Popsicle stick to hold while singing.)

Twinkle, twinkle little star,
How I wonder what you are.
Up above the world so high,
Like a diamond in the sky.
Twinkle, twinkle little star,
How I wonder what you are.

When the blazing sun is gone,
When he nothing shines upon.
Then you show your little light,
Twinkle, twinkle all the night.

Twinkle, twinkle, little star,
How I wonder what you are.
Up above the world so high,
Like a diamond in the sky.
Twinkle, twinkle, little star,
How I wonder what you are.

I Am Sleepy

(Tune: Oh My Darlin' Clementine)
(Suit actions to words.)

I am sleepy, oh so sleepy,
Watch me stretch and stretch and
  yawn.
I'll close my eyes and just pretend,
That the sunshine now has gone.

I'll breathe so softly, lie so still,
A little mouse could even creep,
Right up to me because he thought,
That I was laying here sound asleep.

(Snore loudly.)

Big Yellow Moon

(Suit actions to words.)

Big yellow moon shines so bright,

(Hold your arms above your head in a circle shape.)

Glides across the starry night.

(Move your arms from left to right.)

Looks down at me,

(Use your hands to shade your eyes.)

Asleep in bed,

(Pretend to sleep.)

and whispers, "Good night
  sleepyhead."
Big yellow moon your turn is done,

(Move your arms down in front of your body.)

Here comes Mr. Morning Sun!

(Move your arms above your head in a circle shape again.)

Four Little Stars

 (Use your fingers to represent the stars.)
Four little stars winking at me.
One shot off, now there are three.
Three little stars with nothing to do.
One shot off, then there were two.
Two little stars afraid of the sun.
One shot off, then there was one.
One little star thought being alone was
   no fun.
It shot off, now there are none.

5 Crescent Moons

 (Use your fingers to represent the moons.)
5 yellow crescent moons,
How the sleepy one did snore!
He went away to bed
and then there were 4.

4 yellow crescent moons,
Shining bright as could be.
One went to find the stars
and then there were 3.

3 yellow crescent moons
Now what could they do?
"I'm off to play" said the bright eyed one
and then there were 2.

2 yellow crescent moons
Out came the sun.
"It's much too bright", one complained
and then there was one.

1 yellow crescent moon
Alone so way up high.
Shines and shines for all the earth
Can you see it in the sky?

Sleeping

 (Tune: Mulberry Bush)
(This is a great song to get the whole family in-volved.)
 This is the way a baby sleeps,

(Curl up with your knees at your chest.)
Baby sleeps, baby sleeps,
This is the way a baby sleeps,
In his little crib.

This is the way a daddy sleeps,

(Lie on your back with your arms outstretched.)
Daddy sleeps, daddy sleeps.
This is the way a daddy sleeps,
In his big bed.

This is the way a doggy sleeps,

(Lie on your side.)
Doggy sleeps, doggy sleeps.
This is the way a doggy sleeps,
On the floor.
This is the way a ducky sleeps,

(Stand on one leg with your head down.)
Ducky sleeps, ducky sleeps.
This is the way a ducky sleeps,
In the tall grass.

Now you show me how you go to
   sleep,

(Let the children choose a position.)
Go to sleep, go to sleep.
Now you show me how you go to
   sleep,
When it's time for bed!

Rockets Away!

Materials

1 toilet paper roll per person

Aluminium foil (enough to cover the rockets for your whole group)

Tissue paper, red, yellow, orange

Bristol/poster board, any colour

Scissors

Decorating supplies: markers, glue, glitter

Scotch tape

Instructions

1. Cover the toilet paper roll with the aluminium foil and secure it with tape or glue.

2. Cut a 1-inch or 2.5 cm slit anywhere at the top of the roll and another directly across from it.

3. Photocopy and trace the triangle template onto the Bristol/poster board and cut it out.

4. Fit the triangle into the slits at the top of the roll.

5. Cut the tissue paper into 5-inch or 13 cm strips .

6. Let the children attach as many strips at the bottom of the rocket as they would like once they are done with decorating, and the rockets are ready to fly!

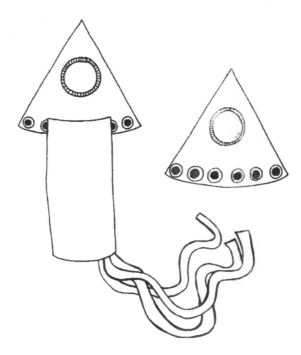

Program 2
Family Fun: Enchanted Evening

Have you ever dreamed of what life would be like living in a castle? Who hasn't? This evening will be especially enchanting when you announce the theme. Kings, queens, fairies, and dragons will fill the thoughts and dreams of the children in your group as you sing of royal families and mystical creatures. In this program, the caregivers and kids alike get a chance to sing and participate in group time, and then get to take a "Puppet Palace" storytime souvenir home so the magic can be repeated over and over again. The best storytime souvenirs are the ones that enhance your program in a way that the children are sure to remember. It's a great storytime extension!

Plan Ahead Note

Make sure you have plenty of room for this lively program. Get your parents and caregivers involved by having them participate in a song or rhyme. One song you could start with would be *There Was a Princess Long Ago*. We have found this song to be a big hit with children. In fact, they may like it so much it may be the only song you get to sing!

The storytime souvenir for this program requires that the programmer do a moderate amount of preparation ahead of time. If possible, you may wish to recruit a volunteer to help out with the cutting; if not, begin preparing this craft a week or so in advance to give yourself plenty of time to complete it.

Books to Share

Princess Prunella and the Purple Peanut, by Margaret Atwood

Good Night, Princess Pruney Toes, by Lisa McCourt

I Am Really a Princess, by Carol Diggery Shields

More books to share with families can be found in the bibliography at the end of this chapter.

Family Fun: Enchanted Evening

Rhymes and Songs

There Was a Princess Long Ago

(Tune: Mary Had a Little Lamb)
(Choose a child to play each part in this song. You may have to repeat this one a few times so everyone gets a turn. A magic wand is also a great addition!)

There was a princess long ago,
Long ago, long ago.
There was a princess long ago,
Long, long ago.

(Princess stands in the centre of the circle.)

She lived up in a big tall tower,
Big tall tower, big tall tower.
She lived up in a big tall tower,
Long, long ago.

(Children raise their arms above their heads.)

The wicked witch she waved her wand,
Waved her wand, waved her wand.
The wicked witch she waved her wand,
Long, long ago.

(Wicked witch goes around the outside circle waving her wand.)
Additional verses:

The princess slept for one hundred
years . . .

(Princess pretends to sleep on the floor.)

A great big forest grew all around . . .

(Children stand around the princess.)

A handsome prince came galloping by
. . .

(Handsome prince gallops outside the circle.)

He took his axe and chopped it down . . .

(Children sit down one by one.)

He took her hand and woke her up . . .

(Prince takes princess's hand—she awakes.)

Everybody's happy now . . .

(Children dance and clap.)

Did You Ever See a Dragon?

(Tune: Did You Ever See a Lassie?)
(Suit actions to words.)

Did you ever see a dragon, a dragon, a
dragon?
Did you ever see a dragon breathe hot
fire and smoke?
Breathe hot fire and grey smoke?
Breathe hot fire and grey smoke?

(Have children pretend to be dragons.)

Did you ever see a dragon breathe hot
fire and smoke?

Little Fairies

(Use your fingers to represent the fairies.)
(Suit actions to words.)

Said this little fairy, "I'm a tired as can
be."
Said this little fairy, "My eyes can
hardly see."
Said this little fairy, "I'd like to go to
bed."
Said this little fairy, "I want to rest my
head."
Said this little fairy, "Climb the stairs
with me."
Tiptoe, tiptoe, one, two, three . . .
Be as quiet as can be.
Pull up the covers in your bed,
Good night little sleepyheads.

218

Dopey the Dragon

 (Use an old clock as a visual aid with this rhyme.)
I had a little dragon and Dopey was his
  name.
At 1 o'clock he ran away,
At 2 o'clock he came.
At 3 o'clock he bothered me,
At 4 o'clock he stopped.
At 5 o'clock he fetched the leash
and took me for a walk.

If You're a Dragon

 (Tune: If You're Happy and You Know It)
(Suit actions to words.)

If you're a dragon and you know it
  breathe hot fire.
If you're a dragon and you know it
  breathe hot fire.
If you're a dragon and you know it,
Then your breath will surely show it.
If you're a dragon and you know it
  breathe hot fire.

If you're a dragon and you know it
  swish your tail.
If you're a dragon and you know it
  swish your tail.
If you're a dragon and you know it,
Then your tail will surely show it.
If you're a dragon and you know it
  swish your tail.

If you're a dragon and you know it
  ROAR! out loud.
If you're a dragon and you know it
  ROAR! out loud.
If you're a dragon and you know it,
Then you're ROAR will really show it.
If you're a dragon and you know it
  ROAR! out loud.

I'm a Little Dragon

 (Tune: I'm a Little Teapot)
(Suit actions to words.)

I'm a little dragon, strong and stout.
Here is my tail and here is my snout.
If I get all steamed up you better watch
  out.
I can give you something to shout about!
ROAR!

5 Queens

 (Use your fingers to represent the five queens.)
There were 5 queens on a quest,

 (Hold up five fingers.)
To see who was the very best.

(Wiggle fingers.)
The first queen went to take a test,

(Touch thumb.)
The second said, "I'll go out west."

(Touch index finger.)
The third queen climbed Mount
  Everest.

(Touch middle finger.)
The fourth queen made a beautiful
  vest,

(Touch ring finger.)
The fifth queen said, "I'll just take a
  rest."

(Touch little finger.)

5 Green Dragons

 (Use your fingers to represent the dragons.)
5 green dragons making such a roar,
1 danced away and then there were 4.
4 green dragons dancing around a tree,
One danced away and then there were
  3.
3 green dragons dancing around you,
1 danced away and then there were 2.
2 green dragons dancing in the sun,
1 danced away and then there was 1.
1 green dragon having lots of fun,
She danced away and then there were
  none.

219

Puppet Palace

Materials

1 photocopied queen per person

1 photocopied king per person

1 photocopied palace per person

1 medium brown paper lunch bag per person

Popsicle sticks (enough for your group)

Masking tape

Cardstock or Bristol/poster board

Decorating supplies: glitter, glue, markers, crayons

Instructions

1. Photocopy the king and queen to approximately 6 inches or 15 cm and the castle template large enough to fit onto the paper bag. Back them onto cardstock or Bristol board to make them more sturdy.

2. Cut out the king and queen and tape a Popsicle stick onto the back of each.

3. Cut out the castle and glue it to the front of the paper bag.

4. Let the children decorate each piece; when they're ready to go, they can simply put the king and queen in the castle to carry home.

Program 3

Family Fun: Monster Mash

Why wait until Hallowe'en to sing about monsters? Children have a natural fascination with monsters. They live in closets, under beds, virtually anywhere dark and unexplored. So . . . why not take something scary and make it something silly instead? This program is jam-packed with fun and interactive songs that will have your group growling and stomping in no time. Monsters . . . they aren't just for Hallowe'en anymore!

Plan Ahead Note

The storytime souvenir for this program requires that the programmer do a moderate amount of preparation before the program. Since this craft requires a large paint stirrer or stick for each person in your group, take a trip to your local home and garden store. Retailers in this business will give away paint sticks free of charge (as long as you don't request too many of them too often).

Books to Share

The Beast in the Bathtub, by Kathleen Stevens

The Monster Who Ate My Peas, by Danny Schnitzlein

Monster Munchies, by Laura Joffe Numeroff

More books to share with families can be found in the bibliography at the end of this chapter.

Family Fun: Monster Mash

Rhymes and Songs

5 Little Monsters

 (Use your fingers to represent the monsters.)

5 little monsters by the light of the moon,
Stirring chocolate pudding with a
   wooden spoon.
The first one says, "It mustn't be runny."
The second one says, "That would
   make it taste funny."
The third one says, "It mustn't be
   lumpy."
The fourth one says, " That would
   make me grumpy."
The fifth one smiles and hums a little
   tune,
and licks all the drippings from the
   wooden spoon.

Monster Stomp

  (Tune: Camptown Races.)
(Suit actions to words.)

Monsters stomp around the house,
Boom boom, boom boom.
Monsters stomp around the house,
Boom boom boom boom boom!
With their eyes shining bright,
They stomp with all their might.
Monster stomp around the house,
Boom boom boom boom boom!

Additional verses:

Monsters clap, growl, yell,

If You're a Monster

 (Tune: If You're Happy and You Know It)
(Suit actions to words.)

If you're a monster and you know it
   wave your arms,
If you're a monster and you know it
   wave your arms,
If you're a monster and you know it,
Then your arms will surely show it.
If you're a monster and you know it
   wave your arms.

Additional verses:

. . . Show your teeth
. . . Stomp your feet
. . . Growl out loud

Old McMonster

 (Tune: Old McDonald)
(Suit actions to words.)

Old McMonster has a house
Oo-ee-oo-ee-oo.
and in this house there lives a witch,
Oo-ee-oo-ee-oo.
With a cackle, cackle here,
and a cackle, cackle there,
Here a cackle,
There a cackle,
Everywhere a cackle, cackle.
Old McMonster has a house,
Oo-ee-oo-ee-oo!

Additional verses:

Skeleton—rattle, rattle
Bat—screech, screech
Ghost—boo, boo

Five Little Monsters

 (Use your fingers to represent the monsters in this rhyme, similar to This Little Piggy.)

This little monster has a big red nose,
This little monster has purple toes.
This little monster plays all night,
This little monster gives such a fright.
This little monster laughs,
  "Tee-hee-hee,
I'm not so scary, I'm just silly me!"

5 Silly Monsters

 (Tune: 5 Little Monkeys)
(Have the children pretend to be the sleeping monsters.)

5 silly monsters sleeping in my bed,
1 crawled out from under my spread.
I called to Mama and Mama said,
"No more monsters sleeping in your
  bed!"

4, 3, 2, 1,

No silly monsters sleeping in my bed,
None crawling out from under my
  spread.
I called to Mama and Mama said,
"THERE ARE NO MORE
  MONSTERS,
NOW GO TO BED!"

If You Ever See a Monster

  (Tune: Did You Ever See a Lassie)
(Suit actions to words.)

If you ever see a monster,
A big ugly monster,
If you ever see a monster,
Here's what you should do.
Make this face . . .

(Make different faces.)

and this face . . .
and this face . . .
and this face . . .
If you ever see a monster
Be sure to shout . . . "BOO!"

Horns and Fangs

  (Tune: Head and Shoulders)
(Suit actions to words.)

Horns and fangs,
and knees and claws,
Knees and claws,
Knees and claws.
Horns and fangs
and knees and claws,
Eyes, ears, tails and paws.

Wild Thing

Materials

1 sheet each of light green, dark green, and brown construction paper per person

1 paint stick per person

1 photocopied "Wild Thing" per person

4 pipe cleaners per person (10-inch or 25 cm)

Cardstock

Glue sticks (enough for your group)

Scissors

Decorating supplies: crayons, markers

Instructions

1. Photocopy the "Wild Thing" (to fit an 8½-by-11-inch sheet of paper) template, glue it onto cardstock to make it more sturdy, and cut it out.

2. Take two pipe cleaners and twist them together. Take the other two pipe cleaners and twist them together. (These are the arms.)

3. Tape one end of the pipe cleaners onto the back of the "Wild Thing" and bend the other end of the pipe cleaners to form the hands. Set the "Wild Thing" aside.

4. Out of the light and dark green construction paper cut leaf shapes. Out of the brown construction paper cut or tear brown strips. (These are the branches.)

5. Provide the leaf shapes and the branches for the children to glue onto one side of the paint stick.

6. Let the children decorate the "Wild Thing" and once they are finished, hook the hands onto the decorated paint stick and watch him swing!

226

227

Program 4

Family Fun: Loony Tunes

The name says it all! Not every family program has to have a sleepy, bedtime, or quiet-time theme. If you get the people in your group up and moving, they'll be ready to sit down and listen to a good story when your minutes in motion are over. But don't be surprised if you only get to sing a few of the songs we have listed here. In our experience, songs like *Sticky, Sticky, Sticky Bubble Gum* become favourites so fast that the kids want to keep making up places to stick the gum!

Plan Ahead Note

The storytime souvenir for this program requires little preparation on the part of the programmer. The cutting will be the most time-consuming part. About a week in advance (or more if you choose), you'll need to take a trip to your local dollar or discount store to purchase the party blowers you'll need (you'll find them in the party section).

Books to Share

Incredible Ned, by Bill Maynard

How Do Dinosaurs Say Goodnight?, By Jane Yolen

Giggle, Giggle, Quack, by Doreen Cronin

More books to share with families can be found in the bibliography at the end of this chapter.

Family Fun: Loony Tunes

Rhymes and Songs

5 Little Fingers

(Tune: Skip to My Lou)
(Suit actions to words.)

What can I do with 5 little fingers?
What can I do with 5 little fingers?
What can I do with 5 little fingers?
What can I do today?

I can shake my 5 little fingers.
I can shake my 5 little fingers.
I can shake my 5 little fingers.
I can shake them today.

Additional verses:

I can wiggle my 5 little fingers
I can wave my five little fingers
I can clap my 5 little fingers.

Sticky, Sticky, Sticky Bubble Gum

(Have the children/caregivers give suggestions as to where the bubble gum could be stuck.)

Sticky, sticky, sticky, bubble gum,
Bubble gum, bubble gum.
Sticky, sticky, sticky, bubble gum,
Sticking to my head!

(Stick your hand to your head.)

Is it stuck?
Unstick it!

(Pull your hand from your head.)

Additional verses:

Sticking to my . . . nose, knees, feet

Ain't It Great to Be Crazy

(Suit actions to words.)

Boom-boom, ain't it great to be crazy?
Boom-boom, ain't it great to be crazy?
Giddy and foolish all day long.
Boom-boom, ain't it great to be crazy?

A horse and a flea and three blind mice,
Sat on a corner shooting dice.
The horse he slipped and he fell on the flea,
"WHOOPS!" said the flea,
"There's a horsey on me!"

Boom-boom, ain't it great to be crazy?
Boom-boom, ain't it great to be crazy?
Giddy and foolish all day long.
Boom-boom, ain't it great to be crazy?

Old Mother Hobble Gobble

(Suit actions to words.)

Old Mother Hobble Gobble sent me to you.
What can you do? What can you do?
Can you shake your right hand like I do?

Additional verses:

Can you tap your left foot like I do?
Can you spin around and around like I do?
Can you clap and clap your hands like I do?
Can you rest a little while like I do?

Shake My Sillies Out

(Suit actions to words.)
   I'm gonna shake, shake, shake my
      sillies out,
   Shake, shake, shake my sillies out.
   Shake, shake, shake my sillies out,
   and wiggle my waggles away.

Additional Verses:
   Clap, clap, clap my crazies out.
   Jump, jump, jump my jiggles out
   Yawn, yawn, yawn my sleepies out
   Stretch, stretch, stretch, my stretchies
      out

Underneath the Monkey Tree

(Suit actions to words.)
   Come and play a while with me,
   Underneath the monkey tree.
   Monkey see and monkey do,
   Just like monkeys in the zoo.

   Swing your tail one, two, three,
   Underneath the monkey tree.
   Monkey see and monkey do,
   Just like monkeys in the zoo.

   Jump up and down one, two, three,
   Underneath the monkey tree.
   Monkey see and monkey do,
   Just like monkeys in the zoo.

Stretching

(Tune: Twinkle, Twinkle Little Star)
(Suit actions to words.)
   Everybody reach up high,
   Stretching, stretching to the sky.
   Swaying left and swaying right,
   Blinking in the sky at night.
   Everybody reach up high,
   Stretching, stretching to the sky.

Itsy Bitsy Monkey

(Tune: Itsy Bitsy Spider)
(Do as the actions indicate.)
   An itsy bitsy monkey climbed up a
      coconut tree,

(Make a climbing motion with your hands.)
   Down came a coconut and hit him on
      his knee—Ouch!

(Slap your knee.)
   Out came a lion shaking his mighty
      mane . . . AND..

(Sway your head back and forth.)
   The itsy bitsy monkey climbed up the
      tree again.

(Make a climbing motion with your hands.)

Silly Monkeys

Materials

1 photocopied monkey face per person

Brown construction paper for each person

1 party blower per person

Decorating supplies: crayons, markers, etc.

Exacto or matte knife

Instructions

1. Enlarge and photocopy the monkey face onto brown construction paper to the size of a large paper plate.

2. Use an Exacto knife to cut the "X" where the monkey's mouth should be.

3. Have the children decorate the monkey face.

4. Insert the plastic part of the blower through the monkey's mouth. Have the children hold the end of the blower and blow. It will look like the monkey is making a silly face.

Program 5

Family Fun: Family Favourites

It is important to remember that the songs and rhymes listed here are only a guideline. Every group is going to be different, and every group will have their own set of favourites. That's why we chose to include a program called "Family Favourites." The idea with this theme is to include the most popular or most requested songs of your group into one fun program.

Plan Ahead Note

If you write down a couple of songs or rhymes each week, starting at the beginning of your program, you can end your session with a "Favourites Only Sing-Along" and have a whole lot of fun!

Books to Share

Is Your Mama a Llama?, By Deborah Guarino

What Moms Can't Do, by Douglas Wood

What Mommies Do Best/What Daddies Do Best, by Laura Joffe Numeroff

More books to share with families can be found in the bibliography at the end of this chapter.

Family Fun: Family Favourites

Rhymes and Songs

Family Fingerplay

 (Do as the actions indicate.)
> This is a family,

(Hold up one hand, fingers spread.)
> Let's count them and see.
> How many are there?
> and who can they be?
>
> This is the mother,

(Touch index finger.)
> Who loves everyone.
> This is the father,

(Touch middle finger.)
> Who is lots of fun!
>
> This is the sister,

(Touch ring finger.)
> She helps and she plays.
> and this is the baby,

(Touch pinky finger.)
> He's growing each day.
>
> But who is this one?

(Touch thumb.)
> He's out there alone.
> Why it's Ruffus the dog!
> and he's chewing a bone!

(Wiggle thumb.)

Momma Don't Allow

 (Suit actions to words.)
> Momma don't allow no hand clappin'
>   'round here.

(Clap your hands as you sing.)
> Momma don't allow no hand clappin'
>   'round here.
> Well we don't care what momma don't
>   allow,
> We'll just clap our hands any old how.
> Momma don't allow no hand clappin'
>   'round here.

Additional verses:
> Momma don't allow no foot stompin',
> Knee slappin'
> Loud shoutin'—HOORAY!

Grandma, Grandma

 (Suit actions to words.)
> Grandma, Grandma you're sick,
> All you need is a peppermint stick.
> Hands up . . . shake, shake, shake.
> Hands down . . . shake, shake, shake.
> All around . . . shake, shake, shake.
> Put them down . . . shake, shake,
>   shake.

Additional verses:
> Hands up . . . clap, clap, clap
> Hands up . . . snap, snap, snap

5 Little Monkeys

(Use your fingers to represent the five monkeys or have the children be the monkeys.)

5 little monkeys jumping on the bed,
1 fell off and bumped his head.
Mama called the doctor and the doctor said,
"NO MORE MONKEYS JUMPING ON THE BED!"

(Repeat with 4,3, and 2.)

1 little monkey jumping on the bed,
He fell off and bumped his head.
Mama called the doctor and the doctor said,
"PUT THOSE MONKEYS STRAIGHT TO BED!"

Imagination Station

(Suit actions to words.)

Bring your imagination inside,
There's nowhere here for it to hide.
Bring it out to play,
Let it twist and turn throughout the day.
We'll hold it way up high,
High enough to touch the sky.
We'll dance it way down low,
So low it will touch your toes.
We'll spin it round and round and round,
and then we'll sit right down.

Bend and Stretch

(Suit actions to words.)

Bend and stretch, reach for the stars,
There goes Jupiter, here comes Mars.
Bend and stretch, reach for the sky,
Stand on tippy toes, oh so high.
Turn around and around once more,
Then everybody sit down on the floor.

The Wheels on the Bus

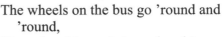

(Suit actions to words.)

The wheels on the bus go 'round and 'round,
'Round and 'round, 'round and 'round.
The wheels on the bus go 'round and 'round,
All through the town.

Additional verses:

Doors on the bus go—open and shut
Money on the bus goes—clink, clink, clink
Driver of the bus says—"MOVE ON BACK!"
People on the bus go—up and down
Babies on the bus they—cry, cry, cry
Mommies on the bus say—"shh, shh, shh,"
Daddies on the bus go—"yak, yak, yak,"

If You're Happy and You Know It

(Suit actions to words.)

If you're happy and you know it clap your hands,

(Clap, clap.)

If you're happy and you know it clap your hands.

(Clap, clap.)

If you're happy and you know it,
and you really want to show it,
If you're happy and you know it clap your hands.

(Clap, clap.)

Additional verses:

Stamp your feet—stamp, stamp
Shout Hooray!—Hooray!

Storytime Souvenir

I Spy Telescope

Materials

1 paper towel roll per person

Coloured cellophane, enough to cover the paper towel rolls

Construction paper

Rubber bands (enough for your group)

Scotch tape

Decorating supplies: stickers, foam pieces, glitter, ribbons, yarn.

Instructions

1. Cover one end of the paper towel roll with the coloured cellophane. Attach the cellophane either by taping it or using a rubber band to secure it.

2. Cover the whole tube by wrapping a sheet of construction paper around it and fastening it with tape.

3. Let the children decorate the tube, being careful not to cover the ends.

4. Encourage the children to look into the tube and see how different things look.

 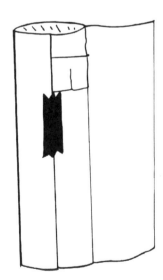 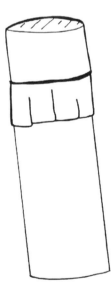

Program 6

Family Fun:
Inside-Outside, Upside-Down

Children love active songs that they can be silly to or jump around for, as well as changing clothes. Children at any age certainly require a lot of action. From the time they wake up in the morning until they go to bed at night, kids can go through a lot of changes. Of clothes that is! So they'll know all the moves (and so will their families) and be ready and willing to sing along with you.

Plan Ahead Note

A few of the songs and rhymes in this program require that you use pictures or props. Decide at least a week before your program which rhymes and songs you would like to use so that you can plan your program accordingly. This should give you plenty of time to gather the necessary ingredients to help to make your program a success.

Books to Share

Jesse Bear, What Will You Wear?, By Nancy White Carlstrom

Red Is Best, by Kathy Stinson

Froggy Gets Dressed, by Jonathan London

More books to share with families can be found in the bibliography at the end of this chapter.

Family Fun: Inside-Outside, Upside-Down

Rhymes and Songs

A Journey to Japan

 (This rhyme requires a bit of preparation. It works best if you have a picture or the actual object mentioned to show your group.)

I'm taking a journey to Japan,
My jet is leaving soon.
I'm packing up my J things,
You'd think I was off to the moon.

I'm taking a jack-o-lantern
and plenty of juice and Jell-O.
Of course, I will take my jewellery
and my jacket that is sort of yellow.

I'm planning to take my jellyfish,
Who speaks perfect Japanese.
He taught me how to jitterbug
Jeepers, that hurts my knees!

I packed a jigsaw puzzle
and a book about how to juggle.
I didn't forget my jackrabbit,
The toy I love to snuggle.

Now I'll just pack my jump rope
and a jar of jam if I can.
Then I think I'll have all my J things,
For my journey to Japan.

Cloudy Days

 (Have your group pretend to get dressed and undressed right along with you in this fun rhyme.)
(Do as the actions indicate.)

The day is cloudy and the wind is bold.
Dress up warmly, you mustn't get
cold.
Put on your coat and zip it up tight,
Put on your left boot, put on your right.
Put on your scarf and put on your hat,
Put on your mittens and clap, clap,
clap!
Go outside and play, play, play,
Come in again and then we'll say—
Take off your coat that was zipped up
tight,
Take off your left boot, take off your
right.
Take off your scarf, take off your hat,
Take off your mittens then take a nap!

Tony Chestnut

 (Slowly sing these words and touch the body part that is mentioned. Repeat this song a little faster each time and listen for the giggles that will follow.)

Tony Chestnut knows I love you,

(Touch your toes, knees, and head.)
Tony knows, Tony knows.

(Touch your toes and knees.)
Tony Chestnut knows I love you,

(Touch your toes, knees, and head.)
That's what Tony knows.

(Touch your toes and knees.)

238

Eeny Meeny Miney Mo

 (Suit actions to words.)

Eeny meeny miney mo, let me hear
   your hands go,
Clap, clap . . . clap, clap, clap,
Clap, clap . . . clap, clap, clap.

Sounds so good, sounds so fine,
Let me hear them one more time.
Clap, clap, . . . clap, clap, clap,
Clap, clap, . . .clap, clap, clap.

Additional verses:

Let me see your lips go—kiss
Let me hear your feet go—stomp
Let me hear your fingers go—snap
Let me see your mouth go—shhhh

Getting Dressed

(Tune: The Farmer in the Dell)
(Suit actions to words.)

I'm getting dressed myself,
I'm getting dressed myself.
Hi-ho I'm growing-o,
I'm getting dressed myself.

Additional verses:

I'm pulling on my shirt
I'm slipping on my socks
I'm tying up my shoes
I'm zipping up my coat

I'm ready to go out,
I'm ready to go out.
Hi-ho just watch me go,
I'm ready to go out.

Old Shoes, New Shoes

(Suit actions to words.)

Old shoes, new shoes,
Who is wearing red shoes?
One, two, three, four,
Stomp, stomp, stomp them on the floor!

(Replace red with other colours.)

Last verse:

Old shoes, new shoes,
Everyone is wearing shoes!
One, two, three, four,
Let's all stomp them on the floor.

In My Pocket

 (Plan ahead for this rhyme. It works best if you have picture of these things in your back pocket to take out and show the group.)

The things in my pocket are lots of fun,
I will show you one by one.
The first thing in my pocket is a frog,
I found him sitting on a log.
The second thing in my pocket is a car,
It can race off very far.
The third thing in my pocket is a ball,
I can bounce it off the wall.
The fourth thing in my pocket is a bunny,
She twitches her nose and looks so funny.
The fifth thing in my pocket is a dog,
He's a friend of my little frog.
In my pockets my thing hide,
Do you have pockets with things inside?

All Kinds of Shoes

 (This is a great rhyme to use with the flannel board.)

There are all kinds of shoes,
For all kinds of feet.
To wear at home,
Or out on the street.
There are boots for splashing,
and sneakers for dashing.
There are slippers for napping,
and tap shoes for tapping.
There are cowboy boots for riding,
and ice skates for gliding.
But the best shoes of all
Are the ones that fit you
While you're doing the things
That you love to do!

Hats Off to You!

Materials

1 paper plate per person

Pipe cleaners, any size (enough for your group)

Scissors

Glue sticks (enough for your group)

Tape

Decorating supplies: glitter, stickers, pom-poms

Instructions

1. Cut the inside of the paper plate out so that you are left with only the rim and a flap to fold up. (This is a perfect fit to the heads of most children.)

2. Bend the pipe cleaners around pencils to make coils, or in any wacky direction, and tape them onto the hat.

3. Provide the children with the decorating supplies; let them decorate their hats and they can wear them home.

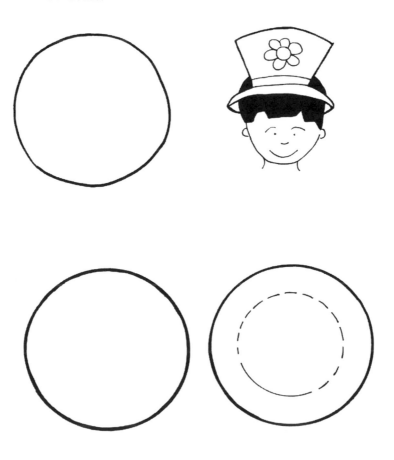

Program 7
Family Fun: Bunnies and Bears

We were very excited to include this program, not only because the songs and rhymes are great, but because the storytime souvenir is simply amazing. It really works! Kids will think it's one of a kind, and caregivers won't know how you did it. You'll keep them busy and guessing for a while. This is a program sure to be remembered and a souvenir that will be a permanent fixture on the fridges and in the keepsake boxes of many in your group.

Plan Ahead Note

To prepare this craft, the first thing you will need to do is visit any home improvement or paint retailer to purchase your blackboard/chalkboard paint (you will need to decide on a colour; there are a few). Once you have your paint, you are ready to move on to the photocopying and preparing for the finished product.

Books to Share

Bear Snores On, by Karma Wilson

Grumpy Bunnies, by Willy Welch

It's Not Easy Being a Bunny, by Marilyn Sadler

More books to share with families can be found in the bibliography at the end of this chapter.

241

Family Fun: Bunnies and Bears

Rhymes and Songs

Bears

 (Get the children to participate by making the noises of the bees, fish, etc.)

Big bear, big bear,
Hunting near the trees.
Feasting on the honeycomb
Made by busy bees.

(Bzzz, bzzz, bzzz,)

Big bear, big bear,
Wading in the lake.
Fish is your favourite dish,
Which one will you take?

(Swish, swish, swish.)

Big bear, big bear,
Resting in your den.
Sleeping through the winter
Before you're out again.

(Zzz, zzz, zzz.)

I Am A Little Bunny

 (Suit actions to words.)

I am a little bunny,
Eyes on the sides of my head.
I see to the left and right,
Behind me and ahead.

I am a little bunny,
These are my very long ears.
They help me to hear many sounds,
I can hear from far and near.

I am a little bunny,
My strong legs are for jumping.
I warn others of danger,
When I use my feet for thumping.

I am a mother bunny,
With a white and fluffy tail.
I lift it up into the air
and my babies will follow my trail.

Did You Ever See a Teddy?

 (Tune: Did You Ever See a Lassie)
(Let the children help to decide which way teddy should move.)

Did you ever see a teddy bear,
A teddy bear, a teddy bear?
Did you ever see a teddy bear
Go this way and that?

(Move teddy bears side to side.)

Go this way and that way,
and this way and that way.
Did you ever see a teddy bear,
Go this way and that?

5 Little Bears

 (Use your fingers to represent the bears.)

5 little bears were dancing on the floor,
1 fell down and then there were 4.
4 little bears climbed up a tree,
1 fell down and then there were 3.
3 little bears wondering what to do,
1 chased a bunny and that left 2.
2 little bears were looking for some
    fun,
1 took a swim and that left 1.
1 little bear sitting all alone,
Had no one to play with so he went
    home.

242

Grizzly Bear, Grizzly Bear

 (Do as the actions indicate.)
> Grizzly bear, grizzly bear,
> Where have you been?
> Over the mountains

(Place one hand over your eyes and pretend to be looking over the mountains.)
> Such things I've seen!

> Grizzly bear, grizzly bear,
> What have you done?
> Eaten fresh blueberries

(Pretend to be eating.)
> Made ripe by the sun.

> Grizzly bear, grizzly bear,
> What have you found?
> Ice-cold spring water

(Pretend to drink.)
> Deep from the ground.
> Grizzly bear, grizzly bear,
> What do you dream?
> Sweet tasting salmon

(Make a swishing motion with your hands.)
> Swimming upstream.

> Grizzly bear, grizzly bear,
> Where do you creep?
> Into my dark cave alone,

(Pretend to creep into a cave.)
> Now let me sleep!

This Little Bunny

 (Use your fingers to represent the five bunnies.)
> This little bunny has two pink eyes.
> This little bunny is very wise.
> This little bunny is white as milk.
> This little bunny is as soft as silk.
> This little bunny nibbles away,
> At cabbages and carrots all through the day!

Here Is a Rabbit

 (Suit actions to words.)
> Oh, here's a fluffy rabbit,
> With two ears so very long.
> See him hop, hop, hop about,
> On his legs so very strong.
> He nibbles, nibbles carrots
> For his dinner every day.
> and as soon as he has had enough,
> He hops, hops, hops away!

Robbie the Rabbit

 (Suit actions to words.)
> Robbie the Rabbit is fat, fat, fat.

 (Pat your tummy.)
> His soft little paws go pat, pat, pat.

(Tap your feet lightly.)
> His soft little ears go flop, flop, flop.

(Hands behind your head—wave hands up and down.)
> and when Robbie runs he goes hop, hop, hop.

(Feet together—tap them on the floor.)

Blackboard Bear

This is a great craft, and it works!

Materials

Black chalkboard paint (small can)

1 photocopied bear per person

String, any colour

Cardstock or Bristol/poster board

Decorating supplies: markers, crayons, sequins

Chalk, 1 stick per person

Instructions

1. Photocopy the bear template (to fit an 8½-by-11-inch sheet of paper) and the circle for his tummy.

2. Back them both onto cardstock and cut them out.

3. Paint the circle with the blackboard paint and let dry.

4. Once dry, glue the circle onto the bear's tummy.

5. Let the children decorate the bear and provide each child with a piece of chalk to take home.

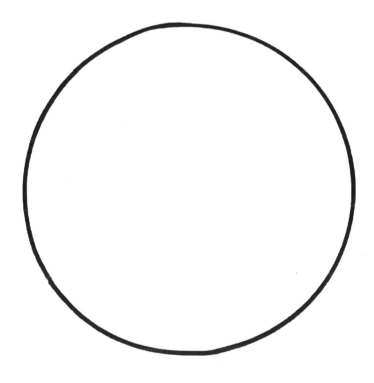

Program 8

Family Fun: Farmyard Fun

We would like to end this chapter with one of our favourite themes: the farm. Many of the songs listed here may be new or different than what you're used to singing for a farm theme, but that's the point! We hope that you have learned how and will continue to think in obscure ways in regard to your programming. Make it a challenge to yourself to try a little something new in each of your programs. To fail or succeed, you have to try. Good luck, and remember to have fun!

Plan Ahead Note

As an extension for the songs and rhymes in this program, make multiple copies of the farmer and farmyard animals and tape them onto Popsicle sticks. When you sing your songs (such as *Farm Flurry*), let each of the children pick an animal to be, and when you say the name of an animal the children with that particular animal get to respond. Children love it when they get to chime in and sing along. This program is especially great for doing so.

Books to Share

Farmer Brown Goes Round and Round, by Teri Sloat

The Little Red Hen, by Paul Galdone

Sitting on the Farm, by Bob King

More books to share with families can be found in the bibliography at the end of this chapter.

Family Fun: Farmyard Fun

Rhymes and Songs

All Around the Barnyard

 (Have pictures of barnyard animals available. This allows the children to participate by naming them as you say the rhyme)

All around the barnyard,
The animals are fast asleep.
Sleeping cows and horses,
Sleeping pigs and sheep.

Here comes the cocky rooster,
To sound his daily alarm.
"Cock-a-doodle-doo!
Wake up sleepy farm!"

Farmer McDonald

 (Have pictures of the things mentioned in the rhyme or give the children a chance to fill in what item the animals eat, drink, etc.)

Old McDonald had a goat,
It ate his winter overcoat.

Old McDonald had a sheep,
It ate his big red four-wheeled jeep.

Old McDonald had a cat,
It ate his furry winter hat.

Old McDonald had a goose,
It drank his can of apple juice.

Old McDonald had a duck,
It liked to drive his big green truck.

Old McDonald had a pig,
It ate his sister's brand new wig.

Old McDonald had a horse,
It ate his rubber boots, of course!

Here Is the Barn

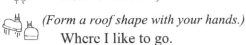 *(Suit actions to words.)*
Here is the barn,

(Form a roof shape with your hands.)
Where I like to go.

(Walk in place.)
It's as tall as a tree,

(Point up overhead.)
and cosy you know.

(Hug your body with your arms.)
Here is the barn,

(Make a roof shape with your hands.)
I'll go there with you.

(Point to children.)
To pet a sweet lamb,

(Pretend to pet a lamb.)
and cuddle it too!

(Pretend to hug the lamb by wrapping your arms around your chest.)
(Substitute other barnyard animals for the lamb.)

247

5 Friendly Farmers

(Use your fingers to represent the farmers.)
5 friendly farmers
Wake up with the sun,

(Stretch and yawn.)
For it is early morning
and the chores must be done.

The first friendly farmer
Goes to milk the cow.

(Pretend to milk a cow.)
The second friendly farmer
Thought he'd better plow.

(Pretend to hoe a field.)
The third friendly farmer
Feeds the hungry hens.

(Pretend to feed chickens.)
The fourth friendly farmer
Puts the piggies in their pens.

(Pretend to shoo piggies into a pen.)
The fifth friendly farmer
Picks the ripe corn.

(Pretend to pick corn.)
and waves to the neighbour
When he blows his horn.

(Wave and pretend to blow a horn.)
When the work is finished
and the evening sky is red,
5 tired farmers tumble into bed!

(Pretend to go to sleep.)

5 Crows

(Tune: 5 Green Speckled Frogs)
(Use your fingers to represent the crows.)
5 crows all shiny and black,
Sat on a scarecrow's back,
Eating some most delicious
    corn—Caw! Caw!
Scarecrow jumped and
  hollered—BOO!
Scared one crow and away he flew,
Now there are 4 black shiny
    crows—Caw! Caw!

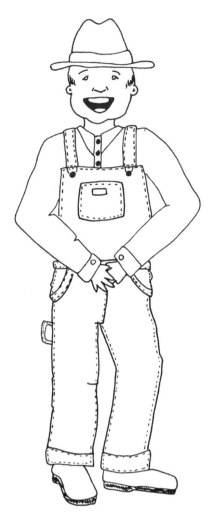

The Animals on the Farm

(Tune: The Wheels on the Bus)
(Let children participate by volunteering to be an animal, a farmer, etc.)
The animals on the farm,
The animals on the farm,
Heigh-ho the dairy-o,
The animals on the farm.

The tractor works the fields,
The tractor works the fields,
Heigh-ho the dairy-o,
The tractor works the fields.

Additional verses:
The pigs roll in the mud
The chickens lay their eggs
The duck swim in the pond
The horses run and play

Farm Flurry

 (Make a farmer and animals to accompany this rhyme.)

The farm is in a flurry
The rooster caught the flu.
His cock-a-doodle-doo,
Has changed to cock-a-doodle-choo!

The farm is in a flurry
The cow has caught the flu.
His moo, moo, moo,
Had changed to moo, moo-choo!

The farm is in a flurry
The pigs have caught the flu.
Instead of saying oink, oink, oink
They now say oink, oink-choo!

The farm is in a flurry,
The ducks have caught the flu.
Their waddle, waddle, quack, quack,
    quack
Had changed to quack, quack-choo!

The farmer's in a flurry
For he has caught the flu.
He's stuck in bed with a cloth on his
    head,
ACHOO! ACHOO! ACHOO!

Six Little Ducks

(Suit actions to words.)

Six little ducks that I once knew,
Short ones, skinny ones, tall ones too.
But the one little duck with the feathers
    on his back,
He led the others with a quack, quack,
    quack!
Quack, quack, quack! Quack, quack,
    quack!
He led the others with a quack, quack,
    quack!

Down to the river they would go,
Wibble-wobble, wibble-wobble to and
    fro.
But the one little duck with the feathers
    on his back,
He led the others with a quack, quack,
    quack!
Quack, quack, quack! Quack, quack,
    quack!
He led the others with a quack, quack,
    quack!

Up from the river they would come,
Wibble-wobble, wibble-wobble, ho
    hum-hum.
But the one little duck with the feather
    on his back,
He led the others with a quack, quack,
    quack!
Quack, quack, quack! Quack, quack,
    quack!
He led the others with a quack, quack,
    quack!

Storytime Souvenir

Peekaboo Barn

Materials

1 photocopied barn per person

Cut out animals

Coloured construction paper

Glue sticks

Scissors

Decorating supplies: markers, crayons, animal stickers

Instructions

1. Photocopy the barn template (to the size of an 8½-by-11-inch sheet of paper) and cut it out.

2. Cut along the dotted lines. (This will give you the barn doors.)

3. Glue the barn onto a piece of coloured construction paper, being careful not to get any glue on the barn doors. (This will give you the background.)

4. Photocopy and cut out the animal templates.

5. Let the children decorate their barn scenes with the animals, and using markers and crayons.

6. Bibliography of Books to Share

Atwood, Margaret. 1995. *Princess Prunella and the Purple Peanut.* New York: Workman.

Boynton, Sandra. 1995. *The Going to Bed Book.* New York: Little Simon.

Carle, Eric. 1979. *The Very Hungry Caterpillar.* New York: Philomel Books.

Carlstrom, Nancy White. 1996. *Jesse Bear, What Will You Wear?* New York: Aladdin Paperbacks.

Cronin, Doreen. 2002. *Giggle, Giggle, Quack.* New York: Simon & Schuster.

Dickinson, Rebecca. 1996. *The 13 Nights of Halloween.* New York: Cartwheel Books.

Faulkner, Keith. 1999. *The Big Yawn.* Brookfield, CT: Millbrook Press Trade.

Fox, Mem. 1993. *Time for Bed.* San Diego: Harcourt Brace.

Galdone, Paul. 1985. *The Little Red Hen.* New York: Houghton Mifflin.

Guarino, Deborah. 1992. *Is Your Mama a Llama*? New York: Scholastic Trade.

Joffe Numeroff, Laura. 1998. *What Mommies Do Best/What Daddies Do Best.* New York: Simon & Schuster.

Keats, Ezra Jack. 1962. *The Snowy Day.* New York: Viking Press.

King, Bob. 1992. *Sitting on the Farm.* New York: Orchard Books.

Leuck, Laura. 1999. *My Monster Mama Loves Me So.* New York: Lothrop, Lee & Shepard.

Lindbergh, Reeve. 1987. *The Midnight Farm.* New York: Dial Books for Young Readers.

London, Jonathan. 1992. *Froggy Gets Dressed.* New York: Penguin USA.

Maynard, Bill. 1999. *Incredible Ned.* Toronto: Puffin Books.

McBratney, Sam. 1995. *Guess How Much I Love You.* Cambridge, MA: Candlewick Press.

McCourt, Lisa. 20012. *Good Night, Princess Pruney Toes.* Memphis, TN: Troll Communications.

Moulton, Mark Kimball. 1999. *A Snowman Named Just Bob.* Milwaukee, WI: Lang Books.

Numeroff, Laura Joffe. 1998. *Monster Munchies.* New York: Random House.

Pearson, Tracey Campbell. 1999. *Where Does Joe Go?* New York: Farrar Straus & Giroux.

Rosen, Michael. 1989. *We're Going on a Bear Hunt.* London: Walker.

Sadler, Marilyn. 1983. *It's Not Easy Being a Bunny.* New York: Random House.

Schnitzlein, Danny. 2001. *The Monster Who Ate My Peas.* Atlanta, GA: Peachtree Publishers.

Shields, Carol Diggery. 1996. *I Am Really a Princess.* Toronto: Puffin Books.

Sierra, Judy. 1999. *House That Drac Built.* Minneapolis, MN: Econo-Clad Books.

Sloat, Teri. 2001. *Farmer Brown Goes Round and Round.* Toronto: DK Publishing Merchandise.

Stevens, Kathleen. 1985. *The Beast in the Bathtub.* Milwaukee, WI: Gareth Stevens.

Stinson, Kathy. 1988. *Red Is Best.* Toronto: Firefly Books.

Van Allsburg, Chris. 1985. *The Polar Express*. Boston: Houghton Mifflin.

Welch, Willy. 2000. *Grumpy Bunnies*. Watertown, MA: Charlesbridge Publishing.

Williams, Linda. 1988. *The Little Old Lady Who Was Not Afraid of Anything*. New York: HarperTrophy.

Wilson, Karma. 2002. *Bear Snores On*. New York: Margaret McElderry.

Wood, Audrey. 2000. *The Napping House*. Lake Worth, FL: Red Wagon.

Wood, Douglas. 2001. *What Moms Can't Do*. New York: Simon & Schuster.

Yolen, Jane. 2000. *How Do Dinosaurs Say Goodnight*? New York: Scholastic Trade.

Appendix

Suggested Reading

Emergent Literacy and Reading-Readiness

Baker, Betty, et al. 1998. Reading Awareness: An Evolving Success. *Illinois Libraries* 80:2 (Spring): 84-86.

Berg, Leila. 1977. *Reading and Loving.* London: Routledge & Kegan Paul.

Butler, Dorothy. 1998. *Babies Need Books: Sharing the Joy of Books with Children from Birth to Six.* Portsmouth, NH: Heinemann.

Carlson, Ann D. 1985. *Early Childhood Literature Sharing Programs in Libraries.* Hamden, CT: Library Professional Publications.

Carlson, Ann D. 1992. *The Preschooler and the Library.* Metuchen, NJ: Scarecrow Press.

Crago, Maureen, and Hugh Crago. 1983. *Prelude to Literacy: A Preschool Child's Encounter with Picture and Story.* Carbondale: Southern Illinois University Press.

Cullinan, Bernice E. 1992. *Read to Me: Raising Kids Who Love to Read.* New York: Scholastic.

Ernst, Linda L. 1995. *Lapsit Services for the Very Young: A How-To-Do-It-Manual.* New York: Neal-Schuman.

Ernst, Linda L. 2001. *Lapsit Services for the Very Young II: A How-To-Do-It-Manual.* New York: Neal-Schuman.

Flatow, Kathleen M. 1997. Programs for Babies in Public Libraries. *Illinois Libraries* 79 (Summer): 107-9.

Fox, Mem. 2001. *Reading Magic: Why Reading Aloud to Our Children Will Change Their Lives Forever.* San Diego: Harcourt Brace.

Glazer, Susan Mandel. 1980. *Getting Ready to Read: Creating Readers from Birth Through Six.* Englewood Cliffs, NJ: Prentice-Hall.

Greene, Ellin. 1991. *Books, Babies, and Libraries: Serving Infants, Toddlers, Their Parents and Caregivers.* Chicago: American Library Association.

Kropp, Paul. 2000. *How to Make Your Child a Reader for Life.* New York: Broadway Books.

Kropp, Paul. 1996. *Raising a Reader: Make Your Child a Reader for Life.* New York: Doubleday.

Ontario Early Years Study. 1999. *Reversing the Real Brain Drain: Early Years Study: Final Report.* Toronto: Canadian Institute for Advanced Research.

Preschool Services and Parent Education Committee, Association for Library Service to Children. 1990. *First Steps to Literacy: Library Programs for Parents, Teachers, and Caregivers.* Chicago: American Library Association.

Program Plans and Collections of Songs and Rhymes

Batluck, Naomi. 1993. *Crazy Gibberish: And Other Story Hour Stretches (From a Storyteller's Bag of Tricks)*. Hamden, CT: Linnet Books.

Bauer, Caroline Feller. 1992. *Read for the Fun of It: Active Programming with Books for Children*. New York: H. W. Wilson.

Beall, Pamela Conn. 1994. *Wee Sing Children's Songs and Fingerplays*. Los Angeles: Price Stern Sloan.

Briggs, Diane. 1997. *52 Programs for Preschoolers: The Librarian's Year-Round Planner*. Chicago: American Library Association.

Cobb, Jane. 1996. *I'm a Little Teapot!: Presenting Preschool Storytime*. Vancouver, BC: Black Sheep Press.

Dailey, Susan. 2001. *A Storytime Year: A Month-to-Month Kit for Preschool Programming*. New York: Neal-Schuman.

Davis, Robin Works. 1998. *Toddle on Over: Developing Infant & Toddler Literature Programs*. Fort Atkinson, WI: Alleyside Press.

DeSalvo, Nancy. 1993. *Beginning with Books: Library Programming for Infants, Toddlers, and Preschoolers*. Hamden, CT: Library Professional Publications.

Friedes, Harriet. 1993. *The Preschool Resource Guide: Educating and Entertaining Children Aged Two Through Five*. New York: Plenum Press.

Jeffery, Debby Ann. 1995. *Literate Beginnings: Programs for Babies and Toddlers*. Chicago: American Library Association.

Kladder, Jeri. 1995. *Story Hour: 55 Preschool Programs for Public Libraries*. Jefferson, NC: McFarland.

Lerach, Helen. 1993. *Creative Storytimes*. Regina, SAS: Regina Public Library.

MacDonald, Margaret Read. 1995. *Bookplay: 101 Creative Themes to Share with Young Children*. North Haven, CT: Library Professional Publications.

MacDonald, Margaret Read. 1988. *Booksharing: 101 Programs to Use with Preschoolers*. Hamden, CT: Library Professional Publications.

Marino, Jane, and Dorothy F. Houlihan. 1992. *Mother Goose Time: Library Programs for Babies and Their Caregivers*. New York: H. W. Wilson.

Miller, Karen. 2000. *Things to Do with Toddlers and Twos*. rev. ed. West Palm Beach, FL: Telshare Publishing.

Nespeca, Sue McCleaf. 1994. *Library Programming for Families with Young Children*. New York: Neal-Schuman.

Nichols, Judy. 1987. *Storytimes for Two-Year-Olds*. Chicago: American Library Association.

Oakes, Susan. 2001. Animal Crackers, Milk, and a Good Book: Creating a Successful Early Childhood Literacy Program. *Public Libraries* 40:3 (May/June): 166-69.

1001 Rhymes & Fingerplays for Working with Young Children. 1994. Everett, WA: Warren Publishing House.

Reid, Rob. 1995. *Children's Jukebox: A Subject Guide to Musical Recordings and Programming Ideas for Songsters Ages One to Twelve.* Chicago: American Library Association.

Reid, Rob. 1999. *Family Storytime: Twenty-Four Creative Programs for All Ages.* Chicago: American Library Association.

Ring a Ring O' Roses: Stories, Games and Fingerplays for Preschool Children. Revised Edition. 1977. Flint, MI: Flint Public Library.

Sierra, Judy. 1997. *The Flannel Board Storytelling Book.* New York: H.W. Wilson.

Silberg, Jackie. 2002. *The Complete Book of Rhymes, Songs, Poems, Fingerplays, and Chants: Over 700 Selections.* Beltsville, MD: Gryphon House.

Sitarz, Paula Gaj. 1990. *More Picture Book Story Hours: From Parties to Pets.* Englewood, Colorado: Libraries Unlimited.

Van Vliet, Virginia. 1987. *Time for Tots: Library Service to Toddlers.* Ottawa, Ontario: Canadian Library Association.

Warren, Jean. 1983. *Piggyback Songs: New Songs Sung to the Tunes of Childhood Favorites.* Everett, WA: Totline Press; Warren Publishing House.

Weissman, "Miss Jackie." 1991. *Higglety, Pigglety, Pop! 233 Playful Rhymes and Chants for Your Baby.* Overland Park, KS: Miss Jackie Music Co.

Woboditsch, Mary. 1995. *You Asked for It: A Guide to Storyhours.* Lively, ONT: Walden Public Library.

Works, Robin. 1992. *Promoting Reading with Reading Programs: A How-To-Do-It Manual.* New York: Neal-Schuman.

Yolen, Jane. 1989. *The Lap-Time Song and Play Book.* San Diego: Harcourt Brace Jovanovich.

Child Development

Allen, K. Eileen, and Lynn R. Marotz. 2000. *By the Ages: Behavior & Development of Children Pre-Birth Through Eight.* Albany, NY: Delmar Thomson Learning.

Bredekamp, Sue, ed. 1987. *Developmentally Appropriate Practice in Early Childhood Programs Serving Children from Birth Through Age 8.* Washington, DC: National Association for the Education of Young Children.

Leach, Penelope. 1997. *Your Baby & Child: from Birth to Age Five.* 3d ed. New York: Alfred A. Knopf.

National Network for Child Care. 1999. *Child Development.* Washington, DC: United States Department of Agriculture. Available: http://twosocks.ces.ncsu.edu/cyfdb/browse_2pageAnncc.php?subcat=Child+Development&search=NNCC&search_type=browse. (Accessed April 9, 2003).

Nespeca, Sue McCleaf. 1999. Bringing Up Baby. *School Library Journal* 45:11 (November): 48-52.

Schaefer, Charles E., and Theresa Foy DiGeronimo. 2000. *Ages and Stages: A Parent's Guide to Normal Childhood Development.* New York: Wiley.

Shelov, Steven. 1998. *Caring for Your Baby and Young Child: Birth to Age 5.* rev, ed. New York: Bantam Books.

What a Child Will Be Depends on You and Me: A Resource Kit for a Child's First Five Years. 2001. Toronto: Invest in Kids Foundation.

White, Burton L. 1985. *The First Three Years of Life.* rev. ed. New York: Prentice Hall Press.

Woolfson, Richard C. 2001. *Bright Baby.* Hauppauge, NY: Barron's.

Library Children's Services

Fasick, Adele. 1998. *Managing Children's Services in the Public Library.* Englewood, CO: Libraries Unlimited.

Gerhardt, Lillian, ed. 1997. *School Library Journal's Best: A Reader for Children's, Young Adult and School Librarians.* New York: Neal-Schuman.

Reif, Kathleen. 2000. Are Public Libraries the Preschooler's Door to Learning? *Public Libraries* 39:5 (September/October): 262-68.

Rollock, Barbara T. 1988. *Public Library Services for Children.* Hamden, CT: Library Professional Publications.

Sackowski, Inge. 2000. The Buck Stops Here: Charging for Programs. *School Library Journal* 46:11 (November): 29.

Steele, Anita T. 2001. *Bare Bones Children's Services: Tips for Public Library Generalists.* Chicago: American Library Association.

Teale, William H. 1999. Libraries Promote Early Literacy Learning: Ideas from Current Research and Early Childhood Programs. *Journal of Youth Services in Libraries* 12:3 (Spring): 9-16.

Children's Literature

Bettleheim, Bruno. 1977.*The Uses of Enchantment.* New York: Vintage Books.Hilman, Judith. 1999. *Discovering Children's Literature.* 2d ed. New York: Prentice Hall.

Lynch-Brown, Carol, and Carl M. Tomlinson. 1999. *Essentials of Children's Literature.* 3d ed. Boston: Allyn and Bacon.

Sutherland, Zena. 1997. *Children & Books.* New York: Longman.

Bibliographies and Booklists

Association for Library Service to Children. 2001. *The New Books Kids Like.* Chicago: American Library Association.

Cullinan, Bernice E. 1993. *Let's Read About . . .: Finding Books They'll Love to Read.* New York: Scholastic.

Cullum, Carolyn. 1999. *The Storytime Sourcebook: A Compendium of Ideas and Resources for Storytellers.* New York: Neal-Schuman.

Landsberg, Michele. 1986. *Michele Landsberg's Guide to Children's Books: With a Treasury of More Than 350 Great Children's Books.* Markham, ONT: Penguin Books.

Lipson, Eden Ross. 2000. *The New York Times Parent's Guide to the Best Books for Children.* New York: Three Rivers Press.

McGovern, Edythe M., and Helen D. Muller. 1994. *They're Never Too Young for Books: A Guide to Children's Books for Ages 1 to 8.* Buffalo, NY: Prometheus Books.

Thomas, James L. 1992. *Play, Learn, and Grow: An Annotated Guide to the Best Books and Materials for Very Young Children.* New Providence, NJ: R. R. Bowker.

Other

Statistics Canada, 2002. *2001 Community Profiles.* Ottawa, Ontario: Statistics Canada. Available: http://www12.statcan.ca/english/profil01/PlaceSearchForm1.cfm. (Accessed April 9, 2003).

U.S. Census Bureau, Demographic Surveys Division. 2002. *American Community Survey.* Washington, DC: United States Department of Commerce. Available: http://www.census.gov/acs/www/. (Accessed April 9, 2003).

Author/Title/First Line Index

Subject Index

About the Authors and Illustrators

BETH MADDIGAN is Coordinator of Children's Services at Cambridge Libraries & Galleries, Cambridge, Ontario.

ROBERTA THOIMPSON is Head of Children's Services at The Clemens Mill Branch of the Cambridge Libraries & Galleries, Cambridge, Ontario.

STEPHANIE DRENNAN is Early Childhood Educator/Children's Programmer at Cambridge Libraries & Galleries, Cambridge, Ontario.